Teaching and Advocacy

Teaching and Advocacy

EDITED BY

Denny Taylor

Debbie Coughlin

Joanna Marasco

Stenhouse Publishers
York, Maine

Stenhouse Publishers, 431 York Street, York, Maine 03909

Copyright © 1997 by Stenhouse Publishers.

Library of Congress Cataloging-in-Publication Data
Teaching and advocacy / edited by Denny Taylor, Debbie Coughlin, and
    Joanna Marasco.
        p. cm.
    Includes bibliographical references.
    ISBN 1-57110-045-8
    1. Special education—United States—Case studies. 2. Exceptional children—Government policy—United States—Case studies. 3. Literacy—United States—Case studies. 4. Language arts—Social aspects—United States—Case studies. 5. Teaching—United States—Case studies. 6. Educational change—United States—Case studies.
I. Taylor, Denny, 1947– . II. Coughlin, Debbie. III. Marasco, Joanna.
LC3981.T42 1996
371.9′0973—dc20
                                    96-38946
                                    CIP

Cover and interior design by Ron Kosciak, *Dragonfly Design*

Cover illustration by Carolyn Latanision

Typeset by Technologies 'N Typography

Manufactured in the United States of America on acid-free paper
01 00 99 98 97   9 8 7 6 5 4 3 2 1

"Finally," she says. "I trust you now. I trust you with the bird that is not in your hands because you have truly caught it. Look. How lovely it is, this thing we have done—together."

TONI MORRISON

CONTENTS

ACKNOWLEDGMENTS

We would like to express our special gratitude to Dr. Kenneth Goodman and Dr. Yetta Goodman for their constant support, inspiration, and wisdom.

Our thanks go to the faculty and students in the Department of Language, Reading, and Culture at the University of Arizona who provided the forum for our advocacy, especially the students who participated in the courses that are the foundation of this book. We are grateful for their commitment and passion as teachers and researchers, and for the friendships we made as we discussed some of the difficult issues surrounding teaching and advocacy.

We would also like to thank Philippa Stratton and Tom Seavey at Stenhouse for creating a very modern, old fashioned press that has made publishing fun again. Martha Drury, the production editor, was always easy to reach, she listened to our ideas, and remained calm when we became a publisher's worst nightmare and wanted to make changes when the book was well into production.

Lastly, we would like to offer special recognition to the children and families whose stories we have told. It is our hope that we will all learn from them.

We *Do* Language: That May Be the Measure of Our Lives

DENNY TAYLOR

When academics take a sabbatical, most of them go off somewhere quiet to write; but on my sabbatical, I went to teach in a university. I already lived a quiet life so I could write. I wanted to share some of my research with students, so for one year I became a visiting professor in the department of language, reading, and culture at the University of Arizona. During the first semester I taught two courses.

One was a weekend course that focused on family, community, school, bureaucratic, and workplace literacies. Most of the participants were teachers, some working on doctorates. It was an amazing group, filled with vitality and willing to adopt a kindergarten format for our graduate class. For five hectic weekends we came loaded with bags of print that we noisily sorted, analyzed, and organized into displays that filled the walls. Let's go back to the class . . .

Many of my students say the ideas we are considering in class are new to them. So I question them: How are these ideas new? What questions are you asking yourselves? How can you expand your understanding of what it means to be literate in American society? What are the pitfalls? Do the ways in which you are thinking about literacy have an impact on the ways in which you might teach? Does advocacy enter into your literacy configurations? What do you think of the proposition, "If we change the ways we use print, we change the system"?

"Come ready to talk, to share your ideas about the course," I say, "about the readings, and about the ways in which you are constructing your portfolios."

We are in disequilibrium. Documenting literacy shakes us up, challenges old beliefs, makes us question. Even though I have been researching and writing for over twenty years I feel that I am in the same situation. We are surrounded by boxes of stuff—otherwise known as "data." We explore the possibilities.

"As you are studying literacy in communities, you might want to consider applying the types-and-uses categories,"[1] I suggest. "Or, you might want to think about what you are observing from the perspective of practical intelligence. You know, the stuff on the complexity of problem solving in everyday life."² Becoming more obscure, I add, "A third possibility would be to think about the sociological, cultural, or political significance of the literacies that you are observing in use."

"Don't be overwhelmed by these suggestions," I add. "They are *only* suggestions!"

At the next weekend meeting the tables are piled high with print. Students bend over, sifting and sorting, talking to one another about the significance of the artifacts they have collected. They are analyzing the bureaucratic texts they have brought with them from the social agencies they have visited since our last session. In front of them are regulations, applications, forms, contracts, invoices, signs, identification cards, licenses, letters, and memorandums.

They haven't just collected these documents, they have observed them *in use*, seen what happened as people tried to use them. "Does everybody agree that literacy can be esthetic," I ask, "but that it is *always* political?"

Every document has a story. Some of the stories are so urgent that students vie to tell them. We listen. There is the legal documentation gathered by a woman who developed cancer from contaminated drinking water and the medical documentation from another woman who was denied a medical procedure because it was not covered by her HMO.

The stories are rich in the details of discriminatory practices and the violations of peoples' rights. The class has become serious. Literacy has a new face with a jagged edge. Developing profiles of our own literacy configurations helps us broaden our understanding of who we are as literate adults. Developing biographic profiles of families makes us rethink what it means to be literate. Our explorations help us build community. We laugh a lot. But our study of official documentation is no laughing matter. We spend time simulating the situations in which the texts were used: Who writes the text? Who reads the text? Who can interpret the text? Who can interrupt the text? Who can change the text? Where does the power lie?

These are new questions. The ways in which we transact with the text are changing. Students talk of their own lives, their vulnerabilities, their personal experiences of the ways in which texts have been used unjustly. Some texts have silenced them or a member of their family. A student talks about her mother, another about a situation where he works. For some of them it is the first time they are questioning the role of authoritative texts in their own lives. The personal connection increases their awareness of literacy as problematic in the places they have been observing.

Debbie Smith talks about her own experiences in school as she begins her research into the literacies of adolescents who are not allowed to make it in "the system." She is working with a young mother of three small children, doing everything she can to help her graduate from high school. The administration at the high school the young woman attends does not see graduation in her future. Debbie talks about the official documentation she is powerless to change.

We discuss the power of print. How come I've never thought about this before?

Why haven't we learned to question? Another shift takes place in the ways in which the students position themselves within their observations. They become advocates.

Melanie Uttech talks about her border crossings. She has been moving back and forth between Arizona and Sonora, which is just across the border in Mexico. She can cross the border to go to a restaurant, to buy fresh vegetables. The border guards joke with her. She is an American. Her documentation is a formality. She is treated with partiality. Not so the family she visits in the shantytown that has grown up along the edge of Sonora. The mother she visits cannot cross the border, even though all she wants to do is visit a supermarket in Nogales, Arizona, where the canned goods are cheaper then they are in Nogales, Sonora.

Melanie explains that the woman has to be able to show she has been a resident of Sonora for six months before she is allowed to cross the border. An electricity bill or a water bill would do. But there is no electricity in the cardboard shacks of the shantytown, and there is no running water. "And even if there were," Melanie continues, "there is no mail delivered where she lives."

For Melanie it is the beginning of her essay in this book and the beginning of her doctoral research. She helps us take an activist stance. Literally and metaphorically we stand beside her. Politicized. Each one of us reexamines our assumptions about literacy.

The other course I taught during that first semester focused on ethnographic approaches to literacy assessment in schools. There were twenty students in this advanced seminar, and they were all well into their doctoral studies. This class was much more intimidating. During the first class they scared me silly. But by the second meeting I relaxed a bit. (It helped when I found out that some of them were as intimidated by me as I was by them.)

Teaching as advocacy was central to our research. Every participant was asked to find a child or an adult for whom reading and writing were problematic based on traditional assessment procedures. No one had any difficulty finding someone. Debbie Coughlin worked with Valerie, a little girl in her fifth-grade class who was recovering from brain cancer. Caryl Crowell worked with Francisco, who had been placed in a self-contained special education classroom. And Joanna Marasco worked with Serena, who at sixteen was having a baby and living in a home for pregnant teenagers.

Each student was asked to become a participatory activist, to advocate for the person with whom they were working, by developing an intensive analysis of (1) his or her personal literacies and (2) the official version of these literacies that was contained in the bureaucratic documentation that shaped their lives. We used *Learning Denied* and *From the Child's Point of View*[3] as our course books, and supplemented them with the writings of Ann Haas Dyson, Richard Figueroa, Jean Lave, Ray McDermott, Hugh Mehan, Mary Poplin, Barbara Rogoff, and Nadeen Ruiz.

Again, each week students brought in "stuff" and then spent time working together developing critical analyses of the literacy skills of the person with whom they were working and juxtaposing their findings with the pronouncements of official texts. Here's what it was like . . .

Early in the course we discuss the notion of "human pathology." "What do you mean by pathology?" Alan asks. It is the question that is central to his essay in this book.

"Whose pathology is it?" I respond.

We talk of the "ascription of internal states." This is heavy duty. Using a paper by Joe Kincheloe and Shirley Steinberg[4] we try to locate pathology from a post-formalist perspective.

"These are Ph.D. questions," I say. Then to lighten the load, I add, "But as Emma Thompson says about her acting, 'I like to stretch!' I hope you like stretching, too."

The real-life importance of the questions we are pursuing are not lost on any of us. Valerie's official files are riddled with the "pathologies" that have been ascribed to her, Francisco is supposed to be mildly mentally retarded, and Serena's "deviant" social behavior is blamed on her lack of education. To counter these official positions, to advocate, we need more than our personal opinions. Our expertise as teachers is not enough. We have to be able to deconstruct the official texts and build alternative explanations that we can document in more authentic texts.

We talk about the "situatedness" of our explanations.

We study the writings of Ray McDermott. His article on inarticulateness is particularly helpful.[5] "From the commonsense point of view, we can separate the articulate from the inarticulate and wonder why respectively they are the way they are," Ray writes. Then he states, "From the sociocultural point of view, we can only wonder how full members of the culture can come together and arrange for each other to look differently able."

How have Valerie, Francisco, and Serena become "differently able"? Where do we locate "their" pathologies? How have they become so inarticulate?

"Inarticulateness is a dance in which we all engage," Ray writes, as if in answer to our questions. "Either by suffering it ourselves or by arranging for others to carry the burden." Patiently he explains, "If we cannot tell the dancer from the dance, it is certainly unfair to complain about the dancer if there is no music."

"I want to make the connection," I say, "between Ray McDermott's article on inarticulateness and the use of literacy in everyday life."

We discuss how we can gain an in-depth understanding of a particular person's articulateness or inarticulateness. We decide that we need to do more than analyze his or her language production. We need to know something about the opportunities that the person has to speak.

"We need to ask, What's happening?" I say. "What's going on?" I remind them of something Ray says, "'It's not the utterance alone that makes a difference, as much as the conditions for its being delivered, heard, acted on, remembered, and quoted.'"

We raise other questions. What are the constraints on literacy? Who writes to whom and for what purpose? How do our students learn to read? How do they learn not to read? How are "disabilities" organized? How do we separate the "literate" from the "illiterate"? How do we orchestrate reading failure? Where do we locate pathology? (This question haunts us.) What are the literacy resources available for transforming the situation?

Asking these questions pushes us to ask a different set of questions. We talk about the kinds of learning environments educators can create that provide both teachers and learners with the maximum opportunity to explore the functions, uses, and forms of written language. How do we create environments for people that provide opportunities for them to articulate their situation? How can we develop conversations about the ways in which we use print? How can we change the conditions that limit the opportunities that our students have to use and learn about print? How can we learn to advocate?

Alan Flurkey is deep into theory. He is greatly impressed by the work of Ray McDermott, and he spends most of the semester just playing with Ray's ideas. The Kincheloe and Steinberg article has turned him on to postformalism. Thanks to Alan, postformalism becomes a topic of conversation in the corridors and in other classes. Students and even a couple of professors ask for copies of his paper.

Writing and publishing are second nature to me. It is my chosen form of advocacy. By the end of that semester *Teaching and Advocacy* was in the works; we began discussing the possibility of a book. I was excited at the prospect of collaborating with my students. A number of students reworked their papers into essays, but we didn't yet have enough to fill a book. Fortunately, I had more courses to teach the following semester.

In my course on reading, writing, and text, each student explored a person's literacy development from the perspective of a major literacy theorist's research . . .

At our first weekly meeting I tell the students, "There is an essay by Eduardo Galeano in which he says, 'One writes out of a need to communicate and to commune with others, to denounce that which gives pain and to share that which gives happiness.'"[6]

"Who we are and what we do," I continue, "is often explained through reading, writing, and texts. In this course we will explore how we come to read and write, how we come to mean through print, and how print shapes the meaning of our lives. It is the *activity* of reading, writing, and producing texts that will be of importance to us."

We shift our lens. We take a worldview, building overarching configurations of written language in use. Nan Jiang tells us that he has never done any research above the "word" level. He has never had the opportunity in class to contemplate worldviews of literacy. He embarks on the study of Ty's Chinese and English literacies. Nan talks about literacy use in China.

How is print used in other societies with which we are familiar? How is print used in the society in which we live? Who influences the reading, writing, and interpretation of texts? Who is included? Who is excluded? We talk about news-papers, television, political campaigns, public information, official documentation, advertisements, junk mail.

Our lens shifts. We talk about the literacies of communities, of families, and the personal and shared literacy configurations of community and family members. Again we question. When and why do people read and write? What types and uses of literacy are found in the community? the family? the school? day care? the workplace? What are the characteristics of the texts that people use? Are their literacy practices emancipatory? Which texts are accepted? Which texts are re-jected? Who writes? Who reads? For what purpose?

Again we shift. We reach Nan's "word." We talk about texts. We discuss the language of written discourse. How do the forms of written discourse affect the person's reading of the text? What about different languages? different orthogra-phies? cultural differences? How do you locate meaning? Whose meaning? How would you describe the language of the texts you have collected from the person who is helping you with your study? How does the study of semantics help us with our ethnographic descriptions? pragmatics? grammatical and syntactical in-terpretations?

We continue to shift our lens as we discuss the theorists whose work we are studying. Some of them have one-legged models. They are stuck at the level of words. Others have reached the sentence level. Divorced from the world, they are unable to shed any light on the ways in which language is used.

Nan is now at the world level. Even though he has never participated in any research where the units of analysis are larger than words, he persists. He tells us that in a matter of weeks, Ty has lost his ability to write in Chinese. He has become more competent as a writer in English, but at what cost? Nan becomes an advocate for Ty, for his family. He raises our consciousness about the problems of first-language loss, and his study becomes an essay in this book.

The other course I taught that second semester was a methods course in language research. I found the prospect particularly unnerving. I had spent the previous summer trying to find a textbook to use. Not easy. In the end I decided to use several supplemental texts, with the excessively expensive *Sociolinguistic Metatheory*, by Esther Figueroa,[7] as the principal text. I loved it. My students didn't . . .

I know I am in trouble when one young woman walks to class with me and asks me if I have actually *read* the book. What a struggle! Debbie Smith and Melanie Uttech, who have been in my other classes, are both generous enough to give it a try. Students who don't know me are less charitable. One student writes, "Well, I don't know whether to laugh or to cry. This book just does absolutely nothing for me."

In my memos to the class I try to convince everyone that Figueroa's book will help us. Whether we are doing research in communities or teaching in schools, our ability to advocate depends on our understanding the underlying philosophical and theoretical differences between competing paradigms. It is not an easy concept to get across.

When the class meets for tutorials, we talk about Esther Figueroa's metatheories. But for the most part we are intent on understanding how our theoretical orientation helps or hinders us as we develop frameworks for our studies of teaching and advocacy.

Debbie Smith has begun her work with adolescents in an alternative high school and has become interested in their tagging (a kind of graffiti). She wants to understand their tags and she is beginning to see them as an alternative form of language. Esther Figueroa's deconstructions of the theories of Dell Hymes, William Labov, and John Gumperz push Debbie more deeply into the sociolinguistic significance of her students' tagging.

Melanie Uttech's border crossings have led her to her earlier study of a Mexican family in Nogales. She is spending much of her time writing proposals to obtain funds to pay for a year of ethnographic research in rural Mexico. The study of one family will lead to the study of another and, in Melanie's case, to the study of a whole village.

LaFon Phillips's questions revolve around the language development of her young hearing-impaired students. LaFon is studying their pictorial representations as responses to stories. Esther Figueroa helps her develop a theoretical frame for her study. LaFon also starts to write about her son, Mark, and his experiences at school. She tries to understand what is happening to him, how the school can view Mark and his learning so differently from his family's view of his progress. She is experiencing the clash of paradigms in very concrete ways. Her personal life is caught up in educational metatheories. In our conversations about Esther Figueroa's book, LaFon often talks about Mark. Her paper about his schooling eventually becomes an essay in this book.

"I am trying to create a context in which you can discuss the theoretical framework of the language researchers we are studying," I tell everyone. "But at the same time I want you to become critically conscious of your own philosophical and theoretical orientations and how these orientations frame both your research and practice."

Where is language located? Where is language located in our own research? We discuss the critical relationship between our theoretical positioning of this question and the ways in which we define our critical sites of inquiry.

"Push," I say. "Don't give up on this question. I want to encourage you to be critically conscious of the ways in which your own philosophical and theoretical framework shapes your research, your reading of other people's research, and your practical interpretations of both your own research and teaching."

Figueroa is getting easier, but some sections are difficult to take. A student jokes that it "beats reading Chomsky's minimalist theory," but we are all struggling.

At the end of the course *Sociolinguistic Metatheory* remained an anathema for some students, but for many it became the foundation for much of their research. About

six months after the course ended, I ran into one such student.[8] We talked for a
few brief moments as we passed each other on the fifth floor of the education
building.

"I just want you to know that Figueroa really helped me," she said, as if she
knew how troubled I had been by students' reactions to the book. "That book
made me think about my own paradigm. I thought she laid out very clearly the
different paradigms and in such a way that it helped me think about my own beliefs
and where they fit in. I think it helped me put into words what I believe, and to
describe that using the vocabulary." She then added as a qualifier, "It's the language
that's in the field, and so to be able to take it and make it one's own is important."

Also about that time the student[9] who had joked about Chomsky's minimalist
theory wrote me a note while I was sitting in on the course he was taking taught
by Luis Moll: "I began reading *Sociolinguistic Metatheory* overwhelmed and confused
and I finished it feeling inspired. It's the one book on my shelf that I refer to again
and again."

I smiled. It really does make a difference when we have some understanding of
the nitty-gritty of one another's worldviews.

My sabbatical is over and I am back in a quiet place, writing. I still see many of
the students who were in my classes. Teaching is a wonderful way to make friends.
For a while a few of us continued to meet regularly, until doctoral dissertation
research and graduations split us up. We called ourselves the Milagro Coffee
Group, after a Tucson coffeehouse popular with medical and law students. For
several hours on Friday afternoons we would sit in Milagro's at a table for eight,
surrounded by anatomy texts and books on tort law . . .

The Milagro Coffee Group, which includes Debbie Coughlin, Joanna Marasco,
and Alan Flurkey, is interested in encouraging the development of emancipatory
literacy practices in many different settings. How can we advocate for the students
we are teaching or for the participants in our research studies? We talk of *participatory, activist, and transformative* teaching and research. *Participatory* because each
one of us believes in working closely and sharing problems with people. *Activist*
because we are convinced that to make a positive and lasting difference, we must
engage in activities that help people help themselves overcome the difficulties they
face in their everyday lives. And *transformative* because we believe that to foster
opportunities for our students, it is essential that we identify the problems existing
resources have overcoming the barriers that make us unresponsive to peoples'
needs. The transformations we are seeking are in the situations in which people
find themselves.

Ordering another Diet Coke, we come full circle. Remember what Ray McDermott wrote? "Inarticulateness is a dance in which we all engage, either by suffering
it ourselves or by arranging for others to carry the burden."

Again we ask. What are the constraints on literacy? Who writes to whom and
for what purpose? Who can read the text? How do our students learn to read?
How do they learn not to read? How are "disabilities" organized? Where do we

locate pathology? What literacy resources are available to transform the situation? How can we change the conditions that limit the opportunities that our students have to use and learn about print?

We believe it is of the utmost importance that we make visible the strengths of those who struggle. We want to focus on what people can do and how they cope, so that we have a chance of making changes in public policies that will enable all people to use their skills and abilities to participate in what we would like to think can be a fully democratic society. And so we spend our time discussing how literacy is used to both enable and disable functional behavior.[10]

Four basic questions are the center of our conversations, which are intense:

1. How is literacy used to facilitate functional behavior? mentor? support? pave the way? encourage growth?
2. How is literacy used to disable functional behavior? create interference? block growth? build barriers? provide negative responses to positive action?
3. How is literacy used to enable dysfunctional behavior? support the behavior? cover it up? deny the problem?
4. How is literacy used to transform dysfunctional behavior? provide opportunities? support efforts? encourage personal decision making?

These are hard questions to explore in the abstract, but each of us has concrete experiences working with individuals in schools and communities, and that helps us ground ourselves in more than Milagro coffee and the hot air of our own talk. With the understanding that comes from these discussions, we simplify our questions:

1. How is literacy *learning* enabled and disabled?
2. How is literacy *used* to enable and disable?

I tell the group about Marge Knox, who teaches in California and is doing an independent study with me. Marge is advocating for Tom, a seven year old in her classroom who has lived in many places, attended many schools, and never had a permanent home. Eventually, Marge writes an essay and we invite her to publish it in this book.

Debbie Coughlin shares her work with Valerie, the little girl in her class who is recovering from brain cancer. She talks about the opportunities Valerie has at home to participate in events that enable her to read and write, and of the reading and writing that Valerie does in the classroom with Debbie. She also talks about how Valerie's literacy learning is disabled by the inappropriate requirements of her IEP. Until Debbie started to advocate for her, Valerie was continually having to leave the classroom to take special education classes that she did not want to take. Debbie also talks about how literacy was used to disable Valerie's ability to cope with her everyday life. Debbie tells us that Valerie's family was also disabled. She describes the school's negative response to Valerie's cancer—mostly in toxic texts. Insurance hassles. Conflicting medical information. The guidelines of social agencies that do not cover Valerie's situation. The lack of support.

Joanna talks about Serena and the complexity of the literacies that are a part of her daily life. She tells us that Serena writes letters and keeps a journal and that these are important aspects of her personal literacy development. Joanna also talks about the ways in which literacy is used by the bureaucratic institutions that control Serena's life. She shares examples of the many ways in which literacy—reports, forms, regulations—is used to discourage Serena from continuing her education or from taking care of her baby. She is encased in the military rules of the institution in which she lives, and she is denied any opportunity to become a productive member of society.

Listening to Debbie and Joanna as they talk about their activist research and the ways in which they are advocating for Valerie and Serena helps us get a handle on the problem of teaching and advocacy.

There is so much in what they say that at one of our editorial meetings, I suggest to Debbie and Joanna that we follow each chapter in *Teaching and Advocacy* with a conversation with the author. We all agree it will add another dimension to the book.

It is clear that teachers are advocates for their students but that it's rarely talked about. Teachers often stand alone when they advocate. For most teachers there are no courses available on teaching and advocacy. We rarely talk about the role that literacy plays in providing opportunities for teachers to work as advocates. Exploring how literacy learning is enabled and disabled, and how literacy is used to enable and disable, provides us with that opportunity.

In her Nobel acceptance speech Toni Morrison says, "We die. That may be the meaning of life. But we *do* language. That may be the measure of our lives."[11] The *doing* of language is the essence of the work that the authors write about in this book. We are using written texts to uncover the hidden assumptions that shape our perceptions about what happens to people in everyday life—children in school who have cancer, who speak other languages, who are told they are different, who know they don't "fit"; adolescents who are kicked out of "regular" high school, who end up under the control of the social welfare system, belong to gangs, whose friends are killed by gunfire; families who live at borders, both physically and metaphorically, who are trying to make it, somehow, someway, anyway that they can. We are studying how language is done, what we do with it, how we define ourselves in print, and how our students are defined—often reinvented—in obscure documents of bureaucratic print. We are using print to search for particular connections in the larger patterns of our human existence: how we *do* language but also how language is *done* to us.

Endnotes

1. Denny Taylor and Catherine Dorsey-Gaines, *Growing Up Literate: Learning from Inner-City Families* (Portsmouth, NH: Heinemann, 1988). **2.** Jean Lave, *Cognition in Practice: Mind, Mathematics, and Culture in Everyday Life* (Cambridge, UK: Cambridge University Press, 1988); Barbara Rogoff and Jean Lave, eds., *Everyday Cognition: Its Development in Social Con-

text (Cambridge, MA: Harvard University Press, 1984); Barbara Rogoff, *Apprenticeship in Thinking: Cognitive Development in Social Context* (New York: Oxford University Press, 1990). **3.** Denny Taylor, *Learning Denied* (Portsmouth, NH: Heinemann, 1991); Denny Taylor, *From the Child's Point of View* (Portsmouth, NH: Heinemann, 1993). **4.** Joe Kincheloe and Shirley R. Steinberg, "A Tentative Description of Post-Formal Thinking: The Critical Confrontation with Cognitive Theory," *Harvard Educational Review* 63 (3): 296–320 (1993). **5.** Ray McDermott, "Inarticulateness," in *Linguistics in Context: Connecting Observation and Understanding*, edited by Deborah Tannen (Norwood, NJ: Ablex, 1988). **6.** Eduardo Galeano, "In Defense of the Word: Leaving Buenos Aires, June 1976," in *The Greywolf Annual Five: Multicultural Literacy* (Minneapolis: Greywolf, 1988). **7.** Esther Figueroa, *Sociolinguistic Metatheory* (Oxford, UK: Elsevier Science, 1994). **8.** Lauren Freedman, Personal communication, June 6, 1996. We reconstructed Lauren's earlier comments. **9.** Steve Bialostock helped me reconstruct the comments he had made in class and excerpts from the note he wrote that I have put in a safe place. **10.** Denny Taylor, *Toxic Literacies* (Portsmouth, NH: Heinemann, 1996). **11.** Toni Morrison, *The Nobel Lecture in Literature* (New York: Knopf, 1994).

Maybe I Should Have Died:
Learning from Valerie

DEBBIE COUGHLIN

QUESTION: What makes you sad?

VALERIE: When I have a bad day, when people yell at me, and if someone dies.

QUESTION: What scares you?

VALERIE: That I will get cancer again; heights, and having to stay in fifth grade because I had cancer. I liked school last year but I wished I could have learned more.

QUESTION: What helps you learn more?

VALERIE: A kind, helping teacher has helped this year. Talking slowly, softly, and clearly. Explain [directions and misunderstandings] to me by myself—not in front of everybody.

VALERIE CLARIE'S DIALOGUE JOURNAL[1]

This story is really two tales. It is a look at what happens to a child when the school does not pay attention, and what happens to a teacher who does.

The first tale is about Valerie Clarie and her return to school. It is a story of brain cancer,[2] childhood dreams, and a school district's systematic treatment of children who do not fit the norm. It is a disturbing look at how a school system's humanity, integrity, and common sense gives way to procedure, personalities, and power struggles. Lost in the middle is Valerie Clarie: unsupported, disregarded, and nonvalidated. She is a child working without a net.

The second tale is about advocacy and the school system. It is a look at the manner in which school systems control and silence educators and parents through the bureaucracy and social structures imposed within the school community. The social dynamics within a school system that both embrace and disempower educators also dictate and control the education that each child will receive. Educators who do not fit the expected norm within these social structures and constraints face parallel anxieties of doing something wrong or not being liked. Nevertheless, advocacy on any level is political.[3] When teachers weigh the risks of advocating, they should also remember that even by taking no action they are still involved. Not taking a position still has consequences; and although ignoring a difficult situation may be an educator's first choice, it is always considered questionable from a moral and ethical point of view.[4]

There are many ways to tell this story. My first instinct was to present a thorough case study of Valerie as a learner. I would love for you the reader to get a clearer view of Valerie as not only a capable student but as a kind, loving child. I believe you would find samples of her work both informative and fascinating, and I would love to validate her abilities and experiences. However, it is impossible to do justice to Valerie and her strengths in one chapter. Rather than portray Valerie modestly or incompletely (which is precisely the problem), I decided it might serve Valerie best to focus on the nature of advocacy. Therefore, the story will unfold for you as it did for me: chronologically. I have no doubt that you will have some questions and confusion about certain events, as I did at the time. (About some I still do.) However, choices need to be made without the benefit of hindsight and subsequent knowledge. We do what we believe to be best at the time.

Background

In June of 1993 my husband and I relocated. I was fortunate enough to secure a teaching position and spent a great deal of time over the summer moving into my new classroom: organizing, planning, but mostly decorating. The classroom environment is extremely important to me. It is our home, and it needs to reflect that.

At six-thirty the evening before school began, I decided to call it quits. Packing one last bag of materials to take home and work on, I left my classroom—confident that all was finally in place and ready for the big day.

The school was nearly deserted as I headed for the parking lot. Crossing the courtyard, I ran into Sarah, one of the four fifth-grade teachers in our pod.[5] Sarah informed me that a new student, Valerie Clarie, was being added to my class list. Valerie was originally scheduled to be in Sarah's classroom, but Sarah was not comfortable with the placement and asked that she be moved. Valerie had brain cancer, and Sarah had her own issues with cancer and did not feel up to dealing with it. "Besides," Sarah added, "her mother is supposed to be a real nuisance."

I had no problems with receiving an additional student. I only questioned why the school had not notified me earlier in the day so that I could adequately prepare for her. I turned and went back to my classroom. After reorganizing the desks and pulling additional materials, I quickly made Valerie a name tag and left for the evening. I would have to remember to add Valerie's name to my checklists and attendance records. Why hadn't anybody told me?

I received official notification of Valerie's placement the next morning. It was in my mailbox, along with several articles from Mrs. Clarie, Valerie's mother, regarding children with cancer. I also found a message to call Valerie's hearing specialist, Mrs. Sheraton, as soon as possible. Unfortunately, it would have to wait until lunch. The children would be arriving in fifteen minutes.

Sarah stopped by just before the first bell to deliver a box of equipment assigned to Valerie Clarie. It had been given to Sarah by the special education resource teacher, Mrs. Dorsey. Sarah said that Valerie and I were supposed to wear it. I opened the box and looked inside. It was filled with wires, transmitters, attachments, and a battery pack charger. My confusion was interrupted by the first bell of school. Sarah hustled to her classroom and I closed the lid and placed the equipment with my other papers. Children and parents began wandering into the classroom. I walked out front to greet my students.

By the time the second bell rang, most of the children were sitting quietly and expectantly in their seats. I have rarely seen children be as dutiful and angelic as they are on the first day of school. I was just noticing that two of our seats were still empty when the back door of our pod opened. It was Mrs. Taylor. With her was a tiny, blue-eyed, blonde-haired little girl who looked on the verge of tears. It was Valerie. She had wandered into Mrs. Taylor's fifth grade by mistake. Now she was confused and unsure where she was supposed to be.

I welcomed Valerie warmly and showed her to her seat. I was turning to introduce myself to the children when we were abruptly interrupted by Mrs. Dorsey, the special education resource teacher, who came bustling into our classroom to see if I had received Valerie's equipment. I told her that a box had just arrived but that I had not had a chance to really look at it. Mrs. Dorsey informed me—and the class—that Valerie must wear this equipment right now or she would not be able to hear a word I said. The children were now staring at Valerie quietly. Mrs. Dorsey quickly shuffled Valerie and me out of the classroom and into the central pod area to get Valerie's equipment. (My new class was now totally unattended.)

Mrs. Dorsey opened the box and explained how the equipment worked. Valerie and I were both hooked up to transmitters. I wore a microphone, and Valerie wore earplugs. Valerie could adjust her transmitter as needed throughout the day. Both Valerie and I could turn our transmitters off when they were not needed.

Once the transmitters were in place, Mrs. Dorsey herded us back into the classroom. She introduced herself and proceeded to tell the children about Valerie's hearing equipment. She suggested that the children all take turns listening through Valerie's earplugs. Valerie, who had been very quiet through the entire ordeal, said, "No, it's not going to work." She still looked very much on the verge of tears. She sat very small and low in her seat, and I believed her to be embarrassed. Mrs. Dorsey then suggested that we try this another time and said she would come back later in the day. (She never did.) After Mrs. Dorsey's ten-minute interruption I finally began our first day.

Throughout the day, Valerie helped me learn how to use the transmitter. My role was mostly to remember when to turn it on and off. Valerie's job was to adjust the volume and watch for feedback. She adjusted hers frequently.

At lunch time I found two messages from Mrs. Sheraton in my mailbox asking me to contact her at the end of the day. Another teacher saw my transmitter and commented about "Mom" being a pain. I decided to skip lunch and headed toward the playground. I still did not know my way around the school.

As the day wound down, Valerie and I began to talk; mostly about Florida. Her mother had told her that I had just moved from Florida, and Valerie had been in

Florida a year ago courtesy of the Make a Wish Foundation. Valerie had photographs to show me of her trip to Disney World. Would I like to see them? Valerie pulled out her photographs and showed me a picture of her and her family. In the posed shot, they are huddled around Mickey Mouse. It looks like they are standing in Candy Land. Valerie explained the photo. Originally, she and her family were scheduled to reside in Cinderella's castle, "but somebody was supposed to die before I was, so we got to stay in the Gingerbread house instead." She is bald in all of her photos. The bell rang. It was the end of our first day.

The Classroom

The classroom contained twenty-seven students, all diverse, all with individual needs. Some needs were more obvious than others. Nadia had cerebral palsy, Greg was Samoan and had recently relocated from Hawaii, Nari was Cambodian and had spent time in a refugee camp. This was his third school in two and a half years. Jackson had a grandfather and uncle who disappeared during a vacation to Mexico the previous year. They were still searching for the bodies and some answers. Valerie had brain cancer. Although the tumor on her brain stem was discovered when she was in second grade, this would be her first full year back in the school system since being in remission. There were fourteen boys and thirteen girls. The ethnic/racial breakdown included one first-generation Mexican, two Hispanics, one Samoan, one Cambodian, one African American, and twenty-one Caucasians. Three students were pulled out of the classroom for the "gifted" program, four for "learning disabled" instruction, one for a remedial reading program, five for band, and two for student council.

The Curriculum

I am a whole language teacher.[6] My students spend a great deal of time reading and writing in an integrated workshop setting for authentic purposes. I rarely use prepared materials. The curriculum I create is based on my past experiences, professional readings, the grade level I am teaching, district mandates, and any known information regarding my students and their interests. It is usually negotiable and always flexible.

As the children begin their classroom inquiries and explorations the curriculum becomes predominately created and generated by the students.[7] In planning my curriculum, my main objectives are to be accountable for the school and district mandates, provide experiences and materials that accommodate each individual child's needs, to start each child where she or he is ready to begin, and to assist each child to go as far as he or she wants to go.

My curriculum is individualized.[8] I can usually accommodate any "level," interest, or circumstance. Social studies is integrated with language arts and presented predominately through literature-based instruction.[9] The morning is occupied with a daily picture book and discussion, personal journals, writing workshop,[10] and literature discussion groups.[11] The afternoon is set aside for individual inquiry, predominately in the field of science; however, science and math content are also integrated into the literature-based social studies curriculum.

Assessment and evaluation are based on portfolios, journals, projects, presentations, participation, essays, and informal teacher-made "tests," which usually take the form of a culminating activity using and demonstrating our explored content. My main criteria with my students are that effort, growth, and risk-taking are to be evidenced in their work throughout the school year. Anybody who tries, let alone tries their best, will have a personally and academically successful year.

The diversity of this classroom format allows us to remain united as a community, yet each child can pursue individual interests while working at her or his own academic pace and performance. I have worked within this framework for the past five years; always changing, always modifying.

Before moving from Florida, I piloted a mainstreamed multiage fourth/fifth-grade program using this same basic format. The class contained thirty-two children, who ranged in age from eight to twelve. Four of the children were "gifted" and six were "learning disabled." The "learning disabled" children were placed in a monitoring IEP (individual educational program) and mainstreamed, by parental request, for the first time in their academic careers.

The school, the children, the parents, and I were all pleased with how the class functioned and with individual results. I had no doubts that the same format, with modifications, would work with my new class here. My only concern was the population. Were these fifth graders different from fifth graders in Florida? What did they like? What was cool? I would eventually learn these things the same way I learned about each child . . . one day at a time.

Valerie

First Week of School (August 23–27)

Throughout the first week of school Valerie seems unsure of the role and expectations of the morning personal journals. Although it is always "free writing," an opened-ended prompt for those children who either request more focus or believe they have absolutely nothing to say that day is provided. Valerie is not generating her own topics. She has thus far responded only to the prompts. Her responses are very short, typically just one or two sentences. She appears to like drawing, and she draws frequently. Many pictures are copied or traced directly from a text. She has also stated that she does not like to write a lot in writing workshop: her arm gets tired and she does not know what to say.

I decided it best to start our literature discussion groups with Jon Scieszka's *Time Warp Trio* series. I could coordinate the chapter books with his picture books. I have yet to meet a child who does not appreciate Jon Scieszka. His books are perfect for modeling the procedures and expectations of the literature discussion groups. The chapter books are fairly short and very interesting, and most fifth graders can read them comfortably. Valerie chose Jon Scieszka's *The Knights of the Kitchen Table*.[12]

Valerie

Valerie has begun creating pictures for me at home. Some are crayon-colored drawings of flowers and rainbows. Others are collages of fabrics and textures. She has also created some stapled books containing drawings of scenes traced from *The Knights of the Kitchen Table.*

It is apparent that she loves the poetry and illustrations of Shel Silverstein. She has copied and illustrated three of his poems to share with our class. Her illustrated posterboards are hanging from the ceiling and on the walls of the classroom.

In math, we are working in small groups with cooperative group problems.[13] Each child has an integral role to play in completing the group's activity. Valerie not only participates fully, but quietly protests when her turn is skipped. She takes the group's directions and reminds them of the rules. The next day she is the group leader and shares her group's findings with the rest of the class. She is also working on completing our math chart of patterns. She is beginning to raise her hand to participate and guess at patterns during class instruction.

Valerie has noticeable difficulty remembering directions and multistepped instructions. Thankfully she is not afraid to ask me to repeat—four or five times, if necessary—what she needs to do or to reword instructions in a way that she can better understand. Frequently she will come up to me smiling and say, "What was that again?"

In the afternoons when we return from lunch, we take afternoon attendance before I read to the children from our ongoing chapter book. We don't begin reading until our attendance monitor returns so he or she does not miss any of the story. However, we've discovered that with her transmitter on, Valerie can walk to the office, deliver the attendance, and still hear our story. The kids think it's neat. The class has therefore appointed Valerie the official attendance monitor, responsible for taking the afternoon attendance to the office every day. She has also taken it upon herself to make sure that our lunch box basket gets returned to our classroom from the cafeteria. It apparently annoys her that everybody forgets.

She hates recess and says she gets too hot. She cannot wear her transmitter during PE or music because of the noise. She has also begun to shut it off when she is writing and I am working with other children.

Valerie finishes her first story in writing workshop this week. She shares it from the author's chair.[14] It is called *The Nosy Pig let*.

August 24, 1993

The Nosy Pig let

(first draft)

There once lived a pig let that was so nosy he didn't have any time to do anything else. when he did his math he was done at the same time because he saw all of the answers. at reading time he wanted to read after his friends. his name is Charlie. But people call him nosy! He is sad sometimes because people don't relly like him even no they pretend to. His friend's pretend to like him to! One day a girl named Sue was skating she fell down and hert her leg she couldn't get up. There was nobody around when she fell. Good thing Charlie was walking to school. Charlie found her laying on the ground. He picked Sue up he took her to his house and told his parents and he called the hospitle. The hospitle took good care of her! They found that she broke her leg, and sprang her rist. After every body found out what he did! Every body thanked him! The parent's thanked him to. Every body was Charlie's friend now, But Sue was Charlie's best friend.

The End

She is the first student to share her work. She is becoming very social, although she is quiet. It is the end of our first full week and I am pleased at her adjustment and proud of all my students.

Second Week of School (August 30–September 3)

Special education services begin this week. Valerie is pulled out for special education resource classes. She is gone frequently. She is no longer with us for literature discussion groups, although she has chosen to keep up her reading journal on her own. She compares her journal notes with her other group members, and she always shows me her responses to the text before she leaves for special ed. She is missing our morning picture books (we are reading Jon Scieszka and Lane Smith). Occasionally she is here for the latter part of writing workshop, but she leaves again prior to sustained reading.

I have twice had to leave my lunch to unlock our classroom door so that Valerie and Katie (classified as educable mentally handicapped [EMH]) can get their lunch boxes. Both children attend the same resource classes and they have gone over schedule. Valerie has also begun getting to PE about fifteen minutes late. She is no longer with us for science and social studies. I am told that this is noted on the IEP and that I am not accountable. That really is not the issue. How can I integrate curriculum when the children themselves are not integrated? They have a right to this education.

Whenever Valerie returns to the classroom she attempts to join our classroom activities. She is always helped by both me and her peers, but she appears frustrated, often not understanding what to do. Being removed from the classroom is causing Valerie to loose the context for her learning. There are too many gaps we are unable to fill in. She does not perform confidently nor to her ability when she is not participating and learning along with the other children. Oral directions and quick "catch-up" descriptions of what she has missed upset her. Twice, in frustration, she has cried. Although it is not required, she is insistent about wanting to do her regular class work. Currently she is working on making a geography book with a small group of her friends. Her group is almost finished and Valerie considers herself behind. She appears very concerned about this.

Because I do not teach specifically from the math text, my students are out of sync with the other fifth grades. For example, my class is not on page 16, problems 1–12. In fact, we are not in the text at all. This makes it difficult for Mrs. Dorsey to work with Valerie in her remedial math class. For the convenience of Mrs. Dorsey, all the learning-disabled students in Valerie's fifth-grade group need to be in the same place at the same time. Therefore, Mrs. Dorsey has decided that Valerie needs to go to Mr. Dale's fifth-grade class for math.

Wednesday, September 1, is the first day Valerie goes to Mr. Dale's for math. She leaves hesitantly. I don't think she likes changes. Although I assure her it will be fine, she has tears in her eyes when she leaves the room. She has so much to carry that one of her classmates offers to help her with her books. On September 2, her second day going to Mr. Dale's for math, she begins to cry. She is obviously very upset, and asks not to go. I send a note to Mrs. Dorsey informing her of the situation, saying that I am more than willing to keep Valerie with us for the afternoon. I explain Valerie's mental state and ask Mrs. Dorsey what she would like me to do. I can see no reason why Valerie should be forced to participate in an environment she finds threatening. She is not going to learn anything, and it is certainly not worth her getting upset. Mrs. Dorsey agrees that Valerie can stay with us for the day.

Valerie has also begun complaining about being tired and about leaving for resource classes in general. She says she is tired from all of the moving back and forth and would like to stay in one place. She is always lugging an armful of stuff (textbooks, notebooks, pencils, jacket, transmitters). She's actually very good-natured about the situation. Never have I observed her to be whiney or angry. She simply states her case and goes off on her rounds.

Mrs. Clarie calls me regarding this issue after school on September 2. (It is our first contact.) She is concerned because Valerie has so much to carry back and forth to resource classes. She wonders if it would be possible for Valerie simply to leave most of the materials in Mrs. Dorsey's room. Although Valerie is in remission, she still gets very tired. I assure her that I will speak to Mrs. Dorsey, but I am sure it will not be a problem.

Mom's second concern is Valerie's emotional state. Valerie has also begun crying at home. Her mother believes it is because Valerie does not like going to resource classes. Valerie comments on how little she sees me or is in class anymore. The friendships she has begun to establish in the classroom have had to be put on hold.

Although it may not be the first priority to most families or educators, friends are a new commodity for Valerie. Mrs. Clarie alludes to Valerie's postcancer school years as miserable and unhappy. When Valerie has been able to be with other children, she has been shunned and ridiculed. She has found little support from the school or the teachers. In fact, it appears that Mom considers the school's apathy one of the biggest problems. I assure Mom that I will work with Valerie whenever possible. I find Mrs. Clarie to be pleasant, reasonable, and concerned.

For a child that dislikes resource classes, Valerie masks her dislike very well. She is responsible for going back and forth to her classes on time. Often she reminds the other students when they are supposed to leave. She has also taken responsibility for putting both of our transmitters on the charger at night and handing mine to me in the morning when she enters the classroom.

In the afternoon, I am reading Roald Dahl's *Matilda*[15] to the children. Valerie laughs frequently. She especially likes the scenes that include Miss Trunchbull. She also enjoys our morning picture books. On the days that Valerie is with us she continually joins in the discussion and predictions. She particularly likes Alexandra Day's *Good Dog, Carl*.[16] She enjoys describing the scenes and creating the text for this wordless picture book with her classmates.

I have been notified that Valerie has a routine IEP meeting scheduled for September 14. This meeting will be attended by Valerie's IEP committee: the principal, resource teacher, classroom teacher, speech pathologist, hearing specialist, and parents. It is my understanding that Valerie's parents are divorced and that although there is joint custody, Valerie resides with her mother. Dad is expected to attend the meeting too. The purpose of the meeting is to review Valerie's work with the intention of formatting and modifying a plan of education for this year. Her IEP meeting is unfortunately scheduled for the afternoon that I have my first doctoral class of the semester at the university.

Valerie has been very successful in the regular classroom. Her portfolio shows that she is beginning to write consistently in writing workshop. She has participated in projects, group events, and presentations. Other than participating in literature discussion groups, which she is not present for, she has completed all of our regular class work, including math. Her work is as thoughtful and well prepared as, if not better than, that of her classmates. It puzzles me why this child needs to be pulled out for special education classes.

Socially, she has become one of the class favorites. She is usually one of the first children her classmates choose to sit by or work with in small groups. Many of the children inquire about the time of Valerie's return throughout the day. They have also become very protective of Valerie. In the classroom they have invented the "silent clap," a method of moving their hands so they can applaud their classmates' efforts without hurting Valerie's ears. On the playground they watch out for her.

When I ask Valerie what she does in her special education class, she shows me some papers and tells me she is in spelling group C, which is not as good as spelling group B, and she also does vocabulary flash cards. After thinking about it, she states that she is pretty good with the flash cards; she knows all of her words, but if she stops going there would be nobody else to flip the flash cards for her partner because everybody works in pairs.

Her pull-out instruction concerns me. Her resource papers predominately reflect isolated skill and drill in spelling and grammar. Valerie is also unable to elaborate verbally about her readings other than that they are little short stories she does not remember. Considering the richness of her work in the regular classroom, I feel Valerie is being cheated. She is capable of doing so much more.

When Mrs. Sheraton, the hearing specialist, arrives in the afternoon to work with Valerie I speak to her of my concerns and observations. Since Mrs. Sheraton was Valerie's hearing specialist last year as well, I expect she will be able to offer some perspective and insight into the growth and competence I have noticed. Her knowledge of the situation is certainly more extensive than mine, and I value her opinion. I would like to keep Valerie in the classroom full-time and I want her impressions. I believe Valerie's work is evidence of her ability. The classroom community provides her with support both socially and academically.[17] Rather than working on isolated skills, I prefer that we empower Valerie to formulate lifelong learning strategies she can employ every day. Mrs. Sheraton thinks it is a wonderful idea. She has noticed an extremely positive difference in Valerie's behavior this year, both socially and academically. I tell her that I will speak to the principal about it as soon as possible.

The following morning, I speak to the principal about my observations, Valerie's demonstrated class work, and her emotional well-being. The principal agrees with me 100 percent. She is pleased with my work so far, and has heard wonderful comments from both parents and their children. I point out that the IEP meeting has been scheduled for the afternoon I attend classes. Unless the date is changed, I will be unable to attend. Unfortunately, this is the best time for the majority of the others. I assure the principal that I will document Valerie's class work and behavior to support my recommendations to the IEP committee. I leave her office encouraged and pleased by the support and reinforcement I am receiving from the school.

Third Week of School (September 5–9)

On September 7 I type a two-page letter documenting Valerie's demonstrated growth based on her classroom work and behavior thus far. As accurately as possible, stating specifics, I portray Valerie as a conscientious learner and leader within our classroom community. In light of Valerie's excellent work and effort and her requests not to leave the classroom for resource instruction, I highly recommend that Valerie be placed in a monitoring IEP and mainstreamed into our regular classroom full-time.

I am more than willing and able to adhere to IEP guidelines. Individualization is built into our classroom format and curriculum. I have an elementary education degree and a masters degree in reading. I have relocated in order to pursue a Ph.D. in language, reading, and culture. I am taking courses while I teach. According to the IEP, Valerie's biggest "weakness" is in language arts, specifically reading. I feel more than confident that I will be able to help Valerie in this domain. I am certainly concerned about the type of special education instruction that Valerie is receiving compared to her demonstrated needs.

I submit a copy of my recommendation to the principal and the special education teacher, Mrs. Dorsey. The principal states that she wishes more teachers felt the way I do about keeping special-needs children in the classroom. I receive no feedback from Mrs. Dorsey. However, I pass Ms. Turner (Valerie's speech patholo-gist) in the courtyard. She mentions only that the principal has shown her a copy of my IEP letter. I also mention to Mrs. Sheraton that I have written a letter for the IEP committee and have submitted a copy to the principal and Mrs. Dorsey. I tell her that I am encouraged by the principal's support.

In the meantime, Valerie is becoming increasingly more unhappy when she leaves the room. Her tears when she returns are escalating.

Fourth Week of School (September 12–16)

On the morning of the IEP meeting I stop by the principal's office to discuss the afternoon's agenda. I sincerely hope that all will go well. It is becoming more important and more necessary with each passing day that Valerie remain in the classroom. I hope that tomorrow we will have good news. The principal again praises my position and assures me that things should work out fine. I leave for my university class feeling extremely hopeful.

I cannot wait to get to school the next morning. I am eager to find out what has transpired. Reaching my mailbox, I am disappointed and concerned. There are no copies of an IEP document for my signature or review. There are no memos nor messages. The principal and Mrs. Dorsey are not anywhere to be found. I have a previously scheduled meeting with the principal for ten-thirty. Its purpose is to give me feedback from my recent classroom observation. I will have to wait until then. Valerie demonstrates no noticeable difference in her behavior or conversation when she enters the classroom on first bell. Neither of us broaches the subject, and she leaves for resource instruction at her usually scheduled time.

At ten-thirty (my scheduled break time) I go to see the principal. I find out that the IEP commitee has determined that Valerie can stay with me for math but because she has missed so much school in the past, she still needs pull-out instruction in the language arts. I am extremely disappointed.

Two days later, on September 16, Mrs. Sheraton arrives at her scheduled time to work with Valerie in the classroom. All of the other children have left for the day and Valerie is sitting on the carpet, waiting. On entering, Mrs. Sheraton asks

Valerie to please leave the room with her book for a few minutes because she wishes to speak with me privately. Mrs. Sheraton then asks me if I know what happened at Valerie's IEP meeting. I repeat what the principal told me.

Mrs. Sheraton says that the principal's version is not quite accurate. According to Mrs. Sheraton, when she arrived at the IEP meeting at the scheduled time, the IEP was already filled out. After some pleasantries and introductions, Mrs. Dorsey went over the document with Valerie's parents. She explained what Valerie's weaknesses were, what her educational program would look like for the school year, and how it would be measured. Mrs. Sheraton sat quietly, waiting for my letter to be distributed and discussed. Mrs. Dorsey finished explaining the IEP to Valerie's parents and asked them to sign it, thereby agreeing to the proposed plan. At this point, Mrs. Sheraton quietly turned to the speech pathologist and asked about my letter. The speech pathologist shrugged her shoulders. The IEP continued. Documents were signed. Mrs. Sheraton left the meeting believing that either she had totally misunderstood me or that the school had intentionally buried my statement to the IEP committee and Valerie's parents.

The latter is true. They have buried my letter. I am confused and furious.

Fifth Week of School (September 19–23)

Over the weekend, I speak with many colleagues and professors about Valerie's situation. Everyone agrees that Mrs. Clarie had a right to full disclosure of the information. I dwell on it constantly. This is more than just an ethical situation regarding Valerie. This has to do with trust between me and the principal. It will mean confronting my peers and supervisors about lies and deceit. It is about placing my loyalties on the line. I am not sure I am prepared to do that. Apparently, Mrs. Clarie is comfortable with the situation. Perhaps it is not my place to make waves.

Our class has a field trip scheduled in two days that Mrs. Clarie will be chaperoning. I will be meeting her in person for the first time. I decide to keep an eye on Valerie and play it by ear. Personally, I am sickened by the hypocrisy and deceit I have been prey to. All the smiles and praise I have received from the principal now appear putrid. I will never again believe anything the principal says. My support crumbles. Regardless of my personal feelings, I decide it is best to remain quiet. This entire situation may blow over. Valerie's persona and well-being will have to be the deciding factor.

The day of the field trip arrives. Mrs. Clarie comes in to chaperone Valerie and Valerie's group. Other than some brief small talk when we are introduced, she hardly speaks to me. In fact, she appears a little perturbed. I am immediately relieved that I have not mentioned anything to her about Valerie and her IEP. There is no reason to have everybody angry with me.

The defining moment occurs the very next day. Valerie returns from resource instruction at the end of the day in tears. Mrs. Dorsey has told her that she needs to make up all the work she missed when she went on the field trip, plus the work she has missed while participating in DARE (the school drug prevention program) and BAT (the school first aid program). How can she keep up with her regular class work with all of this makeup? The thought of falling behind her classmates scares her.

On top of that, Ms. Turner, the speech pathologist has yelled at her. Valerie says it was a mistake. She was confused and didn't mean to do anything wrong. Apparently they were playing a game in a small group. Ms. Turner was asking questions, and each child was answering in turn. Valerie was not wearing her transmitter and could not hear well. The speech pathologist directed a question to Gina, and Valerie, mistakenly thinking it was her turn, answered the question. Valerie was yelled at for being rude and disrespectful and made to sit out the remainder of the afternoon session.

Valerie adds that Ms. Turner is frequently rude to Gina, an EMH child. She hurts her feelings; once she made Gina cry. Valerie says there is no way she would intentionally do anything to hurt Gina's feelings. People pick on Gina, and it makes Valerie feel bad. Valerie is one of the children who frequently protects her. This is the final straw. Valerie has had it. She does not want to leave the classroom anymore. I ask Valerie for Mom's phone number and tell her that I will call her mother that evening. She leaves the classroom, still crying.

I call Mrs. Clarie when I get home and leave a message on an answering machine. Mrs. Clarie promptly returns my call. Valerie has returned home in tears, the third time in less than a week. Mrs. Clarie is also concerned about Ms. Turner's apparent lack of compassion. This is not the first instance Valerie has reported. Mrs. Clarie says she has been so encouraged at the beginning of the year. It was the first time in Valerie's postcancer school career that she was happy and excited about going to school, but as she continued to be pulled out for resource instruction, her mood darkened. And, if the truth be known, Mrs. Clarie is a little disappointed in me, as well as in Valerie's teachers before me. She had hoped that I would want to keep Valerie in the classroom. She cannot understand a teacher being unwilling to work with her child. "Isn't that what teachers are for?"

I tell Mrs. Clarie the story behind the IEP. She knows nothing of my recommendation to keep Valerie in the classroom; nor has she been at all informed about Valerie's progress.

Mrs. Clarie adds that she is tired of fighting with people. She has to fight with doctors, agencies, and educators regarding the well-being of her daughter. This has not been her first run-in with the school. People are afraid of Valerie and her cancer. Last year, in an attempt to get services and support for her child, she became involved in a heated argument with the principal in which she had suggested the principal look up the word *educator* in the dictionary. After our extended conversation I tell Mrs. Clarie that I still want to keep Valerie in the classroom full-time. If this is what Mrs. Clarie and Valerie want, I will support their position. I believe it to be in Valerie's best interest socially, mentally, and academically. We agree to sit down and meet the following morning in my classroom.

Susan Clarie arrives at 8:30 A.M. I give her a copy of the IEP letter I had written requesting that Valerie be placed in the regular classroom. Mrs. Clarie brings me copies of Valerie's medical records. I inform Mrs. Clarie that as the parent of this child, she has the final say regarding placement, regardless of the school's position. Mrs. Clarie says the school has told her otherwise. She also says that she talked extensively with Valerie the evening before. Valerie is miserable. The child's life has been interrupted enough without this turmoil. It is their decision that Valerie remain in the classroom full-time. She will request another IEP meeting to discuss Valerie's placement immediately. I again assure her that I will support this decision.

Mrs. Clarie leaves my classroom to inform the principal. I wait for the other shoe to drop. At lunchtime I find a notice in my mailbox asking me to see the principal ASAP. She has talked with Susan Clarie and they have decided that it is in Valerie's best interest that she remain in pull-out resource classes. Mrs. Clarie has, however, voiced some concerns about Valerie's resource instruction. Therefore, I am to meet with Mrs. Dorsey so that I can assure Mrs. Clarie that Valerie's needs are being met.

I call Mrs. Clarie on my lunch break. She says the principal made her feel confused and guilty. She was told that it is understandable that she is reacting as a concerned parent. However, the schools are the professionals. They are best qualified to determine what is in Valerie's best interest. Putting her in my classroom full-time will be "pulling the rug out from under Valerie." She will certainly have problems next year when there will not be a sixth-grade teacher to accommodate her. The IEP committee has made a sound decision.

Although Mrs. Clarie still wants Valerie to remain in the classroom full-time, she no longer believes she has the power or the education to make that decision. Perhaps she is so eager to have Valerie happy and "normal" that she is overlooking Valerie's other needs. We agree to meet at three-thirty to discuss the situation.

Mrs. Sheraton is working in the classroom with Valerie when Mrs. Clarie arrives, so she joins our meeting. I have pulled much of Valerie's work from the school year, and I show Mrs. Clarie Valerie's strengths and abilities. Valerie is averaging all As and Bs in her course work. Although there are areas of concern, I feel confident that she will be successful in the classroom. Mrs. Clarie is amazed that Valerie is doing so well. Contrary to the school's position, it is quite obvious that Valerie's education is not being compromised for her happiness. She asks me if the school administrators are aware of Valerie's strengths. I tell her they have been informed; however, nobody has asked to see Valerie's work.

Mrs. Sheraton assures Mrs. Clarie that the parent has the final say regarding a child's placement. She tells her that part of the hearing specialist's services are to provide support and strategies that Valerie can use in tackling her schoolwork. Valerie and she can work on much of her schoolwork together. It is her position that Valerie should stay where she is happy and thriving.

Mrs. Clarie looks frustrated. Although Valerie's education is a priority, it is not the number one priority. Her child has survived a one-in-five-thousand chance of living. She cannot sit by and watch her child be miserable in school. It is Valerie's happiness and quality of life with which she is most concerned. She says she will send a letter to school with Valerie in the morning, again requesting that a new IEP be scheduled as soon as possible. She will also stipulate that Valerie is to remain in the regular classroom until placement is settled.

Valerie arrives at school the next morning carrying two letters from her mother. One letter is addressed to me, the other is addressed to the principal. They both state that Valerie is to remain in the regular classroom until a new IEP meeting is scheduled. The principal is out sick. The letter is left in her mailbox.

Valerie stays with us in the classroom for the entire day. She is particularly exuberant and asks other children if they want to listen through her earphones. In writing workshop she reworks her piece on her trip to Disney World through the Make a Wish Foundation. She has been "done" with it for a couple of days, but in our conference, I point out several places in her story that I would like to know more about. What did Space Mountain feel like? How was the ride? Valerie says that she would rather tell the reader that in person if they ask. She does, however, think she should probably add some details about the castle. She leaves to rework her story.

After reading her story to Mary and checking the spelling with Amy, she shows it to me. Her revisions are minor but encouraging. She has elaborated slightly on the appearance of the castle and corrected most grammatical and spelling errors. I am pleased that she has reworked this spot, even if she is just trying to humor me. She shares her story that afternoon from the author's chair. It is the first time Valerie has addressed the issue of cancer openly among her classmates. It is no longer a taboo subject.

During reading, Valerie chooses *Maniac Magee*[18] as her new literature discussion book. I hear her telling Mrs. Sheraton that she has read four chapters during sustained reading and that she thinks the book is funny.

In math, the children are creating long-division jigsaw puzzles. Valerie completes hers and shares it with her neighbors. She is obviously becoming more social and outgoing. I find her to be less hesitant and reserved. I believe she is allowing herself to become integrated into the community.

Sixth Week of School (September 26–30)

On Monday, September 26, the principal returns to school from her illness. I am feeling extremely nervous about my position with regard to Valerie. I get knots in my stomach as I drive into the school parking lot. The tension takes the form of avoidance. I check my mailbox that morning at times I know the teachers lounge to be quiet and the principal unavailable. I am careful about walking through the courtyard unnecessarily. I eat lunch in my classroom in an attempt to avoid any embarrassing confrontations.

I find it curious that staff members I hardly know are asking me about Valerie. The publicity this situation has received leaves me uncomfortable. I have been at this school for four weeks . . . and I feel like a pariah. I am mostly confused by this feeling of guilt and awkwardness. This conflicts so strongly with how the principal originally presented herself. She apparently fully supported my beliefs on mainstreaming children and holistic education. They had been our main topic of discussion during my interview some two months earlier. In fact, she hired me for them.

My evaluations from the principal's classroom observations have all been excellent. She has gone out of her way to tell me how pleased she is that I have joined their staff. She has even hugged me once and told me that if I ever have any problem at all to let her know. I am doing a great job and she will do what she can to keep her teachers happy.

I decide to approach the principal about this confusion with Valerie. She is obviously annoyed. Entering her office, I can't get a word in. A blur of phrases is spewed in my direction. I am pulling the rug out from under her. Valerie's mother has little to say in this matter. This is an IEP decision and Mrs. Clarie could be found negligent for interfering in what is regarded as Valerie's best interest. Valerie's mother also resides outside the school district. It is Valerie's father who lives within the district, and they were divorced before Valerie entered school. Dad needs to be making the IEP decisions. Perhaps they need to look at the fact that Mom is not paying tuition. I am also told that if Valerie is mainstreamed into my classroom she will no longer be able receive any of the other district services, such as Mrs. Sheraton and Ms. Turner. And Valerie will be out of luck next year, when they won't have a sixth-grade teacher to accommodate her and no services to help her.

I try to tell the principal that Mrs. Clarie only wants Valerie happy. She replies that Valerie is fine and is not going to die in the next couple of years. We have a responsibility to provide her with the services she qualifies for, or we'll be liable. She sarcastically dismisses Valerie's crying. She says the entire situation has been blown out of proportion.

I feebly attempt to explain that I am being made to feel that I am doing something wrong. This is an extremely unhappy child that I can work with in the classroom. I cannot tell a parent or a child that I won't help; especially when it is not only feasible but educationally sound. "This is not about egos," the principal replies. (I'm not sure whose ego she is referring to.) I leave her office. I receive a memo later that day instructing me to contact Mrs. Dorsey and work this thing out.

The hypocrisy is glaring. I have seen it often enough among administrators and whole language teachers with whom I have worked. Principals appear to love whole language teachers. Typically, they create wonderful curriculum, they're loved by the children and the parents, the success of their students is consistent, they write grant proposals, attend conferences, put on productions and events. But most administrators do not support whole language teachers with materials, nor do they like our philosophy or politics once we step out of our classrooms. As long as we remember our place within the school and the community, there won't be a problem. I have obviously crossed the line. The principal cannot even pretend anymore. Fortunately or unfortunately, I find that most whole language teachers live with the same integrity with which they teach. Advocating for a child against the school system is not a smart choice, but it is my only choice. My position here will apparently be short-lived. I write a cordial letter to Mrs. Dorsey suggesting that we meet.

Mrs. Dorsey returns my request to meet, stating that she has a full schedule until the following week. However, the decisions regarding what is best for Valerie have already been made by the IEP committee at the IEP meeting I chose not to attend.

This is fruitless. The only productive thing I can do at this point is prepare for our next IEP meeting and stay within the confines of my classroom. I focus on creating a systematic plan of action.

In order to help Valerie, I need to know more about her. I need to know her school history and her medical history. I also need to find out how and when she qualified for special education resources.

The second thing I need to do is document Valerie as a learner. It's important that I be able to provide a thorough picture of Valerie as a learner in my classroom.[19] This includes documentation of all of Valerie's work, both in and out of the classroom—journals, portfolios, reading logs, photographs, literature digs, field notes, artwork, student-teacher conferences, checklists, anecdotal records.[20] Specifically, I must look to see what it is that special education says Valerie cannot do and attempt to document through authentic classroom experiences Valerie's ability to perform these designated tasks. I need to counter the standardized measures with authentic classroom data.

I also need experienced help and feedback. Someone suggests that I read *Learning Denied*, by Denny Taylor.[21] None of my prior schooling or experiences have ever touched on the awkward situation I am now encountering. Taylor's book validates my experience and centers me. I know that she understands the hidden layers of this conflict: the seemingly senseless tension and intimidation trapped in this gray hypocrisy. I feel as if I am boxing shadows, facing an unknown enemy in a jester's mask. Perhaps I am making something more of this than need be. Can I be imagining things? How can there be animosity when everybody is smiling at me? But as my husband always says, "Just because you're paranoid doesn't mean you're not being followed." *Learning Denied* validates my experience. I pass a copy on to Mrs. Clarie.

Valerie's new IEP meeting is scheduled for October 14. That gives Mrs. Clarie and me two weeks to prepare. The first thing I want to do is view Valerie's school records. This is going to be awkward. All the children's records are kept in an office connecting with the teachers lounge and the secretaries working area. Student files may not be taken from this area, which is locked when school is over. So I have only short periods of time throughout the day to review Valerie's records, in full view of my superiors and colleagues.

I contact Mrs. Clarie. She agrees to request a copy of Valerie's school records the next day. She will pass the records on to me so that I can pore through them in hopes of piecing things together. I have many questions regarding Valerie's special education placement. She is such a strong student. How did this come about? I interview Mrs. Clarie.

This is what I find out:

Valerie was placed in special education at the end of March 1993. This decision was made because Valerie was failing fourth grade. Mrs. Clarie was requesting services and help from Valerie's school. She had missed numerous days throughout the year because of continued weakness and illness. It was becoming difficult for Valerie to keep up with her classmates.

On top of that, Valerie was being tormented in school. Children laughed at her and made fun of her. They would rip off her bandanna to expose her baldness and play Monkey in the Middle with it. Valerie would stand by crying. On several occasions she had been pushed into a bathroom stall and prevented from leaving. Mrs. Clarie demanded that something be done. As far as Mrs. Clarie knew, the situation with the children was never dealt with, although the principal assured Mrs. Clarie that the problem would be taken care of.

Academically, the school posed only two solutions: either Valerie could repeat the fourth grade, or she could be placed in special education pull-out classes. This intervention would prevent her from failing and provide her with additional services. Mrs. Clarie approved the placement.

However, none of Valerie's documentation regarding her special education placement is in her academic school folder. Where is it? I ask Mrs. Sheraton and Ms. Turner about Valerie's placement. Neither has any recollection of how Valerie was qualified. Both reply that the test results should be in Valerie's folder. On further investigation, neither can locate Valerie's documentation or tell me how Valerie's placement came about. Then Ms. Turner tells me about Mrs. Dorsey's personal file. Perhaps Valerie's test results are kept there. They are. I request copies. Valerie's IEP statements and scores for 1993–94 are based on tests that Mrs. Dorsey administered five months earlier, at the end of the previous school year. Valerie was officially tested for special education placement in May of 1993; two months after she was already attending special education classes. The school placed her immediately into special education on the basis of her "traumatic brain injury." Her educational program has been solely determined by, and based on, statements made by the doctors in Valerie's medical records.

While I am poring through Valerie's school records, it becomes extremely evident that this child has missed an incredible amount of school. Valerie's cancer was detected in March of 1991, the fourth quarter of second grade. In that quarter Valerie missed 38.5 days of school, bringing her second-grade absences to 49.5 days total. In third grade Valerie missed 128 days because of vomiting, weakness, and nausea caused by chemotherapy. (She was down to twenty-two pounds.) In fourth grade Valerie missed 65 days of school. Between the fourth quarter of second grade and the fourth quarter of fourth grade, approximately 405 days of school, Valerie had missed 231.5 days, to say nothing of the number of days she attended school incapacitated both before the tumor was detected and during and after treatment.

How much "school learning" has actually taken place in this child's education? Second, third, and fourth grade are critical learning years for school material. Between being sick and being tormented, how much of Valerie's core strategies and curricula has she actually received and/or processed? There is no doubt that Valerie requires some individualized attention. However, pulling her out further is not the answer. She has been out enough. This new information also opens up a whole new set of questions. What if Valerie's difficulties have more to do with her absences than actual dehabilitation from the cancer?

Obviously, removing the tumor caused some trauma and loss of some spatial competency. And the long-term effects of massive radiation and chemotherapy are still unknown. These concerns are predominantly evidenced in her handwriting, layout of math problems, and memory retention. However, these areas can be compensated for by providing Valerie with lifelong skills and strategies to help her continue to function successfully. Valerie also has a 40 percent hearing loss.

It is thus quite possible that Valerie's academic performance is predominately a hearing and an attendance issue. It is certainly not a learning disability issue. The distinction is important. It addresses Valerie's competency and reinforces her right to be educated to her full potential. We cannot dismiss this as the "best she can do because she had cancer," especially since she is showing progress.

The second issue to address is the assessment. I need to provide assessment that will be validated by the IEP committee. Valerie's IEP is particularly concerned with her reading ability. The resource teacher is pulling Valerie out for the following subjects: "Reading," "Spelling," "Written Expression," and "Whole Language English." (I believe the last subject speaks for itself.)

An IEP goal is to have Valerie reading at a mid-fourth-grade level. She has been reading and discussing *Maniac Magee* in literature discussion groups since she reentered our classroom. Although I don't believe in the validity or reliability of reading levels,[22] the school does. *Maniac Magee* is listed on the cover as being reading level 5.

Valerie's work with literature has been progressing nicely. In literature discussion groups she shares her journal entries and laughs with the other children about sections of the text. However, Mrs. Dorsey and the principal both state that because Valerie can read a fifth-grade literature book does not mean she can read a fifth-grade basal and answer the questions at the end. In fact, Mrs. Dorsey comments that "some questions actually place Valerie at a third-grade comprehension."

Unfortunately, accountability and test scores are what schools are about.[23] Yet caution needs to be exercised in the use and interpretation of these test scores.[24] The scores indicate only a small sample of the child's performance at one moment in time. Gardner[25] states that schools should get away from tests and the correlation among tests. Educators need to look at more naturalistic sources of information about how children develop skills that are important to their way of life. And, as Taylor[26] adds, "Thus, theory is balanced with practice to offer the beginnings of an alternative paradigm that can be used as a stepping-stone to the development of more humane evaluation procedures for use in school."

It is also obvious that the school is not valuing my opinion or my diagnosis of the situation. I find it curious that we are in the midst of deciding what is best for a child and not one person from the school has asked to see what Valerie has done or is capable of doing in the regular classroom. Nobody has asked to see her work; and nobody has allowed me to explain her strengths and her competencies. The silencing of my voice is alarming. Michelle Fine[27] writes:

> If the process of education is to allow children, adolescents, and adults their voices—to read, write, create, critique, and transform—how can we justify the institutionalizing of silence at the level of policies which obscure systematic problems behind a rhetoric of "excellence" and "progress."

Jerome Harste[28] echoes these concerns:

> In the past, schools seem to have been better at silencing children and teachers than at hearing them. Silent classrooms have been more than unfortunate; they have been wrong. In a democracy, the role of the school is to hear people, not to silence them.

It is obvious that I need to provide additional assessment. Dr. Prisca Martens, a friend and colleague from the university, agrees to administer a Reading Miscue Inventory[29] to Valerie. I hope that the RMI will not only provide me with information about the strengths and strategies Valerie uses to support her reading but that it may also refute the school's dim view of Valerie as a reader. The RMI proves helpful. Valerie's retelling of the story shows good general comprehension, as well as an ability to recall and state details of the story and story elements. (In fact, Valerie does so well at recalling details that it appears to adversely affect her ability to piece the story together as a whole.) However, only subtle inferences and cause-and-effect scenarios appear not to have been detected. Dr. Martens states:

> Valerie's understanding that reading needs to make sense and sound like language is sometimes overridden by her focus on graphic features in the text and her use of phonics. She would benefit most from an understanding of the reading process and semantic and syntactic reading instruction.

Valerie is very tied to the text, meaning that she is very conscious of *each* word and *every* word. Her only strategy for what to do when she comes to an unknown word is "look it up in the dictionary." It appears that contrary to the IEP statement, Valerie is too focused on details and parts of text. We need to work on how these parts come together to make the whole. As I had suspected, her isolated resource instruction has actually been detrimental to Valerie's learning. She has spent so much time looking at text and flash cards in isolation that she is having difficulty piecing it all together. These observations correspond to Valerie's medical records, which I have just received (the school used only the information in these records that supported their case). Here's the gist:

> In March 1991, after numerous headaches and bouts with clumsiness, a 3 cm tumor located in the region of the medulla was discovered. Valerie underwent a posterior fossa craniotomy with subtotal resection of a medulloblastoma from the fourth ventricle. Subsequently, Valerie received six weeks of radical radiotherapy, which involved maximum radiation to the posterior fossa. Following completion of the radiotherapy, Valerie received chemotherapy until March 1992.
> Effects of the radiotherapy and chemotherapy on Valerie's learning are still unknown. However, Valerie's 40 percent hearing loss is directly attributed to her treatment of the cancer, not the tumor itself.

Brain injury results in extreme problems of organizing, generalizing, integrating, and structuring information.[30] Instruction should therefore focus on how things fit together. Materials should be presented as a whole, not broken up into individual parts. This includes the constant need for associating new information with previously learned information.[31]

A student's language and communication skills may also be deceiving. A child may be able to communicate adequately on a surface level but be unable to provide details or complex explanations that indicate in-depth understanding. However, because a child does not demonstrate these competencies does not mean that these competencies do not exist.[32]

Guidelines also include the optimum classroom environment as well as the classroom curriculum and child's preferred methods of learning. It has been determined that because of the effect brain injury has on affective functioning, curriculum is also needed to meet the emotional and social needs of the brain-injured child, specifically in the areas of self-advocacy, acquiring and maintaining friends, and understanding one's current level of functioning.

Valerie's tiny size is also a result of her cancer treatment. The amounts of radiation and chemotherapy that Valerie received stopped her growth. Her body can no longer produce the hormones that Valerie needs to grow. She is approximately the same size she was in second grade. Daily hormone injections could be given to promote Valerie's growth; however, the injections could cause leukemia or reinstate the cancer.

Seventh Week of School (October 3–10)

The children are working on publishing their snapshot stories. Valerie has finished hers and volunteers to show Nari how to put his together. Valerie uses her book as a model to make sure that she shows Nari correctly. Valerie stays with him until he is finished, showing him where to get the publishing materials and making sure he does it correctly. Nari has missed most of our instruction because of his recent placement in resource instruction for "learning disabilities." (I did question Nari's placement as perhaps being a language and/or cultural issue. I was told that he is learning disabled in Cambodian as well. A person can only fight so many battles at a time.)

In class, Valerie "acts out." She chases Kara around the desks with a ruler. She is intentionally being very funny and silly, making the other children laugh. Bobby and a couple of other children comment on how feisty Valerie's getting. "Boy, Valerie," Bobby says laughing, "you've changed!"

I have again been summoned to a meeting after school with Mrs. Dorsey and the principal. Earlier this week I have been verbally accosted and "put in my place" by my podmate and school leader Sarah. She has heard about the RMI and cannot believe I have had the nerve to bring Dr. Martens into the school. She furiously states that I have absolutely no right to force this issue any further. I have already stepped over my bounds. "Who do you think you are anyway?!" She then storms away. I am shocked and dismayed by her outburst.

The afternoon meeting is more of the same. I am again informed of the error of my ways. Rebuttals are spewed before I can finish statements. Things have been very well choreographed, and it becomes very obvious that I am here solely because they have been forced to deal with me. I could have said that Valerie has a twelfth-grade reading level and it would not have mattered. In fact, I could have sent a stand-in. It apparently does not matter what Valerie is doing in my classroom. I have an "individualized program." In their minds, that apparently negates all credibility for the "real" classroom. Accommodating children assumes that my classroom is easier or compromised. Pabulum. This is not only offensive to me, as the teacher, but to my children as well. It appears we are beginning to negate everybody's learning.

Valerie's unhappiness is again dismissed as an isolated event that "Mom blew out of proportion." The principal states that Mom continually changes her mind regarding Valerie and that this was another such reaction. I am told that Mrs. Clarie runs hot and cold. What she says or insists on today may be different from what she says tomorrow. The school needs to protect itself from her frequently changing points of view and decisions. Decisions that blow with the wind. The school has a legal responsibility that Mom does not care about or recognize. She is only thinking about her child long-term. What happens when Valerie gets sick again or enters sixth grade?

The intent of the meeting is to ensure that we will all enter the IEP meeting on the fourteenth united. It is evident that we are here to become "friends" and work this out. It is also evident that this is an attempt to appease me. Yet not once am I asked about my observations or evaluations regarding Valerie. I sit while I am told what Valerie's needs are and what they are going to do about them.

It seems ridiculous for me even to point out that these people have no idea who Valerie is, nor does their statistical profile of Valerie as a learner have any credibility. Their profile is based on two sheets of standardized test results taken six months earlier under inopportune conditions. I have Valerie's actual work. It really concerns me that they do not want to hear about Valerie's academic or social progress. If they want to see Valerie as a learner they need to look at Valerie's work from this semester or step into my classroom and see for themselves.

It is again determined that Valerie will not be mainstreamed full-time. I can keep Valerie (it sounds like a custody battle) for "written expression," but she definitely needs isolated reading skills. However, the school will compromise. Valerie will go to Mrs. Dorsey two or three times a week. She will be pulled out in the afternoons, so she does not have to move back and forth between classrooms as much.

There is nothing professional, respectful, or academically sound about this. It is patronizing. We have made some gains, but not for the right reasons. This still has nothing to do with Valerie's work or abilities. Unfortunately, I think that the compromise is the best we can do. I call Mrs. Clarie when I get home.

Mrs. Clarie says that Valerie is like a different child. She is happy, she has friends, and she is sleeping nights. Valerie's psychologist has also noted the change, and will be writing a statement to the IEP committee requesting that Valerie remain in the classroom full-time. Both Valerie's doctors and her psychologist recommend that Valerie's placement be the regular classroom. A normal situation, and normalcy in her life, are most important.

I explain to Mrs. Clarie about the meeting with the principal and Mrs. Dorsey. Mrs. Clarie says she will agree to their stipulations if:

1. Valerie is pulled out only at the end of the day.
2. The pull-out totals only one hour a week.
3. Valerie's work in the resource classroom is documented.
4. Valerie's personality does not revert to unhappiness and withdrawal.
5. This new placement is reevaluated in January to establish if it is still deemed necessary.

Mrs. Clarie also tells me that the school has again brought up the issue of tuition. The Claries live in an apartment complex near school. Their apartment is approximately fifty feet short of the district line. Mrs. Clarie has asked other families in her complex whether they had been contacted about tuition. They have not. In the seven years that Mrs. Clarie has had children attending this school, tuition has never been an issue.

We both surmise that this compromise is probably the best we can do. I report Mrs. Clarie's reaction to the school. I am to meet again with school personnel on the thirteenth, the day before the IEP, to finalize times and plans regarding Valerie.

Seventh Week of School (October 13)

The meeting on the thirteenth is held after school in Mrs. Dorsey's room. Present are Mrs. Dorsey and Ms. Turner. Curiously, the principal does not attend. The meeting begins with the usual list of Valerie's deficits and needs. I again interrupt to question the validity of their data. I am stopped. Valerie is no longer going to be pulled out of the classroom. After reviewing the situation, they have determined that Valerie will remain in the regular classroom full-time. She will be placed in a monitoring IEP and continue to receive the services of Ms. Turner (in the regular classroom) and Mrs. Sheraton (after school). She will be monitored by Mrs. Dorsey but receive no instruction from Mrs. Dorsey. In the spring, Valerie will begin to be pulled out for sixth-grade strategies and detail comprehension. Valerie will also need to be drilled for literal comprehension, particularly of content text reading. End of meeting.

The Last Week of the School Year (May 25)

Valerie was officially mainstreamed into our classroom in a monitoring IEP on October 14, 1993. She completed her first quarter of school on the A/B Honor Roll. She has made Principal's List the remaining three quarters. She is ecstatic.

Valerie has been monitored by Mrs. Dorsey in spirit only. Never has she come to observe Valerie in our classroom. Valerie has been pulled out periodically toward the end of the school year by Ms. Turner. Although the pull-out was to be in the afternoons to avoid interruptions, Ms. Turner has not adhered to this schedule. Valerie has been pulled out in the middle of lessons.

It has been determined that Valerie will be in Mrs. Cummings's room for sixth grade. Mrs. Cummings is new to the school also. Throughout the year her classroom has been active with projects and activities. It appears very hands-on. It is hoped that this placement will best support Valerie as a learner. Valerie will remain in a monitoring IEP and will be entering Mrs. Cummings's classroom next year with nine of her current classmates.

Reflection

Valerie is everybody's child. We have more Valeries in our school system than I care to imagine. Oh, your child may not have brain cancer or some other medical condition; perhaps she just has a dialect; perhaps he learns in a different way; maybe you're just "poor." We all have this wonderful fantasy that schools are here to help our children. The reality is that schools have very little to do with the children at all. They are a government institution that is as political and full of bureaucracy as any other government agency. Schools are about numbers and policies and the standards of our children comparatively. They are not about your individual child, just as this situation was not about Valerie. She very blatantly was not even part of the picture.

Taylor[33] points out profoundly that "more than 80 percent of our student population could be classified as learning disabled by one or more definitions presently in use." Furthermore, "Based upon records of those already certified as learning disabled and those not, experienced educators could not tell the difference." In the 1980s, children labeled as learning disabled had grown by 135 percent from the previous decade.[34] The educational paradigm embraced by most special educators is not only suspect but self-perpetuates their field. If something is not found wrong with your child, a lot of people will be unemployed—not to mention the federal funding that each school will not receive for their special education programs.

It is not surprising that special education has become a critical need. It appears that our solution is to label children rather than educate them. We build prisons instead of better schools. Ironically, literacy has been a number one concern in this country. If literacy is a problem, then shouldn't language art specialists be the critical need? It is also not surprising that reading and language difficulty is the most widespread and persistent problem experienced by children labeled as learning disabled.[35] On the whole, most undergraduate education programs (elementary education as well as special education) require and provide only one course in reading and language arts. That educators are designing programs for children with reading difficulties based on outdated paradigms is frightening. Valerie's situation raises some important questions and issues:

• What are the rights of our children and parents within the school system?
• Where do teacher loyalties lie, with the school or with the child?
• How can we maintain quality education in our school system when concerned educators are being silenced and destroyed?

- What resources other than labeling are available in our school system?
- How valid are the special education testing measures that are used to diagnose our children?
- What happens when teachers and parents question the school system?
- What laws are there to support children's learning? Who do you turn to when these laws are broken?
- How do whole language classrooms support children of varying needs?
- How important is community to a child's learning?
- What is it that we really want for our children in the schools?
- What is learning? What is knowledge? What is literacy?
- And most important, what is it that *you* would want for *your* child in the classroom?

I am troubled by school districts and programs that implement standard policy for students but forget about the child. We need educators who will reflect on institutionalized policies and procedures and question their appropriateness for each child. We need to support educators within the school system so that they can use their expertise and experience to provide appropriate education for all children. We need to open up dialogue and communication so that questioning educational decisions is not viewed as threatening and intimidating. School systems appear to be as partisan as the federal government. We need to break down these walls. When we silence our teachers, we silence our children. Educators must rise above the pettiness and truly work for the child.

This is not the end of Valerie's story, for Valerie's story has no end. Problems with the school continue. Valerie's monitoring IEP is not being followed, and her learning style is not being accommodated. State officials have been contacted, and state mediation may be necessary.

Valerie is sitting in school today, still struggling, still negated. Last week, while trying to complete her homework, Valerie put her head down at the kitchen table and cried. "Maybe I should have died," she said.

Last year in her journal Valerie wrote that she wants to be "a lawyer, or artist, or veterinarian, or a baby-sitter, or a baby doctor." This year she just wants to finish sixth grade.

I am no longer at that school. I resigned my position at the end of the school year and am working on my doctorate and teaching an undergraduate language arts methods course at the university. At the principal's request, I amended my resignation to a one-year leave of absence. My end-of-the-year evaluation contained all "superiors"; it is one of the best I have ever received. Yet I cried during that meeting with my principal. I told her that I had never in my life taken so much shit for trying to help one child. I will be searching for a new teaching position in the fall. I cannot return to this school. Fortunately, I am in a position to change my circumstances, take alternative options. Many adults are. Valerie can't.

Endnotes

1. Valerie and I maintained a personal dialogue journal throughout the latter part of the school year. Because Valerie often would not share her feelings or concerns in person, the journal allowed me to ask questions she could choose to answer or ignore. I gave the journal to Valerie in January. Each page contained a question I was curious or concerned about. It was a tool for her to communicate if she wanted to. **2.** Valerie Clarie had a brain tumor when she was seven. Brain tumors occur most frequently in young children and young adults to age twenty (M. Morra and E. Potts, *Choices* [New York: Avon Books, 1994]) and are second only to lymphoreticular malignancies in incidence of all childhood cancers. Over the past twenty years there has been a slow but consistent increase in the rate of survival for children with brain tumors (R. Packer, *Neurocognitive Outcomes in Children with Primary Central Nervous System Tumors* [Rochester, NY: University of Rochester Medical Center, Hematology-Oncology Educational Liaison Program, 1991]). The long-term prognosis for children with brain cancer has therefore improved dramatically (R. B. Noll, *Peer Relationships of Children with Cancer* [Rochester, NY: University of Rochester Medical Center, Hematology-Oncology Educational Liaison Program. 1991]). Valerie is not alone. Over one million children in the United States sustain brain injury each year (Colorado Dept. of Ed., Guidelines Paper: Traumatic Brain Injuries [Denver: Colorado Dept. of Ed., 1991] and M. Mira, J. Tyler, and B. Tucker, *Traumatic Head Injury in Children: A Guide for Schools* [Kansas City: University of Kansas Medical Center, Children's Rehabilitation Unit, 1991]). Many of these injuries are severe enough to leave temporary or permanent damage. Our school systems are the primary and sometimes exclusive provider of long-term services for the brain-injured child, and we are failing these children miserably. Survivors of cancer must now survive the school system. **3.** B. S. Fennimore, *Child Advocacy for Early Childhood Educators* (New York: Teachers College Press, 1989). **4.** T. R. McMahon, "On the Concept of Child Advocacy: A Review of Theory and Methodology," *School Psychology Review* 22 (4): 744–55 (1993). **5.** The school is divided into "pods" by grade level. Each pod contains four separate classrooms of the same grade. These classrooms share a common storage/work area located in the center of the pod classrooms. **6.** For an understanding of whole language philosophy, see K. Goodman, *What's Whole in Whole Language?* (New York: Scholastic, 1986). **7.** Inquiry-based education is discussed in K. Short and C. Burke, *Creating Curriculum: Teachers and Students as a Community of Learners* (Portsmouth, NH: Heinemann, 1991). **8.** H. D. Dell, *Individualizing Instruction* (Chicago: Science Research Associates, 1972). **9.** K. Short, "Moving Towards a Literature-Based Curriculum: Problems and Possibilities," in *Under the Whole Language Umbrella: Many Cultures, Many Voices*, edited by A. Flurkey and R. J. Meyer (Urbana, IL: National Council of Teachers of English, 1994). **10.** For information on writing workshop and journals, see N. Atwell, *In the Middle: Writing, Reading, and Learning with Adolescents* (Portsmouth, NH: Boynton Cook, 1987), and D. H. Graves, *Writing: Teachers and Children at Work* (Portsmouth, NH: Heinemann, 1983). **11.** Literature discussion groups (format and philosophy) are discussed in J. C. Harste, K. G. Short, and C. Burke, *Creating Classrooms for Authors: The Reading-Writing Connection* (Portsmouth, NH: Heinemann, 1988); R. Peterson and M. Eeds, *Grand Conversations: Literature Groups in Action* (New York: Scholastic, 1990); and K. G. Short and K. M. Pierce, *Talking About Books: Creating Literate Communities* (Portsmouth, NH: Heinemann, 1990). **12.** J. Scieszka, *The Knights of the Kitchen Table* (New York: Viking, 1991). **13.** The problems were taken from *Equals* (Regents of the University of California, Lawrence Hall of Science, 1987). **14.** D. H. Graves and J. Hansen, "The Author's Chair," *Language Arts* 60: 176–82 (1983). **15.** R. Dahl, *Matilda* (New York:

Puffin Books, 1988). **16.** A. Day, *Good Dog, Carl* (New York: Green Tiger Press, 1985). **17.** Issues of community are discussed in R. Peterson, *Life in a Crowded Place* (Portsmouth, NH: Heinemann, 1992); and A. Dyson, *Multiple Worlds of Child Writers: Friends Learning to Write* (New York: Teachers College Press, 1989). **18.** J. Spinelli, *Maniac Magee* (New York: Little, Brown, 1990). **19.** D. Taylor, *From a Child's Point of View* (Portsmouth, NH: Heinemann, 1993). **20.** R. S. Hubbard and B. M. Power, *The Art of Classroom Inquiry: A Handbook for Teacher-Researchers* (Portsmouth, NH: Heinemann, 1993). **21.** D. Taylor, *Learning Denied* (Portsmouth, NH: Heinemann, 1991). **22.** See I. L. Beck, M. G. McKeown, and E. S. McCaslin, "Does Reading Make Sense? Problems of Early Readers," *The Reading Teacher* 34: 780–85 (1981); and P. D. Pearson, "The Effects of Grammatical Complexity on Children's Comprehension, Recall, and Conception of Certain Semantic Relations," *Reading Research Quarterly* 10: 155–92 (1974–75). **23.** D. Elkind, *The Hurried Child: Growing Up too Fast too Soon* (Reading, MA: Addison-Wesley, 1981). **24.** J. W. Lerner, *Children with Learning Disabilities* (Boston: Houghton Mifflin, 1971). **25.** H. Gardner, *Multiple Intelligences: The Theory in Practice* (New York: HarperCollins, 1993). **26.** D. Taylor, *From a Child's Point of View* (Portsmouth, NH: Heinemann, 1993), p. 12. **27.** M. Fine, "Silencing in Public Schools," *Language Arts* 64 (2): 157–74 (1987). **28.** J. Harste, Introduction to *Jevon Doesn't Sit at the Back Anymore*, by C. White (New York: Scholastic, 1990). **29.** Y. Goodman, D. Watson, and C. Burke, *Reading Miscue Inventory: Alternative Procedures* (New York: Richard C. Owen, 1987). **30.** Colorado Dept. of Ed., *Guidelines Paper: Traumatic Brain Injuries* (Denver: Colorado Dept. of Ed., 1991). **31.** Ibid. **32.** A. Akmajian, R. A. Demers, A. K. Farmer, and R. M. Harnish, *Linguistics: An Introduction to Language and Communication* (Cambridge, MA: MIT Press, 1993); and N. Chomsky, *Aspects of the Theory of Syntax* (Cambridge, MA: MIT Press, 1965). **33.** D. Taylor, *Learning Denied* (Portsmouth, NH: Heinemann, 1991), p. 6. **34.** S. Forness, "Reductionism, Paradigm Shifts, and Learning Disabilities," *Journal of Learning Disabilities* 21 (7): 421–24 (1988). **35.** J. S. Kuder, "Language Abilities and Progress in a Direct Instruction Reading Program for Students with Learning Disabilities," *Journal of Learning Disabilities* 24 (2): 124–27 (1991).

Denny: Let's try to think of this from the perspective of teachers reading this book; we want them to imagine themselves in the situation you were in. You were a new teacher in the school, with a new classroom and then at the very last minute a new child that you had not had time to prepare for, had not met. You hadn't met the other kids either, but you had their files, you knew who was in your room. You had your list, your books, so you were able to get ready.

DEBBIE: Right. I was able to get all their journals, all their desks put together, everything like that.

Denny: So the classroom is ready for the children to come in and then you learn there's a new child. What was that like?

DEBBIE: It wasn't a problem for me as a teacher to have one more child. It was curious why they did not tell me, because I had been there all day. Especially a child that obviously, as it turned out, had special needs. Apparently, Valerie's mother, Sue, was notified about the change two days before I was. Sue had spent all summer preparing Valerie for her fifth-grade teacher to help assure a successful happy year. And then the teacher Sue prepared her for wouldn't take her. Sue now had to prepare Valerie for her second teacher, which was me. The entire day before school started Valerie and Sue were with Valerie's psychologist, because Valerie was in tears. She did not know me, and she was scared. So the school had time to make arrangements. My only concern was why had I not been told so that I could adequately prepare for this child? Especially since she had problems in school before with peer relationships and feeling as if she didn't belong. Moving her in at the last minute, it didn't seem like she was a part of the community that had been established, even though the children weren't yet in the classroom. There was no care on the school's part to create a welcoming, prepared environment for Valerie. It was given no thought.

Denny: She's in your room and you know that she's a child with special needs and she's working and you're looking at her literacies and her work that she's doing. What were your expectations?

DEBBIE: I didn't have any. In fact I didn't even pay that much attention to the fact that she had cancer or special needs, other than that I didn't want her to feel like an add-on. I had several kids with special needs. I had the child with cerebral palsy; I had Nari, who had been in Cambodian refugee camps. And I believe all children have their special needs. And I don't make any prejudgments. We just started the school year, and I figured things would pan out as the year progressed and I would discover what each child needed as we went along. So, I didn't really focus on

Valerie as, Wow, I have this child with cancer, what am I going to do? I figured I had twenty-some children, all with special needs, and it would just come out in the wash as we worked within the format of our classroom structures. So I didn't really have any concerns. I didn't think there would be any problems. I had worked with children with all different levels of special needs before, so I figured we'd just adapt as we needed to adapt.

Denny: When did you become concerned?

DEBBIE: When I realized that the school had lied to me about their position—about Valerie's education and about her as a learner. That was my first clue that I could not trust the school.

Denny: How was she presented to you as a learner?

DEBBIE: Well, they didn't present her to me as a learner at all, actually. They never presented her to me as a learner until we got into the whole controversy. I never had any records on Valerie that I looked at, and during the second week of school she started to be pulled out for special ed, and that was the first time I even knew she was a special ed student receiving pull-out instruction.

Denny: And her work in the classroom?

DEBBIE: Her work in the classroom was fine. She was doing beautifully. Her hearing issue we were dealing with. Then she started being pulled out for special ed. And when I saw what she was doing in the classroom and talked to the principal about it, I didn't think there was a problem until I realized that those documents weren't talked about at the first IEP meeting. And then the portrait of Valerie was shown to me. It was their handling of that meeting that told me, This is what she does, this is what she can't do, this is what her capabilities are, and this is what we need to do for her. It was the first time anybody had ever presented me with a picture of her as a learner.

Denny: And those interpretations were based on?

DEBBIE: The private neuropsychological report from the doctor.

Denny: So these are all official texts?

DEBBIE: Yes. And then after, they used the neuropsychological report to automatically place her. After she was in special ed pull-out for the two months at the end of the year, she was then tested for special education and qualified. So they used the neuropsychological test to place her, pulling chosen sentences from the report out of context, and then they used their tests to keep her there. And then her test results were used as a diagnosis as to how her school plan would look for the next year. So her curriculum was also being determined based on these official measures and statements. Based on this she will be doing this. So it was all official print.

Denny: And the official print didn't jibe with what was happening in the classroom?

DEBBIE: No. Valerie looked like two totally different people. She looked very deficient and inadequate in the official print. There was nothing that showed any of her strengths or capabilities. It was all about what she could not do. And that was the only picture that Mom had of her as a learner, also. So Mom thought there were obviously deficits that needed to be taken care of in special education.

Denny: So there's the official documentation giving one picture, and then there's the print that Valerie is producing in class that is giving you a totally different picture?

DEBBIE: Right. And it was all informal print—authentic print: her journals, her class work. Nothing was done as official print, like a portfolio, because I didn't realize that was necessary at that time. Fortunately, my classroom is set up so that we use journals and portfolios, and I was able to go back and pull things and say, Well this doesn't make sense according to what I see right here and what is being said over there.

Denny: And this is a form of advocacy. As you're looking at one form of documentation and then looking at another and seeing comparisons as you're moving back and forth between them trying to understand what's happening, that provides, am I right, the opportunity for Valerie?

DEBBIE: As it turns out, that was advocacy. But I do that for all my children. So it's part of my job as a teacher. It got named as advocacy once there was a controversy.

Denny: Which is an interesting statement—you do this for all of your kids and that's what teachers do, yet we don't always think of teachers as advocates.

DEBBIE: Right. It did not get named as advocacy though until the controversy.

Denny: But what you did was advocacy.

DEBBIE: Right. But assessing is apart of advocacy for the children, and it's a teacher's job. It's part of my role. I mean, how can we negotiate curriculum with the children or even help create strategies if we don't look at what they are actually doing now? So it's an ongoing process of kidwatching all year long.

Denny: Not just kidwatching . . .

DEBBIE: And assessing, thinking. And I was watching too, watching her come and leave and the work she was doing in special ed.

Denny: And documenting.

DEBBIE: Unofficial documenting. Other than anecdotal notes, a lot of it was up in my head. I didn't think there was a reason to document most of it in print at that point.

Denny: You documented when you wrote a report. You were taking notes on Valerie when you put the biographical profile together.

DEBBIE: I have field notes on all my students.

Denny: So the field notes are there, you're taking them on all your kids, and here's a situation where you need those field notes.

DEBBIE: I had a reason to use them for purposes outside the classroom. But I had field notes on all the children. This just happened to be a situation where they came in handy for more than informing me, the teacher. It's part of the classroom practice.

Denny: Sometimes when I talk with teachers about documenting kids' learning, I try to emphasize the importance of doing the documentation whether or not you're going to use it in any specific way, because you just don't know if it will become useful. You might have used the documentation on three or four kids that year. But that documentation is there for you to use for instructional purposes as well?

DEBBIE: And I use it because I don't like to use the official school assessments, and I need to find alternative ways to document what the kids are doing when it comes time for the accountability and the report cards and all that school nonsense where you have to give actual numbers. In the school district I'm in, we have to use numerical grades, like a grade of eighty-eight for writing workshop, which is ridiculous. It's contradictory to the philosophy and community of risk-takers I try to create in the classroom. But I have to have documentation in some form to base and support how I came to this report card grade. And without using the official assessments, this is the most accurate way of substantiating and legitimizing how I came to this number on the report card. And actually, it isn't just me. The children and I come to their grade together. But at least it is something to verify how this grade was created.

Denny: So it has multiple purposes.

DEBBIE: It's my way of being accountable for what I'm doing. Not for being accountable in the classroom, but for justifying the fact that there is accountability in the classroom and I'm able to speak about what the children are doing individually and where they seem to be at any given time and what strategies they need to work on. It's kind of my way of proving that I know what I'm doing.

Denny: You used the documentation you were doing to put together a report that you presented at an IEP meeting. How do you think the school used that? Was it as legitimate as the neurological testing?

DEBBIE: No. The school didn't use it. The first letter I wrote inquiring about having Valerie remain in the classroom and questioning why she needed to be pulled out and documenting her strengths based on what I saw, that was the letter that was buried and never presented. At the end of the year I did a major documentation letter for Valerie's sixth-grade teacher addressing what I saw might be Valerie's future needs, and some of the things that I was concerned about, and some of the strategies that had helped. I was told that was not to be placed in her folder. It was not an official document and it could not go in her folder. It was not placed in her folder until her mom insisted.

Denny: So you learned something about which documents count?

DEBBIE: A teacher letter of that nature is not an official document. And if it wasn't for Valerie's mother's insistence, it would not be there. However, her sixth-grade teacher did contact me and said it was the most valuable piece of print she had seen on Valerie because it actually helped her as classroom teacher. She could look at it and say, Oh good, graph paper for math, that's a good idea. Oh, a file box to record steps or procedures in math or outlining, we'll do that. It contained real-life things that could be done for Valerie. The school did not want that in her folder.

Denny: It wasn't just things that could be done for her. It also listed things that Valerie could do?

DEBBIE: It listed all of the books that she read that year. It talked about some of her strengths that I saw, and it also talked about some of the concerns. So it was fairly well rounded. It also mentioned my concern that nobody had asked to see her work all year long except for her special ed work and the official test scores. I think that was seen as being very offensive.

Denny: What did you learn from all of this?

DEBBIE: I learned to approach how I interact with school officials differently. I was very naive about the school situation. I was working from the purest of intents, really, and I assumed the school was doing the same. And what I learned was that the school does not also function with the intent of helping the child. The school is very political and has it s own political situation. And this was a very political situation. There was a lot of animosity in the past between Valerie's mom and the principal. So this was not a professional interaction, it was a personal interaction, and unfortunately, this was what was going to make or break Valerie in the school district. So in the future I won't go naively barreling in thinking that they're all there to help me support this child, because that was not the case.

Denny: If you were sitting down with a teacher who has prepared her class-room and meets someone in the parking lot who says, By the way, you're getting another kid tomorrow who has difficulties similar to Valerie's, what advice would you give?

DEBBIE: I would tell her not to read any of the child's official documents but just to watch and see what she does. I think this is most important: for teachers to make up their own mind, not to go back and look at what the school's record of a child is. Make your own assessment. If there is something you think is harming the child or interfering with her learning, personality, or self-esteem, then approach the school. But I don't look at any of the official records of my children prior to school. I have all of their records available to me, but I don't look at them.

Denny: But doesn't there come a point where you have to go into that folder to show that the information in it is sometimes inaccurate?

DEBBIE: That came up with Valerie, but not with every child. Rarely do I have a need to look through a child's official school folder. Their past is usually not relevant to me. This is a new year, a new situation.

Denny: If you had it to do over . . .

DEBBIE: I wouldn't be that emphatic about meeting with the principal. I would take Valerie's work with me and go to the special ed teacher directly and say, Look at what I see Valerie doing in the classroom. Just rejoice about what she's doing and see what transpires from there. Not go to the principal and say, This is what

I think, what do you think? Because I think things got lost with the principal as go-between. My suggestion was interpreted as me being the authority with a position different from the school, and it was threatening. These were people who had worked with this child since kindergarten, and I had only been at the school for three weeks; what they saw me saying was that what they had deemed best for her was not true, and that offended them. So I need to tiptoe around the next time and not be so offensive. But I don't think I was. I suggested and questioned based on what I saw in the classroom and offered another option, and that in itself was offensive to the school. I questioned their position, and they apparently had a vested interest in putting Valerie in special ed.

Denny: I'd like to come back to official texts. You said you don't read them, and I can sympathize with that because I don't read them either, but you did need to at one point. How would you advise a teacher who lays out the work and tries to celebrate but is met with, This is all very well and good but this is the official text and this is what we need to work on. Because you really deconstructed those texts. Would you advise a teacher to do that?

DEBBIE: Yes. Regardless of what it costs you in terms of your school position, we're talking about the welfare of a child. And seeing Valerie now, she's having a terrible time. But she had one good year. And luckily that one good year is helping her hold on to the fact that she is capable, she can be successful, and maybe she can have other good years. If we can just get her through school she will be okay. But that one good year is very important in the whole scheme of things. I think what you need to do is take what the documents say she can't do, find it in what she's doing naturally, and just present it as an option. You say, You have to address it this way . . . almost as if you're still questioning it yourself, You know I see this here, and the official documents say she is incapable of doing this, and yet I see her doing this, and I don't understand it. You have to act almost naive, as if you don't understand it, to get the person to say, Hey that is interesting, and maybe get her to start questioning the information herself. But to not do anything? I don't think you can ethically do that, regardless.

Denny: There's a balance here. You need to go into the documentation to question it as there's a need. You document, but you don't have to go into writing massive reports on all children unless there's a need. But those are skills a teacher should have, don't you think?

DEBBIE: I can't speak for all teachers, but regardless of who the child is, even with my first graders now, at any given moment I can tell anybody where this child seems to be at, academically and socially. And I think most teachers can do that.

Denny: I think the difference is that if it's spoken, if a teacher talks about a child, it's very different than if the teacher presents a report about a child. It's the weight that we give to text.

DEBBIE: And teacher text is not valued. It's quote, subjective, unquote. It's one person's opinion. And who am I?

Denny: You have to work at it.

DEBBIE: Because we're not treated professionally, we're not treated respectfully, and we're not viewed that way by the parents. And that's another thing. There's no way I could have advocated successfully without her mom. I needed to have the support of Mom because you can't fight the school and Mom at the same time. You shouldn't. It's not your child.

Denny: Which is a good point. If you're going to advocate, then that needs to be within some social framework. And here you were collaborating with the mother.

DEBBIE: Actually, the most important person I needed was Valerie. If this was not what she wanted, then regardless of what I thought, I wouldn't have done it. But I was ready to back off, because it looked like that's what Mom wanted. And this is not my child. I borrow this child. She's loaned to me. So when I saw Mom comfortable saying she wanted her in special ed, I backed off. It wasn't until Valerie came back crying and saying she didn't want to go there that I became a little more assertive. But it was Valerie. Without Valerie and Mom I wouldn't have involved myself further.

Denny: So even though the other teachers offered no support, Valerie and her mother became the support. Valerie trying to support herself, Sue supporting Valerie and you.

DEBBIE: And my colleagues at the university. Because they were the ones who kept reinforcing in me that yes, this is what I should be doing.

Denny: You brought the situation up when we were doing the assessment course. Having that forum was probably helpful as well.

DEBBIE: Yes. Because there is no support for somebody like me in the school system. The other teachers don't support you. They're not going to support a black sheep at the school. So if there isn't a mom or a child telling you this is what she wants done, or a colleague saying this is ethically what needs to be done, who would stick their neck out?

Denny: Which raises all kinds of issues about teachers being isolated, but that's another story.

You Just Hate Me—I Knew It All Along: Mark's Story

LAFON L. PHILLIPS

The harsh sound of forced laughter captured my attention. I glanced over and saw my twelve-year-old son, Mark, writing in his school yearbook. Troubled by the bitterness of his voice, I wondered if he was defacing the contents of his book.

I discovered later that Mark had recorded what he felt were the most memorable aspects of his sixth-grade school year (see Figure 1). These entries were a sad summary of Mark's last year in elementary school. How could a twelve-year-old child conclude that he had no favorite memory of school and that his favorite place to go was "anywhere but school"?

Kindergarten (1987–88)

Mark remembers kindergarten as "being fun." The most memorable event he recalls is "losing my tooth. I was pulling on it in the middle of class, and it fell out right onto the table . . . and I was sent to the nurse's office."

Mark's kindergarten teacher was an earnest woman who had high standards for her pupils. During the second semester, she indicated her concern for Mark's somewhat slow acquisition of letter and letter-sound recognition skills:

2/9/88

I feel Mark is fooling around too much and not working up to the potential that he can. Sometimes he tends to daydream and not do his work before going to centers. I want him to be able to know these letters and sounds for first grade, so he has a great start and will feel good about himself. Last week he received a red dot for bad behavior and it didn't seem to phase [sic] him. Could you please speak to him about behavior, listening, and how important it is to learn these letters.

2/10/88

Mark and I talked [yesterday]. Today he is trying very hard and doing better in listening and behavior.

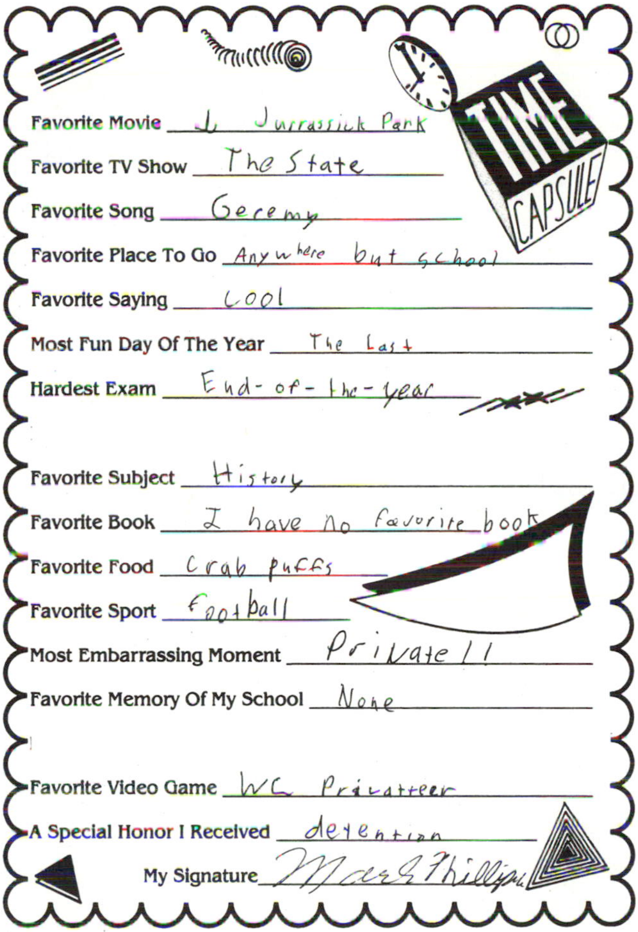

Favorite Movie ___ J. Jurrassick Park ___

Favorite TV Show ___ The State ___

Favorite Song ___ Geremy ___

Favorite Place To Go ___ Anywhere but school ___

Favorite Saying ___ Cool ___

Most Fun Day Of The Year ___ The Last ___

Hardest Exam ___ End-of-the-year ___

Favorite Subject ___ History ___

Favorite Book ___ I have no favorite book ___

Favorite Food ___ Crab puffs ___

Favorite Sport ___ Football ___

Most Embarrassing Moment ___ Private!! ___

Favorite Memory Of My School ___ None ___

Favorite Video Game ___ WC Privateer ___

A Special Honor I Received ___ detention ___

My Signature ___ Mark Phillips ___

Figure 1

Mark's sixth-grade yearbook

Mark's response to me about this situation was, "I *hate* letters and letter sounds!" His reaction combined with the teacher's comments prompted me to request an educational evaluation to determine if Mark had any underlying problem that could be impeding his learning.

As part of the evaluation, a special education teacher observed Mark in the kindergarten classroom. She wrote:

Students were working independently on a numbers sheet, which consisted of copying numbers and a dot-to-dot activity. The next worksheet to be completed independently involved clocks and telling time to the hour. Students were to cut out the clock faces and glue them to the correct time. During the last five minutes, students were allowed to go to the center of their choice.

Mark worked quietly on his worksheet but was slow to finish it when compared to the other students in the class. He also worked slowly on the clock worksheet. He wasn't wasting time, he just moved slowly. When I checked his worksheet his answers were correct. Mark wandered around the room, going from center to center. He appeared to be having difficulty finding something to do.

The diagnostic tests used for evaluation indicated that Mark's "processing abilities" were within the average to high-average range. However, the psychologist noted that there was a discrepancy between Mark's ability and his actual achievement, and she suggested that his achievement should be monitored during first grade.

These observations and test results did not seem to be a cause for alarm. We were optimistic and confident that Mark would do well in the upcoming years of school.

First Grade (1988–89)

Mark's feelings about his first-grade experience were scrawled in purple ink across the cover of a fill-in-the-blank book: "I Love 1st grade." In this book, *All About First Grade*, he wrote:

> My favorite thing about 1st grade was
> my teacher because she is nice.
>
> One thing in first grade that I did not like was
> nothing I like everything.
>
> My best friends were
> Brandon Jared Joey Bradley James Brett Ross jon
> I like them.
>
> My first grade teacher was nice!!!!!!!!!!!

In the comment section of Mark's report card for that year, the teacher wrote:

> Mark is working hard in first grade! I am pleased with his progress. Mark's initial reading skills were a little weak, but are improving as he gains experience and self-confidence. Mark sometimes lacks self-control as far as behavior is concerned. This is an area to focus on as we begin our second quarter.
>
> Mark is making very good progress at school. He is working hard and enjoying first grade. Mark's reading skills are really improving. We will continue working hard in this area.
>
> I *really* enjoyed having Mark in class this year! It has been exciting to watch his progress!

Mark's first-grade year ended on a happy note, and we were relieved and reassured when he overcame his dislike of "letters and letter sounds" and learned to read. It seemed that he was off to a good start in his school career.

Second Grade (1989–90)

In second grade Mark got his first "red light," which meant that "I couldn't go to lunch recess and recess. I was the only one who had one. I stayed in the classroom with the teacher. I put my head down on the desk. It only happened once."

An apple shape-book created by Mark during the first week of second grade states:

My first day in second grade I felt good and nervous.

School

Nice, Prtty, Learning

Playing, walking, Learning

makes me happy.

This week I learned about fire drills and about leters and how to be friends and school rules to put a heading on my paper.

Teacher comments on Mark's report card for this year state:

Mark is a *very* capable student and when he applies himself, he does excellent work. I would like to see Mark consistently do his best. He is making progress in all subjects, but I feel Mark should be putting more effort into his assignments.

I'm pleased with Mark's improved effort in his work; however, I'd like to see consistent good effort from Mark. Mark has shown good progress in his reading and writing skills. I'd like Mark to continue his excellent writing with editing for capitals and punctuation. I'd like for Mark to use his best writing and think about neatness, organization, etc. on all his work.

Mark has shown good progress in all subjects. His writing continues to be a strength. Mark has improved his work habits the last several weeks and is putting more effort and pride into his work.

As these comments indicate, Mark was making good progress in his expressive writing skills. Here are some of his journal entries for this year:

12/13/89

I am so excited I have two book lists ready to be tuned in. 25 on eath list. I am starting one more. I do not have one of the same books on my list. I raed a lot of books. You shoud to.

3/13/90

I got a black eye. I was playing baseball. I almost cot it. I cryed. My mom took me over to the water foten. It felt better. I played on. I hate having a black eye.

3/26/90

I am writing a new book. I have two pages done. I am writing a book about an Airbase. I want to get done soon. I like my book. lots of peple like it to. I hope I get done in a month.

5/31/90

I think second grade was fun because I like learning about a Kit fox and making a Kit fox out of paper masha. My favorit subject in secand grade was science. I laered a lot conting moltaplacation and renaming.

During this year, Mark also wrote a humorous story entitled "The Toy Dinosaur," which was submitted to a local publishing house as part of a schoolwide "Writing Fair." Mark's story was returned with an honorable mention and the following comments: "'The Toy Dinosaur' by Mark Phillips deserves an honorable mention in the fiction category. Mark has an ear for dialog—it's great! I hope Mark continues listening and writing."

Second grade had been a good year for Mark, but there were some indications that trouble lay ahead. The teacher had noted Mark's inattentiveness and restlessness during class. A parent of one of Mark's classmates, who had assisted in the classroom, commented on several occasions that Mark appeared to be bored at times. However, she added that even when he appeared to be inattentive, he would usually respond correctly to teacher questions.

In the spring of that year, second graders were given the Iowa Tests of Basic Skills. During the week of testing, the principal called to tell me that Mark was taking the examination in her office and not in his classroom. Mark had been selecting more than one answer per test item, and when she had questioned him about his actions, Mark had responded that he was doing so "because the test is stupid."

Despite his lack of interest in taking the exam, Mark's scores were in the average to high range. When I spoke about the test results to the principal, she laughingly responded that Mark would never again do as well on any subsequent Iowa Test, because he would not be able to take the exam in her office in the future.

Third Grade (1990–91)

"That's the year that I started to get in trouble."

At the end of the first grading period of this year, I met with Mark's third-grade teacher for a report card conference. She said that Mark was disruptive in class and was the "class clown." She mentioned repeatedly that "Mark is choosing not to work." To emphasize her point she related a classroom incident: Mark had been sitting alone at a table, watching the goings-on of the class. She asked him what he was doing and Mark responded with her words, "I'm choosing not to work."

The teacher also commented that Mark was putting on weight, and she suggested we monitor his diet to see if certain foods could be affecting his behavior. She then recommended that Mark see the school counselor and that we investigate private counseling for him as well.

It dawned on me during the course of this conference that Mark's desk was positioned against a wall in the back of the room, while those of his classmates were clustered in the center of the classroom. It was evident that this arrangement was not a temporary measure, and I was appalled and upset. I felt that Mark was being made a social outcast, but when I brought this up at home, Mark insisted that it did not "bother" him and that he did not want me to intervene. The teacher's comments on Mark's report card for this quarter were:

Mark has been able to choose to quietly do his best work at his seat. As he chooses this more and more often I envision him then having time for other interesting projects of his choice. As this becomes easier to accomplish with practice and success I'm sure he will feel happier and more satisfied.

Shortly after this school conference Mark and I met with a psychologist for several sessions. But neither Mark nor I could establish a satisfactory rapport with her and we stopped going.

In the meantime, the situation was worsening at school. Mark was in a no-win situation. Children taunted him about his weight, and if he reacted angrily to their taunts, the teacher criticized him for "not getting along."

Other report card comments for the year were:

Mark can be an excellent learner with many valuable ideas to share with our class. As he chooses to focus on our projects and work cooperatively with others I envision Mark enjoying the results and the pride he will have in his contributions and the learning growth he will make.

Mark continues to have wonderful ideas to share. It's fun to have his contributions! We will continue to work on behavior. Hopefully January will be repeated in March, April, and May.

Mark was becoming increasingly unhappy with school. We consulted a private social worker who pointed out that by his count, three-quarters of the boys in Mark's class had been recommended for or were receiving counseling for their behavior. The social worker found Mark to be a very personable child, and his regard for Mark was strongly evident in their relationship. Once the school year was over, he stated that he saw no further need for Mark to continue with counseling.

At the conclusion of the school year, we received Mark's scores for the Iowa Tests of Basic Skills (which he had taken in the third-grade classroom). Contrary to the principal's prediction of the previous year, Mark's national ranking on the examination was at the eighty-fourth percentile.

Fourth Grade (1991–92)

"I got a lot of brown slips . . . and I was sent to the office."

Fourth grade was a dismal year. Mark and his male teacher engaged in a never-ending power struggle. On the playground, Mark defied anyone to "mess with him." Anger was evident in his attitude, his tone of voice, and his physical movements.

Mark also became a fixture in the nurse's office—he complained of headaches almost daily. The pediatrician concluded that Mark's headaches were stress related and that he should take extrastrength pain-relievers whenever they occurred.

A note from the fourth-grade teacher states:

11/19/91

Yesterday I sent a note home with Mark regarding his homework and class work time, he lost it. He is not doing his work in class and is not handing in his homework. He does not appear to want to do his work or even care if he doesn't. Please speak to him about this.

During this period we consulted another psychologist, one who was well known and highly regarded in the community. After listening to my account of Mark's school problems and reviewing his school records, the psychologist asked whether Mark had been considered for placement in a class for emotionally disturbed children. He stated that Mark was depressed, hostile, and angry. He recommended counseling, and he said that at some point in the counseling process a determination would be made as to whether or not Mark was emotionally disturbed.

In the meantime, Mark was suspended from school again and again. When I told the principal that suspension was an ineffective measure, she replied that my husband and I were "too easy" on Mark and that we should be more punitive when he was suspended. She stated that "intellectual, professional parents" tended to be too liberal with their children, that I needed to use "tough love" with Mark, and that I should stop "rescuing him." The principal was chagrined when I reminded her that Mark had an older brother who had been raised according to the same standards and that she had never accused us of "liberal parenting" in his case.

Toward the end of the school year, the psychologist concluded that Mark was not emotionally disturbed; he suggested that the school should assume more responsibility for handling "educational problems."

Fifth Grade (1992–93)

"Every little thing that I would do I would get in trouble for, while other people did bigger things and barely, if at all, got into trouble for it."

For fifth grade, the principal placed Mark with a teacher whom she characterized as being "nonconfrontive." I found "Mrs. Smith" to be a small, likable woman who exerted little influence over her class.

At one school conference, Mrs. Smith said that she sent Mark out of the classroom whenever his behavior was inappropriate. She made frequent references to the number of boys with "behavior problems" in the fifth grade, and she bemoaned the fact that there were so few "nice" boys in that group. Curious, I asked, "Just how many boys are there in fifth grade?"

"Eighteen," she replied.

"How many nice boys are there?" was my second question.

"Three," was her immediate answer.

I knew without being told that Mark was not one of the three "nice" boys in the fifth grade.

Mark's grades improved considerably during this year and he was somewhat happier, but I had serious doubts that the improvement on his report card indicated greater efforts on his part.

That spring I took Mark to the pediatrician again. I explained that Mark was still experiencing frequent headaches and that his speech was now becoming unintelligible because of severe stuttering.

The pediatrician was unable to find any physical cause for the headaches or for the stuttering, and he reaffirmed that "frequent headaches in children were mostly stress related." At this point, he agreed to evaluate Mark for a possible attention-deficit disorder.

The results of the evaluation suggested that Mark might have an attention disorder. However, in order to test that diagnosis, Mark would have to take a stimulant drug, such as Ritalin. If the stimulant improved Mark's behavior, he would then be considered to have an attention-deficit disorder.

After considerable thought we finally agreed to have Mark take Ritalin on a trial basis. The teacher reported a "dramatic" difference in Mark's behavior. However, Mark experienced stomachaches with the medication, and he was resistant to taking it. Asserting that he "wasn't crazy," Mark felt that the medication just made him "too tired [to misbehave] and that it didn't do any good." Once school was over for the year I discontinued the Ritalin while I considered various alternatives for the upcoming school year.

Summer 1993

I knew that the principal of Mark's school was planning to assign him to a sixth-grade teacher whom she characterized as being a teacher "who treats sixth graders as adults, and who expects them to behave as such." This characterization and my previous observations of that teacher's manner weighed heavily on my mind throughout the summer. Mark's stuttering, which a speech pathologist felt was probably stress induced, also continued to worry me.

I searched for ways to alleviate the situation. I read books about attention-deficit (hyperactivity) disorder. I investigated private schools in the area. I considered teaching Mark at home.

During this time, a family friend who had retired from public school teaching offered to teach Mark in her home-school along with three other children. We decided that Mark had nothing to lose at this point and that it was worth a try.

Sixth Grade (1993–94)

"The best day of sixth grade was the last day. I knew that I wouldn't have to go back to school for three months."

Mark began his sixth-grade school year in Mrs. J.'s home. Mrs. J. was a very strong-willed and experienced teacher who immediately recognized his strengths and weaknesses as a student. In deference to Mark's keen interest in wildlife and nature, Mrs. J. gave him many opportunities to explore these interests. Mark's reading assignments centered on a collection of texts written by English veterinarian James Herriot. Mark and his classmates were taken on field trips to the Humane Society, the zoo, the Association for the Blind, and a hospital (where they observed newborns being examined after birth).

From the start Mrs. J. predicted that she and Mark would eventually get into a power struggle; she said when it happened she would handle it in her own way. As she expected, it wasn't long before she and Mark locked horns over a minor matter. Mark's normal school hours were from 9:00—1:00, but on that day he did not leave school until 6:00 P.M., and Mrs. J. was declared the winner of their contest.

At Thanksgiving, Mrs. J. invited the parents of her students to a celebration at which the children read aloud or recited memorized pieces to the assembled audience. Mark's lively reading of a tale about a pampered and overweight dog from James Herriot's *All Creatures Great and Small* had everyone chuckling.

Mark made excellent grades throughout his first semester in the home-school. His stuttering subsided and eventually ceased, but he was not happy. He strongly objected to the pervasiveness of the religious teachings in the curriculum and he missed his neighborhood friends. As a result, he lobbied incessantly to return to public school. With strong misgivings, my husband and I agreed to let him return after an upcoming trip to Russia.

After Mark's return from Russia in February 1994, I contacted the principal about reenrolling Mark in school. I was told that he could not be enrolled until everyone (teacher, principal, parents) had met to discuss a "504 plan." We were well aware that this delay was illegal and that Mark should have been allowed to attend school without this prior meeting. However, we agreed to the wait in an effort to demonstrate our desire to cooperate.

I found out later that a 504 plan is intended to address the instructional needs of children determined to be handicapped as outlined by Section 504 of the Rehabilitation Act of 1973. A United States Department of Education Memorandum on AD(H)D (1991) holds that state and local educational agencies should "train regular education teachers and other personnel to develop their awareness about ADD and its manifestations and the adaptations that can be implemented in regular education programs to address the instructional needs of these children." Some examples in the document of possible adaptations in regular education programs are:

> providing a structured learning environment; repeating and simplifying instructions about in-class and homework assignments; supplementing verbal instructions with visual instructions; using behavioral management techniques; adjusting class schedules; modifying test delivery; using tape recorders, computer-aided instruction, and other audiovisual equipment; selecting modified textbooks or workbooks; and tailoring homework assignments.

Mark's accommodation plan mentioned none of these possible adaptations; it simply stated that the sixth-grade teacher

will observe for one wk. & talk w/father regarding need to medicated [sic]. Counselor will talk w/father about private counseling. Mark will use a daily assignment book which will be initialed & sent back by father. Mark will pass rules test w/ 100% accuracy.

The plan goals were:

1. Mark will complete homework each day.
2. Mark will follow school & class rules.

This "plan" spelled out Mark's responsibilities and established the ground rules for his return to school. After a week's delay, these terms were settled upon in the "504 meeting" and Mark was allowed to return to the classroom.

During March and April, matters progressed relatively well. Mark's father had weekly meetings with the teacher to discuss Mark's academic performance and behavior. Mark brought home daily homework assignment sheets, which had to be signed by a parent and returned to school. He also brought home weekly behavior charts that categorized each day's behavior as unsatisfactory, satisfactory, or excellent.

In April, the day before the sixth-grade camping trip, the principal called my husband and informed him that she had "concerns" about Mark's going on the school trip. She said that she had spoken to a group of boys about their conduct on the field trip and that Mark had reacted angrily to her comments, saying, "Yeah. Yeah. I know. You just hate me—I knew it all along."

The principal suggested to my husband that Mark should be kept at home rather than go on the school trip. After he agreed to her suggestion, she reiterated that it was his decision to keep Mark at home and not allow him to go on the excursion.

That evening, Mark was silent and withdrawn. Tears slid down his face as he described how a group of boys had been summoned into the principal's office to discuss their behavior on a trip that hadn't yet been taken. He asserted that the principal was being unfair in her treatment of them, and he said that he was upset at being "embarrassed in front of my friends." Since the trip was scheduled for the following morning, I attempted to obtain the principal's home telephone number in order to discuss the situation. I was unsuccessful; none of the teachers I contacted would give out her number.

The following morning, I waited outside the school to speak to the principal. Excited sixth graders boarded the buses and Mark and I sat in our car and watched them depart. The principal never appeared. The school secretary told me that the principal was in a meeting and would not return to school until late in the day. I went to the school district's administrative offices only to find that the district officials were also out of their offices and unavailable.

I waited at the administration building for an hour until a district official returned. He agreed that given the circumstances I had described, Mark should have been allowed to go on the school trip, but said that he would need to discuss the matter with the principal.

Before long the principal called and gave me a slightly different version of events: Mark was under suspension for his conduct in her office, and my husband had elected to keep him at home rather than send him to school, where he would be supervised in someone's classroom. When I repeated this conversation to my husband, he shook his head disbelievingly and held his hands up in a gesture of helplessness.

In May, four and a half days before the end of the school year, I received a telephone call from the principal. She informed me that Mark was not going to be allowed to participate in the school's sixth-grade graduation exercise because participation in the ceremony was considered to be an honor and Mark had not earned this honor. I asked her if Mark was being retained in the sixth grade, and she answered that he would be "going on to the junior high school."

I was stunned. The graduation ceremony was three days away. I called the superintendent of the school district and explained that Mark was not under suspension and that the school had no grounds to bar him from the graduation ceremony.

After my conversation with the superintendent, the principal called me back: I had "misunderstood" her; Mark was not being passed to seventh grade. Our only recourse was to meet with her and the teacher to see if "we"—the principal and us—could convince the teacher that Mark should be promoted.

This situation was unbelievable. There had been no forewarning that Mark was in danger of failing. By suddenly announcing that Mark was not going to be promoted, the teacher and the principal had disregarded and violated the most common rules and procedures for promotion and retention.

When we arrived for the meeting on the following day, the teacher, the principal, and the same district official who had heard my complaint about the field trip were waiting for us in the principal's office. The teacher and the principal both agreed that Mark did not belong in sixth grade again next year, but the teacher was adamant that Mark had not "earned the honor of graduation." He added that Mark had not been in school long enough nor completed enough schoolwork to justify his promotion. My husband asked if Mark's previous five years of schooling and the time spent at the home-school counted toward promotion.

The teacher responded that Mark did not know sixth-grade subject matter. I pointed out that Mark had taken the school's end-of-the-year English examination and obtained the highest grade in the class. This achievement had led the teacher to recommend that Mark take the junior high school's advanced placement exam for English. I also pointed out that according to the district's educational evaluation, which had been completed *prior to* Mark's sixth-grade school year, Mark had performed at or above the sixth-grade level in all academic areas.

The district official interrupted at that point, stating that the Woodcock-Johnson Achievement Test, which I was citing, was not an achievement test, and that my statement that Mark had performed at the 6.8 grade level in math actually indicated that he had performed as well as a student in the eighth month of sixth grade would have. None of us appeared to grasp the distinction that he was attempting to make here, so I reminded them that Mark had just completed *fifth* grade at the time of the evaluation and that he probably would have performed even better if he had been given medication to improve his attentiveness and/or been a willing participant in the evaluation process. The district official then demanded to know if we had "proof" of Mark's attention-deficit disorder. I responded that we had never been *given* any "proof" and that in my experience, patients rarely received formal documentation from a physician specifying a condition or a diagnosis. I stated that Mark's medication, which was in the nurse's office, should constitute sufficient "proof" for the school district.

The teacher's next tack was to say that Mark did not know the *school's* sixth-grade curriculum and that he would promote Mark only if he completed reading, writing, and math assignments over the coming summer and passed examinations in those same areas.

My husband and I finally agreed to these conditions, and the principal then returned to the issue of the graduation ceremony. She reiterated that graduation was an "honor," and she asked my husband, who is a university professor, if college students participated in graduation ceremonies without having earned the honor of doing so. He laughed and said, "Of course! It happens all the time!" He explained that grades were not due until *after* graduation and the ceremony was simply that—a ceremony.

The teacher replied that the kids in his class had worked hard all year and they were all aware that Mark had not [??]. How could he justify giving Mark a graduation certificate?

At this point, I asked the principal whether Mark would be allowed to participate in the following year's graduation ceremony after he had completed the assigned summer work. Flustered, she finally said, "Well, you know . . . we have concerns . . . the kids really admire and look up to Mark, and you know how he loves to entertain . . ." This confirmed my suspicions about the true issue here, and I stated emphatically that Mark would behave in an appropriate fashion at the graduation ceremony and that he would not "entertain" the graduates.

The final issue to be resolved was the matter of the sixth-grade graduation certificate. Again, according to the teacher, Mark had not "earned" the certificate. Rather than fight any more, we suggested that Mark be handed an interim certificate stating that he would receive a formal graduation certificate upon his completion of the summer work.

At the conclusion of this meeting, the district official (a "neutral observer") snapped his notebook shut and directed the principal to send us a letter stating the conditions that Mark would have to fulfill before he would be allowed to attend junior high school. He added, "And, if he doesn't meet the conditions—he *won't* go."

Fearing that the school would find a reason to suspend Mark and bar him from attending the graduation ceremony, I kept him out of school until the day of graduation. The graduation ceremony was held in the afternoon. Mark was given an interim certificate; he did not entertain the graduates; he did not detract from the occasion.

My most vivid memory of the ceremony involves the principal. At one point she bestowed lavish praise and accolades on a nonverbal, severely handicapped sixth grader. This particular child was lauded for being a "tremendous source of inspiration to everyone in the school"; as he was awarded the prized graduation certificate, members of the audience beamed at each other and wiped away tears. I smiled in return and thought of the irony.

The letter from the school district arrived the next day. It stated that Mark would be promoted to the seventh grade under two conditions: that he satisfactorily complete assignments provided by the teacher in the areas of math, reading, and writing; and that he pass examinations given by the teacher in those subject areas.

Mark arrived home from his final day of school with social studies, English, and mathematics textbooks. He had been given a geography skills workbook to complete; four units of social studies with accompanying tests ("of the style that Mark will be given"); ninety math assignments covering the entire math curriculum; forty writing assignments, each of which involved writing and editing at least two drafts; and nineteen miscellaneous English assignments.

Summer 1994

As I supervised Mark's homework completion, I continued to be upset about the principal's failure to follow correct procedure in Mark's retention. I felt strongly that her actions constituted an abuse of power and I decided to address the issue with the school superintendent. In our meeting, the superintendent stated that he had no control over the situation and that the teacher's decision could be overturned only by the school board. I pointed out that according to the district's promotion and retention guidelines,

> Retention of students is a *process* [emphasis mine] that is followed when the professional staff, in consultation with the parent, determines it to be in the best interest of the student. . . . When circumstances indicate that retention is in the best interest of the student, the student will have individual consideration, and decisions will be made only after a careful study of facts relating to all phases of the student's growth and development. The student's academic achievement level and mental ability are important, but physical and social characteristics are also important factors. A decision should be based on sufficient data, collected over a period of time and motivated by a desire to place the student in the school program where he will be the most successful.

I questioned the motive behind Mark's retention and I called attention to his report card, which was baffling and contradictory (see Figure 2). I pointed out that in almost every instance Mark had been rated satisfactory for subject knowledge, but that in subjective areas—effort, study skills—he had been evaluated as needing improvement; and that in any case, the combination of satisfactory subject knowledge with a less than satisfactory effort did not in my mind equate to a failing grade.

When I pointed out that we had been informed of Mark's retention four days before the end of school and that *none* of the district's stated guidelines had been followed, he responded that we had the right to appeal to the school board (in either a public or private session) to overturn Mark's retention. He stated that we and the teacher needed to present our sides of the argument and that we all had to behave in a "civilized manner." He also stated that neither side should defend "a matter of principle," that we should express our convictions about what was right in this situation. (I construed this to mean that I should not be arguing about the principal's failure to follow procedural guidelines.) He then asked if I was convinced that Mark had the skills necessary for seventh grade. I referred him to the district's educational evaluation (completed after Mark's fifth-grade school year), which indicated that on the Woodcock-Johnson Achievement Test (R) Mark had scored at the 7.6 grade level for reading comprehension, the 8.1 grade level for science, the 7.4 grade level for social studies, and the 6.0 grade level for overall math skills.

At the conclusion of our meeting, the superintendent verified that he had informed me of our legal rights, and he stated that in order to proceed further I would need to send him a letter requesting a hearing before the school board.

Before leaving his office, I asked him about a statement that appeared at the bottom of the pupil retention report with regard to a school board appeal:

> I [we] also understand that any documentation and/or records of this decision and appeal shall be placed in my [our] child's permanent record.

The superintendent asked to see the statement, saying this was the first time this had happened in the years he had been with the school district. After reading it, he acknowledged that such information would become a part of Mark's permanent school records.

In the end, my husband and I gave up trying to fight the system. We were concerned about possible repercussions if we were to go before the school board. We also did not want any evidence about an appeal and a decision to be placed in Mark's school records.

By the third week of August Mark had completed all the homework assignments. He turned the assignments over to the teacher and he took the mathematics, social studies, and writing examinations. He passed all of the examinations and was given a sixth-grade graduation certificate.

Postscript

Mark's junior high school experience was, on the whole, more positive than negative. He enjoyed changing classes and having different teachers for each subject. He found a kindred spirit in his biological sciences teacher, who could "answer questions and discuss" topics, "not just tell you to look it up in a book."

Individual Growth and Development
A - Superior
B - Above Average
C - Satisfactory
D - Below Average
F - Failing
S - Satisfactory Progress
N - Needs Improvement

READING..**F**
    Effort...**N**
    Comprehension (literal and interpretive).............**S**
    Vocabulary (word meaning)................................**S**
    Study Skills..**N**
    Word Attack Skills..**S**

MATHEMATICS..**F**
    Effort...**N**
    Concept (understanding)..................................**S-**
    Basic Skills (knows facts)................................**S**
    Problem Solving (application)...........................**S**

LANGUAGE...**F**
    Effort...**N**
    Written Expression...**S-**
    Sentence Structure..**S**
    Vocabulary Development..................................**S**
    Mechanics (capitalization and punctuation)........**N**

Figure 2
Mark's report card

The chorus teacher gave him numerous responsibilities and opportunities both in and out of class. She was "always smiling" and she was instrumental in involving him in drama where, she insisted, he was one of the most talented students that she had ever encountered. As far as his peers were concerned, Mark was voted the "funniest guy in eighth grade" in the school yearbook.

Mark's junior high school experience lasted for three semesters. His poor organizational skills and insufficient self-discipline finally caught up with him at the midpoint of eighth grade. Several times during Mark's final semester in school, I met and talked with the vice-principal about Mark. It was obvious in the way he spoke and from his efforts to help that Mr. B. had a genuine affection for Mark. His unhappiness was apparent when he told me that Mark would have to repeat the eighth grade if he remained in school. We discussed Mark's latest academic achievement test, which indicated that Mark was performing well into or beyond high school level in reading, social studies, and science and at eighth-grade level in mathematics. He acknowledged that no useful purpose would be served by

```
SOCIAL STUDIES.................................................... F
    Effort........................................................... N*
    Project Work................................................ S
    Understands Concepts.................................. S
    Contributes to Discussions.......................... S
*S is scratched out and N is placed next to it


SCIENCE............................................................. D-
    Effort........................................................... S-
    Cares for Equipment................................... S
    Works on Experiments................................. S
    Understands Vocabulary.............................. S
    Uses Scientific Procedures.......................... S


WORK HABITS AND BEHAVIOR
    Prepares Home Assignments......................... N-
    Follows Directions...................................... S-
    Uses time wisely.......................................... S-
    Accepts Responsibility................................. N-
    Works Independently.................................... S-
    Works well in group activities...................... S
    Respects Personal/Other property................ S
    Is considerate of others............................... S
    Practices Self-Control.................................. S


GRADE LEVEL COMPARISON
              Above    At      Below (Grade Level)
READING                X
LANGUAGE               X
MATH                   X
```

Figure 2

continued

having Mark repeat the eighth grade; shaking his head sorrowfully, he commented, "We put all kids into a school and expect them to learn the same way when, in actuality, it just isn't the case."

At this point we withdrew Mark from school and enrolled him in two high school correspondence courses. Home-schooling has its highs and lows, but it has given me a new perspective and appreciation for Mark. His "adult" side has emerged as he has been able to shed much of his armor of hostility and anger. Now whenever Mark and I discuss some of the events that are included in this story, he displays a wry, philosophic attitude.

Mark's schooling has been achieved at an incalculable cost. Over the years he was called an "underachiever," a "class clown," and a "troublemaker" by those who would not or who could not see beyond the labels that followed him from year to year. We reexperienced the sharp sting of these perceptions recently when a teacher from Mark's school approached us in a restaurant. After all of the introductions had been made she laughingly and unthinkingly said to my older son, "Oh, you must have been good in school because I don't remember you at all!"

These perceptions and the cumulative weight of criticism that accompanied them—"Mark should be putting more effort into his assignments"; "He is choosing not to work"; "He does not want to work"; "He does not care"; "He should be treated with tough love"; "He does not deserve the honor of graduation"—are an indelible legacy of Mark's early schooling.

This should never have been. We entrusted a curious, joyful, and ebullient child to the educational system. He was ready and eager to learn. He believed the lessons he received there. He deserved better.

Denny: Reading what you wrote about Mark's sixth-grade graduation, I thought about my son. Ben finished high school in three years. His third year of high school he took a full load and then he took night courses so he could finish that year, because he hated it. And when it came time to graduate—he had done all of the requirements—they told us that he could not take part in any of the ceremonies because he was not part of the graduating class. Only seniors could take part in the ceremony. And we went, twice, before the school board to ask permission for Benjamin to march in the ceremony, and we had to leave the room while they discussed it. We were told afterward that yes he could march in the ceremony, but he could not take part in any of the other celebrations and that the dinner for graduating seniors and their parents was not something we could attend.

LAFON: I had no idea they could do that.

Denny: It's a real misuse of power.

LAFON: I kept asking myself, was I overreacting? Was it important? Was I just being obstinate? Am I going overboard here? But I just thought that it was important for Mark to go through it.

Denny: It's a ceremony in his life. How would you like teachers to use this paper?

LAFON: I would like them to become sensitive. To be sensitized to these children. Especially the difficult ones. I felt all along that Mark was being pushed aside, he was being told in so many ways that there was something wrong with him, that he wasn't self-controlled or that he was too verbal. They didn't appreciate his wit, his curiosity, his ability to express himself; they viewed it as a threat to their authority. Mark was not a quiet, docile child. I think that's the way we prefer students to be to a large extent.

Denny: Quiet and docile?

LAFON: Yes, to be there to receive our teachings and to observe all the rules, not to disrupt the class. When people walk through classrooms, they should see how orderly they are. I guess it comes down to the issue of authority. And pushing out the kids who don't fit in. Mark is a misfit. He's always been a square peg in a round hole.

Denny: And at home?

LAFON: Well, we adore him—most of the time, anyway! We had no idea that he was overly active. Having two boys, we just thought that's how boys were: active, curious. He always had an ability to communicate with people that I felt was extraordinary. I would take him to the dentist or to the orthodontist and I would swear they looked forward to his coming. They always came out of their offices just laughing and carrying on a conversation with him. He was quite an enjoyable, entertaining child. And it hurt me that teachers couldn't see those qualities.

Denny: And it was a surprise? When Mark was five, if you had predicted his future at school, it probably would have been very different.

LAFON: Well, I never expected this. Never.

Denny: Did being a teacher prepare you in any way? Did that help as you were advocating for him?

LAFON: I don't feel that it did. I felt totally helpless in dealing with these people. I always felt shut down. I was treated like someone who had no sense. They had all the answers and my child was totally at fault. Everything was his fault.

Denny: And you were silenced?

LAFON: Definitely. No question. Anything that I brought up was disregarded. I was effectively silenced, just cut off.

Denny: I was looking at his report card, with a failure, an F, in each of the major categories and then looking at the subcategories. These were satisfactory for the most part, there were some that were not satisfactory, but it seems to me that that document was totally subjective.

LAFON: Definitely. That's what I said, in essence. There was no correlation between the two areas. Mark's grades were Fs when he had satisfactory subject knowledge and satisfactory skills. I felt that the teacher was being punitive. I know that when the principal first called me, she said Mark wasn't going to be going to the graduation but he would be going on to junior high school; I know I did not misunderstand her. And for the story to change after I complained to the superintendent was just mind-boggling.

Denny: So, all those stories changed?

LAFON: Yes.

Denny: And written texts were either used or not used. One of the things I found from my own research was that with bureaucratic texts, if the document supports their case, then they use it. But if it doesn't support their case, such as the testing that was done and he was above grade level, that isn't used.

LAFON: It wasn't sufficient, it wasn't valid. It didn't fit their perception of Mark.

Denny: On the other hand, if those test scores had been low, then one can imagine they would have been used. But because they didn't fit the picture, they weren't used. It really interests me how official stories are invented, and they are inventions. Some documents are used if they fit, or they're discarded, but we end up with this official story that in this case was very harmful to Mark. In your story you're coming back and reminding the principal and the teacher of these other tests that contradict the picture they're building, but they still don't include them. It becomes something that is trivial, a small piece of information.

LAFON: Right. It angered the teacher when I brought it up. I think he felt backed into a corner because the testing clearly contradicted what he was saying. And I knew. Being in special education, I've been at many meetings where this same test is used to demonstrate that a child is one or two years behind grade level, therefore he needs special education. But in Mark's case, because it indicated he was doing as well as he was despite not being taught, it was discounted, it was worthless. In the December testing of his eighth-grade year, Mark's reading level was post-high school, his science and his social studies were tenth and eleventh grade, and obviously he had not had the subject matter, it had not been taught to him. We had to take him out of school because he was going to fail. We're still having a battle right now because we are in a school district that has seventh, eighth, and ninth grade. They don't want to release Mark to go to the high school, because they don't want to pay the ninth-grade tuition. But I don't want him in the junior high.

Denny: What a dilemma, a terrible dilemma.

LAFON: One positive aspect of this situation is that we have always set a high value on education but with Mark we have come to realize that he may not follow tradition. We would like for him to have a traditional high school experience, but we're not optimistic. He could be one of the kids who at age sixteen obtains a GED, or maybe he will take some extra courses, and graduate early, we just don't know yet. We value Mark highly and we would like for him to have wonderful, pleasant educational experiences, but if he has to take another route we will support him.

Denny: How is he right now?

LAFON: He loves being at home. He's become a real computer buff. He's in cyberspace every day. Our phone bill is astronomical, but one thing that has happened as a result is I see how people are drawn to him. Mark would make an excellent counselor or teacher. When I mention this to him, of course he laughs and says no way, but people he has met via the computer call and discuss their problems with him.

Denny: Are these other teenagers?

LAFON: Teenagers, some adults even. He has a marvelous ability to communicate with people which is rather astonishing, I think, for a fourteen-year-old.

Denny: What would you tell other parents, or a teacher who is a parent, in a similar situation?

LAFON: I've counseled parents on what they can expect in dealing with the attitudes of the people in authority.

Denny: Standing up is important?

LAFON: Yes. One thing I think this article has accomplished is that at some point in the future when Mark reads it, he's going to have a better understanding of what happened and he'll realize that we were behind him. He will know that even when we get exasperated with him when he goes overboard, he has our love and our support. We just go day by day with him. There are no long-range plans.

Denny: And there are no answers.

LAFON: No. There aren't.

Denny: Just believing in your son—and yourself. You'll all come through it. We did, we came through it. Benjamin has a bachelors degree and has done a year with Americore voluntary service. I home-schooled him in fourth grade—it's a little different story, but it's really the same story. He had a really tough time in school, and he's always been easygoing and a wonderful person to be with, and we never really understood. He wasn't a behavioral problem. I can't really say what the problem was. His fourth-grade year, four boys were taken out of school by their parents, and many of the boys' parents were told they needed counseling. So it's not just Mark that's in this situation. Then in high school all they were doing was memorization of one test after another test, and David and I worked with Ben. The three of us would work on a paper, we'd share our ideas, edit it, just like a professor would with somebody working on a Ph.D., and then we'd go through it and make sure the grammar was okay, and if we were lucky, the three of us would get a B. But very rarely did we get a B, usually we got a C or a C-. David and I between us have how many years of schooling? A lifetime of schooling, and we never, ever, got more than a B.

LAFON: How is that possible? Did they just see him as being a C student?

Denny: I think there were many students who were in that situation. Whose parents perhaps for whatever reason did not work with their son in ways that we did, they probably worked in different ways, who didn't realize that there's a problem here. Not with my son, or their son, but with the school system and the way that they're being graded. And then when Ben was seventeen he went to Boston University and took one writing course and he said, and he always said this to us, you think I can write because you're my parents, but if I get a good grade on this, I'll go on to college. But if I don't, then I'm not going on to college. And he wrote his first paper—and he wrote it, I don't think we discussed it, he was in Boston, we were in New Hampshire—and he got an A+, and the professor wrote that she hadn't many comments because it was already publishable and she thought that he should think about publishing. And he started writing at college and is actually going to work on a book next year. But he was very angry about all those years they told him in high school he couldn't write. And they were wrong. And it's a very similar story to Mark's.

LAFON: In the early grades, Mark was recognized over and over for his writing. For his teacher to say he needed to work on his writing that summer—and I think it was forty assignments—

Denny: I wanted to ask you about that. He did a whole year's work it seems to me during those few weeks in the summer, so he must have worked every day.

LAFON: The first four weeks went relatively well, but as he realized that his summer was being eaten up and he had to return to school in August, Mark started to become frustrated and angry. And I was very frustrated because I could see that what we were doing was just a rehash. Doing math certainly did not hurt him, but he had no need to write forty stories, a first draft and a second, although that was the most enjoyable for me because I enjoy his writing. The social studies was boring, just answering questions from a textbook, there was no creativity involved. It was certainly a punishment for all of us.

Denny: Amazing. You are an advocate for Mark. There's no doubt about it. I imagine you are his strongest advocate. Did you see yourself in that role?

LAFON: I may not have even been aware of the term at that time. I was just trying to protect Mark from the negative feelings that were being expressed about him; words are very powerful weapons. Mark would come home and he would laugh and he would say, Oh I'm just the class clown, or I'm the troublemaker, and I knew he was starting to believe those statements. I didn't want that to happen to him. Because I know that when Mark becomes an adult, people who were so critical of him will meet him and enjoy being around him because they will value those things about him they didn't value in him as a child.

Denny: I really wanted to ask you about the summer, and we talked about that. But it seemed to me that this was a tremendous imposition not only for Mark but on the family. And reading your story I began to think that this was no longer an issue of whether he should repeat a grade or go on to the next grade, this had become a power struggle, very much in the way of *Learning Denied* when Patrick's parents said, Our son is not disabled, and tried to fight the school district. The school district became more and more entrenched in their position and more and more punitive to the point of saying, You let us test your kid again or he can't go into third grade—which is probably illegal. So the regulations get used in ways that aren't appropriate because the officials have taken a stand and they are not willing to back down from that position.

LAFON: I kept thinking how inequitable it was that Mark had gone to the home-school for the first semester of sixth grade and the teacher said, Well, that's not good enough. He hasn't been here, he hasn't received my teaching, my curriculum. It was totally not good enough. Yet, home-schooling in the summer was sufficient.

Denny: Yes, there's an irony there; I hadn't thought about that.

LAFON: But it was the same thing. He sent the work home. There was no great deal of thought in what he sent home. The writing assignments were dittoed, some stating a problem, some stating pretend you're a scientist and write about this or that. When I think about forty assignments, I doubt that the children in the class wrote forty assignments in a school year. What are there? Thirty-six weeks in a school year? What's that? One assignment per week? I sincerely doubt they covered half the assignments.

Denny: So the assignments become the punishment for Mark?

LAFON: Oh, definitely. We got him through the assignments and then we took him away to a hotel over a weekend to review the material before he took the tests.

Denny: So, not only did he have to do the assignments, he had to study for the tests.

LAFON: Right.

Denny: So, why did you go to the hotel?

LAFON: Just to get away.

Denny: Give him a boost?

LAFON: Yes. It gave Mark a chance to be alone with his dad and it allowed him to focus on the task at hand, which was to review all of the material before taking the tests. I had gotten him through all of the assignments while his dad was away in Russia and Mark and I needed a break from each other! I was weary of dealing with everything.

Denny: I really felt that as an educator I ought to be able to deal with the situation that was happening to Ben.

LAFON: I felt so too. The thing that amazed me was the resentment I felt on the part of the teachers and the administrators. I felt that they should have treated me as a knowledgeable equal, because I felt that I had more insight about my child than they did. And I felt completely helpless in the face of their opposition.

Denny: All the education in the world doesn't make any difference when you're dealing with a bureaucratic institution that has already made up its mind. You can't shift them. And that's what we found, especially in high school.

LAFON: It really bothered me that this district did not follow their own guidelines. I work in a very large school district, and for the most part when it comes to following specific guidelines teachers are very scrupulous, they know that there is a deadline for notifying a parent that a child may need to repeat a grade. We develop intervention plans, we see if we can take care of the problems, and we keep parents informed. In our case there was no notification or documentation that Mark was in danger of failing. Nothing. And then to be told the last week of school, Oh, he's not graduating with the rest of his class, was simply astonishing.

Satiable Curtiosity: The Need to Challenge Learners

MARGE KNOX

September

Thirty-one children were sitting in our morning discussion circle as a thin, tired-looking woman and the sheepish-looking boy clinging to her side waited to be acknowledged. Tom was an unusually tall boy for his seven years, and his face wore a look of total desperation. The woman's opening words confirmed her anxiety. "Tom's your new student. I'm his grandmother. He's had a very hard life and been abandoned several times. He is living with me now, where he'll be loved and have a consistent home and food."

Tom clung closer to her side as she continued, "There are ten people living with me and I'm doing the best I can. Neither of Tom's parents wants him." She patted him on the shoulder, said she would be back after school, and walked down the hall, leaving Tom standing where she left him, just inside the door, facing his new teacher and an unknown world. For a moment he didn't move; then as quickly as he had been introduced, our journey began.

"Our" is a team of six teachers working closely together to turn theory into practice—discussing, planning, talking teacher and kid talk. Support for our practice comes from the work of such educators as Ken and Yetta Goodman, Brian Cambourne, Donald Graves, Kathy Short, Stephen Krashen, Anne Haas Dyson, Denny Taylor, and Sandra Wilde. A major goal of our team is to plan and negotiate with one another and with the children we teach so that our students can experience a more consistent learning environment in which the same holistic beliefs and practices support every child.

Six adjoining classrooms face an enclosed hallway, creating an area for our multiage strand of grades one through six.[1] The school's student population of more than seven hundred is over 70 percent Spanish-speaking. Rick, Stella, and Chris teach grades four through six; Maria, Donna, and I have grades one through three. The children in all six classrooms know they are welcome in any of the rooms, whether they have a specific reason to be there or just want to visit. Big buddies from the upper grades and little buddies from the lower grades share many activities and promote the idea of community. Like the Elephant's Child, we all are "full of 'satiable curtiosity' . . . [asking] ever so many questions."[2] And just as the Elephant's Child discovered in his search for answers, it seems the answers to our questions only lead to more questions.

This is the setting that Tom cautiously entered. His new classmates, who had begun the school year a month before, eagerly invited him to join our circle and vied for him to be their friend. This was not to be, at least not yet. After some wandering and much wondering, Tom sat on the floor just outside the circle, away from the children. He gazed around the room. Almost immediately, he stood up and went to the library area, thumbing through several books. The children, already aware that we all need time to adjust to new things, continued their circle discussion. Here was a child needing time to wonder and wander, to use his curiosity to discover meaning, the same as Anna does in *The Wise Woman and Her Secret*.[3]

Tom took the supplies we gave him and seemed very proud of them all, including a daily journal for writing. He walked around the room observing the children writing. Then the new journal that just moments before had been a prized possession was thrown on the floor. Without a word, Tom scurried under a table and pulled his knees up to his chin. He refused to come out from under the table, and the children and I simply let him have his own space and time. This certainly was a strong indication that writing was not to his liking!

A consistent daily pattern quickly emerged. Tom would enter the room warily, sit just outside the circle, then go to the library area. He found some security in companionship with Pete, his next-door neighbor, whom he followed on a trek through a Spanish session with Maria, an English session with me, and a science/math session with Donna. The slightest unpredictable incident, however, would bring a cloudy look to his face and flight to a place of refuge under a table.

Rob, our new vice-principal, observed one such incident when he came into the room to visit. Tom was under a table sitting very still. Then Mike pointed and said, "Look! There's our new kid under the table." Tom's world suddenly changed. Rob said, "Come out here." Tom didn't move. Rob demanded that he come out. The situation was becoming critical. I desperately wanted to explain to Rob that giving Tom the time and opportunity to feel secure in his new environment was okay, but within seconds, Rob tried to pull Tom from under the table. Tom and Rob tugged at each other, and Tom wrangled to gain control. A chase ensued around the tables, around and around in a constantly changing pattern. Tom lost, and with screams of I hate you, I hate you, and a look of fear on his face, he was tucked under an arm and carried to the office. However, Tom's intuitive or received boundaries showed us one area of his control—he had stayed within the territorial limits of the classroom.

Over an hour later, a very subdued Tom and a victorious vice-principal returned. "He will now stay in the room and do as he is asked." The first part of Rob's statement was correct—Tom stayed within the limits of the room—but the second part didn't happen. Tom sat alone, refusing to join any activities for the remainder of the day.

This traumatic and disastrous beginning was slow to change. Although Tom made sure that we knew he was there (mainly through unexpected but overt and sometimes aggressive actions), he was unusually quiet most of the time. It could be said that he was aggressively passive. He refused to join any activity unless it was his choice and on his terms. We were a little taken aback by Tom's strong determination not to participate but agreed that his needs must be considered and he must come to know that we were on his side.

Literacy events were rare. He occasionally would read a short predictable book, but he refused to write. During music he would hold his hands over his ears and appear to withdraw totally. Later we would discover that he actually was listening and participating in his own aggressively passive way. He would state, "I can't read, and you can't make me." We had to agree—you cannot force a child to do something unless the time is right and the child is ready. Quick-fix answers were not forthcoming. What we could do was provide an environment that we hoped would invite Tom to participate in literacy events involving reading and writing for the purpose of learning.

Chris, Rick, Stella, Maria, Donna, and I, together with our principal, Mark, discussed what we could do to best support Tom. We agreed to make an effort to use only positive statements when talking to him and to document his positive endeavors with examples of his work and through anecdotal validation.

The children continued to be very supportive and understanding. Tom quickly learned that his territory was not limited just to his home room and the rooms of the science and Spanish sessions, but also included the three upper elementary rooms of Rick, Stella, and Chris. Our major concern continued to be his lack of trust in his own learning, even though he had a strong desire to be trusted and an apparent need to trust others.

Soon Tom entered his home room almost eagerly instead of cautiously each day, but he still did not join any group activities. Sometimes he said a few words to an adult and occasionally answered questions. During a brief moment when he allowed himself to have a conversation with me, he identified all of the letter names except R and said he knew two words—*cat* and *to*. Then he read a very short predictable book with very little help. Did the few contextual clues help his reading of the book, or was he just not telling us what he could really do? Probably it was a little of both. He staunchly refused to write anything except his name, the letters carefully drawn, not written.

Science and math provided more positive experiences for Tom. Grandma Jean, a volunteer, when confronted with what she described as his "bizarre behavior," said, "I don't understand why you allow it." We explained that we were not trying to "fix" Tom or his problems, but rather to view the world as Tom saw it and let him take the lead to show us his strengths. Grandma Jean's viewpoint underwent an immediate 180-degree turn, and she became his special safety net.

Grandma Jean, who just happened to be Donna's mother, took great interest in coming to our classrooms almost daily to "grandmother" the children. With her grandmotherly encouragement, Tom began to copy dictated words for illustrations, such as *pinto bean*, *lima bean*, *soil*, and *water*, though he often left out letters. He also began copying short phrases from books into his journal. The small amount of copying he produced was laborious, reminiscent of a much younger child's struggle with uncontrollable squiggly lines.

Still, normally unacceptable behavior was frequent. The causes of Tom's outbursts and withdrawals were very unpredictable, but his actions always reflected limitations. When his frustration seemed to be at its highest, he would spew out hate words and cry crocodile tears. The children, with their innate sense of community and Tom's needs, continued to support and accept him as a full member of our learning community.

The three computers in our room caught Tom's attention. One day as he stood staring at a computer, I asked, "Would you like to use a computer?" His face brightened. "Yes, I've never used one before." He quickly mastered the basics, and the computer offered hours of enjoyment, becoming a new refuge. At first he spent a lot of time using a commercial math program, then he began to explore on his own. Because he was so interested in computers, we tried to make his using them dependent on his participation in other activities. We should have known it wouldn't work.

Other staff members and the school counselor had by now become aware of our problem. Their solutions included "Test him!" "Get rid of him!" "He is a threat to the other children and is interfering with their learning." "He shouldn't be in your room." The counselor added, "That boy needs my help." Others stated, "You probably could have him placed in a special day class." Labels appeared to be very much on the minds of the majority of the onlookers. Several made it clear that they expected "something to be done with him."

On September 22 we received a memorandum: "If you haven't already done so, please see to it that Tom is referred to the student study team ASAP. Thanks, Mark." All of us need our own safety nets, especially when we are challenging systemic traditions and beliefs. We knew we were placing ourselves outside the traditional ways of dealing with challenging learners and were afraid our expectations for Tom would be undermined by those with differing viewpoints. Luckily, an independent study with Denny Taylor made me sit up and take notice of my need to advocate for my students. Denny immediately became our confidant. She encouraged us to document what was happening to Tom. She also suggested that perhaps a discussion with the counselor might be helpful. A meeting was set, but the counselor didn't appear.

We did, however, have a productive meeting with Mark. All of us were familiar with the process of referrals. I had been the chairperson of the school's guidance committee for several years and had observed little real benefit from the testing process. Teachers generally referred students to protect themselves from possible legal implications, but in reality held little hope that children, once labeled, would receive any true or lasting benefits to successfully function in their academic world. Furthermore, many referred children simply tested too low on an extensive test battery to receive any help, which created a sense of "Oh, well, I'll do the best I can, but the child can't learn." The process was also lengthy. We all felt that labels usually created more problems for children and rarely supported their learning.

Current theory about how to challenge learners, as well as our own experiences, had convinced us that all children are learners when they are placed in a caring and literate environment, that they come to school as eager learners with vast knowledge and experience. We maintained that our goal was to support Tom, as we did each child in our classrooms, rather than to view him as a problem child. Concentrating on Tom's needs made it impossible to see him from a deficit perspective, to label him. A proactive advocacy support plan[4] Maria had developed for her graduate studies helped us identify and develop mediation skills. And, using the child-advocacy model described in Denny Taylor's *From the Child's Point of View*,[5] we had already acquired documentary evidence of how Tom's transactions with writing and reading were changing his views and attitudes and bringing about academic growth.

We decided to instigate a weekly study group to investigate the child-advocacy model more thoroughly and use it to understand other children's literacy and learning as well as Tom's. "In adopting this ethnographic perspective of the social construction of behavior (situated practical accomplishments), the oversimplified pronouncements based on traditional evaluative procedures have to be rejected or redefined. Instead of analyzing the 'in-the-head' knowledge of children we have to examine the environments in which that knowledge is applied."[6]

October

Tom knew he was supported in his search for meaning in his world, and he used this freedom to discover and create new spaces within the room where he could watch as a quiet participant. He typically kept four or five short predictable books tucked inside his folder. *The Red Rose*[7] was his favorite, and he held on to it for weeks. Sometimes he copied a bit of text from different books into his journal, but there was no original writing.

The overall theme for the year was Africa. Stories about Africa prompted Tom to draw an elephant—very simple intersecting circles, with straight lines for the legs and trunk. He copied the word *elephant* under the illustration. Then he quickly drew two intersecting circles, no lines, and labeled it *zebra*. Hands-on activities held more lasting interest for him, but projects were often left unfinished. His knowledge of computer technology grew rapidly, and he took great pride in sharing each new computer discovery with both adults and children.

The first time Tom showed interest in a job responsibility in the classroom was an exciting moment, a far cry from his nonparticipant, observational pose. One day he asked if he could be my "special room helper." I replied, "You're already a special helper, and a good one." He accepted this acknowledgment and took this position very seriously. He created a sign that said "Tom is the helper" and asked me to put it on the door. Then he pursued his job on his own terms, reminding children to put things away, returning books to the library, and taking a message to the office. The children seemed to have fun responding to his directives.

Each child had a Life Book in which they recorded things they wanted to remember. Tom decided he now wanted a Life Book to record things he "wanted to remember the rest of my life like the other kids have." He copied the categories in nearly standard spelling—"Temwrk [teamwork], PatEnSF [patience], CFIdEnce [confidence], CAIng [caring]"—then dictated and copied "A long time ago my brother was sad and I made him feel better." The topic of his brother came up frequently. Other than his brother, he talked about his grandma and his friend Pete a lot.

His hand-drawn illustrations were becoming more distinguishable as objects. After hearing a fairy tale, he dictated, "After a thunderstorm, the princess knocked at the palace door." He illustrated this by drawing a door with a window resembling the entrance to a cave and a princess lying horizontally underneath the door. Another illustration showed a line-drawing of Tom at a table making stars, "because I like to make stars." My response to this piece of literacy was, "You are a shining star!" He smiled. Watching and wondering—and having the time to watch and wonder—supported Tom's risk-taking attempts at literacy. He was redefining his place in his school world.

First-Trimester Three-Way Conference

Three-way conferences had proven to be very beneficial as a link between the school and the home. We got the idea from Don Graves:

> First and foremost, I am interested in inviting students . . . to view portfolios as an ongoing process, something they keep in mind every day as they work. . . .
> I also plan to invite parents *and* students to come to parent conferences. I think this would further strengthen the link between school and home.[8]

Parents particularly enjoyed having their children share and talk about their work in this context.

At the end of the first trimester, we asked the children to choose their best or favorite pieces of work to share at their conferences and to prepare an additional fifteen-minute writing and spelling sample. Tom, with gentle nudging, selected a few items from the brief holdings in his folder, but he refused to write a single word and sat under a table as the children composed their writing sample. Later he dictated, "I like math and science. I like the homework. I like playing tennis. I am trying to do math well because I'll learn better. Two things I have done well this trimester are read and copy books. I need to work harder at my homework, write things, and read a book. I am proud I've learned better reading. My goal is math. The hardest things in it are like three numbers on top and three numbers on bottom."

The children also drew pictures of themselves for their portfolios. Tom started a self-portrait by writing his name, but threw it away. Later he said, "I didn't finish the other one" which was his way of saying, Can I do a picture now? He wrote his name, age, and date, then drew a small, quarter-sized circle with a smiling face, and two legs.

The day of Tom's conference arrived. He was very excited and kept asking,

"When is my grandma coming?" The conference was very positive; his grandmother was interested in his portfolio choices and enthusiastic about his improved behavior at home. She told us she was pleased to hear "good news" and see the positive attitude of Tom's teachers instead of being told negatives. Tom didn't lead the conference as planned, but he listened intently to the comments being made.

Tom's grandmother said, "Tom has many problems, but I will talk to him about security." She again volunteered that there were several small children and babies in their "tiny house" and that taking care of the little ones was a job Tom could be depended on to do well. Then she told me, "Tom fell from a second-story window when he was two and landed on his head. Maybe that's why he is so slow." She rubbed his head gently after this statement.

Tom agreed to write something every day at home and bring it to school. (Somehow, however, that writing always got "lost.") He also agreed that he would save his computer efforts onto his disc at school, but as he explained, "I just accidentally erase everything."

November Intersession

A four-week break followed the first trimester. I was off to Arizona to attend my own classes, and I wondered, as we all did, What will happen to Tom? Will he return to school? These were always looming questions. After all, he had attended seven schools in eleven moves during his first three years. His records included only Zoo Phonics and numbers ditto sheets and comments about poor behavior and references to possible testing. (The testing never materialized, probably because he was always moving.)

Donna suggested to his grandmother that Tom attend a two-week quilting intersession to be held immediately following the first trimester. The children would encounter reading, writing, poetry, music, and math within the context of the geometric and scientific attributes of quilting.

Grandma Jean, to whom Tom now felt a special connection, offered to do "grandma reading" with him. A positive, warm relationship sprang up between the two. Grandma Jean reported that she read to Tom the first day, but the next day he asked to read to her. This pattern continued for the two-week session. His favorite book? *The Red Rose.* Donna wrote, "I believe that Tom knows he is safe. He is surrounded by warm and nutritional soil. Add water, the ingredient of caring, and you have the perfect habitat for growth."

He participated in more activities but still found reasons to hide. He attempted to complete all the quilt experiences with Grandma Jean's help and dictated two poems:

Quilts grow from fabric,
to big, to cute, to soft,
and into quilts.

Quilts.
Dark, Big, Cover, Play, Picnic.
Makes me feel good.
Blanket.

It was very evident that Tom (with some gentle nudging from Grandma Jean) was beginning to take more risks and feel more success in his learning.

December

Tom arrived from the remaining two weeks of vacation with a big smile, asking, "Did you miss me?" I replied, "Of course I missed you a whole lot! And I missed your wonderful smile!" Did his eyes take on an added sparkle? I thought so.

Tom seemed in better control of what had previously been problematic situations. He joined more group projects as an interested observer, but still did little writing or reading. He would usually listen to stories from a distance, then later choose a story he had heard and share it with a friend.

However, as the first week back progressed, there were again disruptions. Tom accused children and adults of not liking him. His yelling "I hate you" and kicking at (but not touching) friends and objects became more frequent. He seemed to know intuitively how far he could go with his outbursts without crossing the point of no return. Still, he would interact with various children as long as they didn't require more of him than he wanted to give.

Just before Christmas vacation, Tom's grandmother stopped in and told me she was taking a beauty course in order to make more money and that her phone had been disconnected because the "kids" were making too many long distance calls and not paying for them. When I mentioned that Tom seemed discontent, her comment was, "His mother has been visiting us with her new boyfriend, but she pays no attention to Tom. We are having trouble at home, too."

When the (unacceptable) territorial limits of Tom's periodic self-imposed exiles grew to include the playground and another hallway, we had a serious talk. That is, I talked and he pretended not to hear by covering his ears. Limits were again followed thereafter, but not without a lot of self-imposed isolation and sulking.

Once Mark saw Tom sitting alone, knees up to his chin, and decided to join him on the floor. Soon the two were having a real discussion. Mark seemed rather surprised that Tom had so much to say on a number of different topics! There was a sense that Mark was beginning to appreciate the advances Tom was making.

January

Puppet shows became the vogue this month, and different groups of children produced some very exciting shows. Tom decided to try his hand as a producer. Everyone wanted a part in "Tom's show." He was especially careful to choose good readers for the narration. Tom's only oral contribution was a frequent nasal, twangy "ANNNNG." Tom's friends carried out their parts like real theater troupers, and the other children applauded exuberantly. When Luke asked, "Why did you make that noise?" Tom replied, "To make you laugh." Indeed it had made everyone laugh. For Tom, this was a first and very successful "public" appearance.

Wonderful things began to happen more frequently: more adherence to school regulations, greater coping skills, fewer demanding situations. Tom was evincing a more positive attitude, rudimentary mediation skills, and a greater interest in reading. Whole days went by with only a minor incident or two. Tom also showed more meaningful communication when he tried unsuccessfully to withdraw after an incident. After a brief self-imposed exile and reflection under a table, he joined the adults with a huge smile on his face. Grandma Jean asked, "Why are you here? Do you want something?" His smiling face turned red and he replied, "I'm thinking with my face," and he joined the group. Just as fast as Tom's face would cloud over and he would disappear, he would suddenly return and quietly participate. He was working out ways of solving whatever was bothering him.

January also found Tom more willing to write. Each day the children wrote three items for their work plan. Tom said, "This is a good idea." He buddied up with Chris to discuss their plans, then went to a table by himself and wrote, "1. kmpdr's [computers], 2. math, 3 ridg [reading]." He completed each item on his list. The procedure of writing a daily plan ceased after one day, but Tom continued to follow his schedule. He worked at the computer, did some math papers, copied a bit of text, and began to read his own writing back to us, although spaces were missing. He commented that "It's hard to read with no words." We had a discussion about why words were hard to find.

Next, large dots began to appear between some words. Children's writing shows clearly their thinking at any given time. Here Tom was beginning to understand spaces and their place in the meaning-making of writing. As Anne Haas Dyson writes:

> Learning to write involves figuring out how to manipulate the words on the page in order to accomplish particular kinds of social work; that social work, however, must meet the evaluative criteria of the imaginative universe one is in, and, in school, there are in fact multiple such universes potentially operating at any one moment, each with values not always made explicit.[9]

Science sessions, too, yielded more literacy artifacts. For one project, Tom drew several circles of varying sizes, including the sun with rays and a smiling face. A sense of perspective was evident. Three circles were labeled: "satn [Saturn]," "san [Sun]," and "mls [Mars]."

During one science session Donna witnessed a very sad Tom. She asked him to draw a picture about how he felt. He drew a circle with a frowning face and short lines under the eyes. He added a shark, then dictated, "I felt sad. I cried. See the tears. Here's a shark with sharp teeth."

Literacy evidence continued to confirm that this young man could do far more as he gained his place in our world. Invented spelling surfaced, Tom showed more willingness to complete a few tasks, and he shared more activities with the other children. Security and trust appeared at last to be part of his school and social worlds. One more month of school was left to support his learning before another four-week break.

February

All six teachers of my strand spent the first four days of February at a bilingual conference presenting our view of language acquisition and literacy as we saw it occurring within our student population. My substitute was left to face Tom's uncontrollable kicking and screaming. Although we had discussed his "special case" and I had told her to call the vice-principal—and *only* the vice-principal—in an emergency, she notified the counselor, who strongly opposed the approach we were taking.

On the morning of my return, I was greeted by the counselor: "You have a very serious problem with that boy. He needs my help. I want you to sign these forms requesting that he be referred for testing and counseling." She handed me the papers. I said I would look into the matter. Call Denny! I thought, and I did. Acting on her advice, we again invited the counselor to meet with us and to attend our group discussions so we could clarify our respective viewpoints and share our discoveries about Tom. Although she didn't meet with us, our principal once again supported our stand, notifying the study team that their intervention was as yet inappropriate.

With such support, we grew ten feet taller and continued our enlightening journey with Tom. We offered the counselor a copy of *From the Child's Point of View*, the book we were using as a guide to developing a biographic literacy profile of Tom. She accepted the book graciously, and we suggested she also read some of Anne Haas Dyson's work. She returned the book several weeks later with many marginal notations and the comment, "I've never read anything like it. It was interesting and I enjoyed reading it, but I don't necessarily agree with it."

As the weeks and months went by, Tom appeared to be more secure and at peace in our classrooms; risk-taking attempts also grew. He used more beginning sounds, and recognized some words on sight, and occasionally reread a phrase that didn't make sense to him. The books he read were still short and predictable, but he read more of them.

February 10 was a real celebration. Tom actually participated in every activity all day. Once he retreated to a corner, but within minutes he was back interacting with his classmates. He completed a weather clock and temperature chart in science. Donna said he had done them "all by himself and he seems to be so proud." Later he asked to read to me, but when he noticed that other children were reading he said quietly, "I'll wait until the kids aren't listening." He stood back, waited, and chose the proper quiet moment to read. The book was still short and predictable, but it was a brand-new text and he read it with enthusiasm.

Tom was confirming one of my observations: some children want to share their successes by reading aloud to anyone who will listen, and some prefer the quiet sanctuary of privacy in which to share their new knowledge of the reading process. Many children fall into this latter category, and their needs must be respected. Tom certainly demanded privacy. More than likely he would have refused to read orally if required to do so within a group of readers or to an audience.

We were encouraged by Tom's many positive moments, but all was not smooth sailing. Classroom aides throughout the school were talking about Tom. My own aide stated, "Well, how long are you going to allow this awful behavior. You'll have all the other children start to behave in the same way." She missed the important— and obvious—fact that the children were there for each other and for Tom, the same as the teachers. It was not a matter of the other children learning to violate appropriate behavior, it was a matter of Tom learning to accept appropriate behavior. We talked, and she did make a valiant effort to include him as a working member of our learning community, with very positive results. A few days later she decided to ask Tom to read to her, and to her great surprise, he did. He had refused to acknowledge her up to this point, but now he had one more friend and supporter.

Major changes continued. Tom became a teacher of other kids in reading and writing, although his own writing was still negligible. He overheard Nick say, "Mrs. K., I went through the whole letters and there isn't an R." Tom said, "Oh yes there is. Do you want cursive or printing?" Then Tom showed him the two forms of the letter in a book.

The approach of Valentine's Day brought a look of despair. Tom informed Grandma Jean, "Grandma doesn't have money to buy any valentines and I won't have any for the kids." Of course Grandma Jean bought him cards and sat with him as he copied each name onto a card. He worked very hard at this task. Letter formation was still laborious, but very readable. His mission accomplished, he also created a card on the computer, "TO GAMOM FAM TOM [To Grandmother from Tom]." Valentine's Day was a happy day for Tom and for us all.

The next day Tom met me in the hall, gave me a half-smile, then disappeared. He had discovered new territory—the library. I learned from the librarian that he had been visiting the library frequently "on his way to the bathroom, to look at books." She knew about his outbursts and said, "I'm glad he can come to the library now." She was celebrating his library visits by helping him select books, thinking we had sent him. This time he had found a book about Egypt. He checked the book out for our room library and took it from child to child, sharing information. Each child eagerly awaited "my turn." Luke asked him to help build some clay pyramids that, when completed, were put on display with our African artifacts. How wonderful to observe Tom finding his place, creating new friendships, and sharing new events!

Events is the only possible word to describe Tom's efforts at belonging to a literate classroom. Each time Tom voluntarily wrote, drew, or read, it was an event, shared by his classmates as well as his teachers. He had joined the literacy club:

Learning is a social activity. Learning is a consequence of the way in which you interact with other people. Learning is a matter of your identity. . . . Learning is a consequence of joining clubs, of joining communities, of belonging. Learning is also a consequence of the way people treat you. . . . We get our identity from other people, the people that we see ourselves as being like. . . . You find out what people do with the spoken language. You can't do that until you've joined the club. You've got to be a member of the club first, and then you learn the club activities.[10]

There was a continual and growing acknowledgment by Tom that he could do all the things the rest of the children were doing. As evidence of his membership in the literacy club, he read four never-before-read predictable books with very little help. He held on to them until he knew every word. He also read a fifth book, a very short chapter book. He made more miscues than he usually did, but he persisted and succeeded in completing the entire book.

Another example of his growing literate security happened when Pete, his next-door neighbor and a third-grade literacy learner who challenged us all, observed Tom's self-confidence. He asked Tom to spell *home* for him. Tom looked at different books until he found the word and then insisted that the word be written in neat and precise letters. Pete, happy at being helped, returned to his writing, and Tom returned to copying a book.

We all, children and teachers, felt gratified each time a literacy event occurred in Tom's growing social relationships and learning. Each child understood the power of support and praise, and Tom was learning that he could do what other children could do.

Tom's major disturbances were now almost nonexistent, although minor incidents continued to occur. When Grandma Jean gave him a new pencil, observing that he was writing and reading a bit more, Tom sharpened it and started his copy work. After a few minutes he stopped, tossed the pencil into the air, and watched it fall to the floor. The aide, thinking she was now his friend, picked up the pencil to return it, but added, "Please don't do that again." He ran out of the room crying and disappeared. Checking his usual places of refuge, I found him in the library, where the librarian said he had kicked a boy just to kick him.

This incident needed attention. I said, "Tom, I really care about what happens to you, but we must work things out so that you are happy and everyone else is, too." He was quiet for a moment, then replied, "I was just trying to cool down." I called Rob, our vice-principal. Rob motioned to Tom, saying, "Come here, buddy," and they walked down the hallway to the office, arm in arm. Was Tom expanding the circle of adults who understood him, or was Rob becoming aware of a different frame of reference for dealing with children? I suspect it was a little of both.

A Home Visit

In order to add to Tom's biographic literacy profile, I visited him at home. On the appointed day, Tom was very happy at school. He drew a picture and dictated a story in his journal. "That's me and that's you and that's the rest of the kids. We're all reading." He announced that he could now help the younger children read and called them up one at a time and helped them read one of his short predictable books. As he left school he asked, "Are you coming to see grandma?"

After school, Grandma Jean drove me to his tiny house. A fenced yard full of dogs and puppies meant a tricky walk to the front door. His grandmother had obviously forgotten we were coming, but she graciously invited us in. Adults, children, and diapered babies sprawled on the couch and floor watching television. Others streamed in and out of the house to and from the refrigerator. Tom appeared and stood by his grandmother, who volunteered, "I'm attending beauty college, and trying to hold my family together." Tom smiled a smile of pride, and she continued, "Tom's father has never been in his life. Tom only knows about him and hardly ever sees him. Tom's brother lives with him, but Tom has never once received a present from him for either a birthday or a holiday."

Pam, a twenty-year-old daughter and mother of one of the diapered babies, joined our conversation. She retold the story of Tom's fall. This seemed to be a major issue and an accepted explanation for his lack of academic achievement and behavioral problems in each school. "Tom was looking out of a window on the second floor and fell to the ground. We took him to a doctor, and he didn't find anything wrong with him at the time but told us Tom might have problems later." The grandmother repeated, in a loving tone (as she had on several occasions), "Tom, maybe that bump on your head is why you can't learn."

Pam continued, "Tom's mother was a good mother at first, but when he was three, she abandoned him with different relatives. She was in and out of his life the first year, but when he was four her visits were rare." Grandmother informed us, "the whole first year Tom was with me he didn't open his mouth or say a word. When his mother visited, she would ignore him for the most part, so he would hide in a corner or under a table. She still visits only once in awhile and Tom still runs and hides when she is here."

Cassie, Tom's fifteen-year-old sister, opened the refrigerator door. Grandmother pointed to her and said, "She's the one who really raised him. She protected him and carried him in her arms like a small baby until this year, when we made her stop." Cassie seemed totally oblivious of our conversation.

We were told there were many books in the house, although we saw none. Pam wanted us to know that "Tom likes for me to read to him when I'm here, but I don't always live here." Grandmother continued, "Tom has paper and pencils and draws some, but we haven't saved anything with so many people in the house. He asked me to help him write a letter to you because he likes you." She thumbed through the piles of newspapers and magazines on the table. "He likes to write, and is always asking how to spell words. He won't try on his own." Pam said she was teaching Tom to spell, and that "he knows lots of words." I thought, How I wish I could see some examples!

We learned that Tom watches a lot of TV and sleeps on the couch. "He is really good at helping with the little ones, but he doesn't have any chores. There are just too many people I have to care for."

Tom was listening as his grandmother said, "When Tom loses control at home, he has two options—go to the back room or the strap. I've never had to use the strap, but I do swat him when he loses control, and he comes out of it when he's left alone." His refuge under tables and in other confined spaces was beginning to make sense.

Pam suggested that he "probably has dyslexia or is AD(H)D [attention deficit (hyperactive) disorder]." Tom's grandmother questioned this and suggested the fall from the second story was the cause of "his problems." After our hour-plus conversation ended, we left without a single artifact to show Tom's literacy accomplishments in his home. However, we did feel that we had a much broader perspective of Tom's place in his social, school, and home worlds. We recalled the words of Anne Haas Dyson:

> [The children's] worlds coexisted and intersected. There was the official school world, in which they were "students"; and the peer world, in which they were "co-workers" (and perhaps "friends"); and the world of their respective home communities, which re-formed in the classroom amidst networks of peers. Each world required particular kinds of social work and valued particular kinds of ways with words. . . . In classrooms children are at once members of diverse reference spheres. . . . There are no neat boundaries between "home" and "school," or between the official (teacher-controlled) sphere and that of peers.[11]

Tom was in a very happy mood the next day. He had read by himself, worked on the computer, completed some math papers, and discussed pertinent content issues about Africa with several children. In the science session, he constructed a paper thermometer and wrote an entry in his science log with Grandma Jean's help. "Wan I Blow on The bottom is go sAp [When I blow on the bottom (of a thermometer) it goes up]." There were large dots between some words, indicating space holders. Our prior conversation about spaces had apparently triggered some understanding of the concept of space. Tom had permission that day to stay and help for fifteen minutes, and he was very careful to watch the clock for when the time was up. I wrote a note to his grandmother describing Tom's many productive activities that day. He left, note in hand, saying, "See you tomorrow, Mrs. K." What a joy!

February (continued)

In light of the approaching second trimester of three-way conferences, the children searched their work for items to put in their showcase portfolios. Tom's face turned cloudy, and he said, "I'm dumb and I don't have anything." He finally agreed to look at his work and found more there than he realized he had: "I have lots of things." He chose the thermometer project, dictating, "I chose this piece because it shows that I can do work." On a sheet of tally marks he wrote by himself, "I lik math. IllIk.dheNK HmeWRK [I like math. I like doing homework]."

Mike asked Tom to help him draw a picture of a crocodile for his showcase portfolio; they each drew a large crocodile and Tom added a small picture at the bottom of his illustration. "This is me because I'm dependable and do all of my work. I'm trustworthy, too." I asked, "What does trustworthy mean, Tom?" He responded, "It means always being there to help." In his way, he was being trustworthy by completing some work and helping others. He still refused to do a fifteen-minute writing sample, but as the rest of the children wrote, he noted that the date on the board needed changing. "Can I go and fix the date so the kids can see it?" He looked at the date for a minute, then changed the 7 (in 2/17/95) to an 8 (2/18/95), saying, "All I had to do was change the seven to an eight."

His feeling of security prompted him to produce another puppet show. The only two children he approached turned him down because they were involved in other projects. "No one likes me and they won't do it with me." I suggested, "Have you asked anyone else?" "No, but they don't like me." Several eager friends volunteered. They tried to follow Tom's directives, but one by one they abdicated and the puppet show was left without puppeteers. Five-year-old Nick came up when he saw the children leaving, and observed, "Mrs. K., you know that saying, 'Sticks and stones may break your bones but words cannot harm you?' Well, it's not true. Tom is hurting." Our multiaged learners were truly living and working together.

The annual science fair just before conference time at the end of the second trimester created lots of interest in many projects. The class created a geology display and won a ribbon. Letters were written to parents inviting them to see their winning project at the evening fair. Tom wrote entirely by himself, "DeaR Grandma We weRe WinneRS. We won two 1st prizes and one 2nd prize. PleASe co to the prty to see our winners! Love, Tom." The difference between this communication and earlier attempts at writing was monumental!

Second-Trimester Three-Way Conference

The day of Tom's conference, he met me before school with a smile, ran to get his showcase portfolio, then said, "I can't find it!" He quickly added, "I was just teasing" and produced the portfolio as proof.

Concentrating on school things was difficult for all the children as they waited for their conferences, and Gloria, the substitute, was very understanding. Tom vacillated between the conference area and the classroom until he saw his grandmother. He carefully described each piece of work, and his grandmother offered, "Tom now has some minimal chores to do and he is very dependable." The conference was a total success in Tom's eyes, and a vast success in our eyes.

Conferences continued for two more days. On the second day, Gloria wrote a note about Tom and his day:

He worked all day nicely. At one point he said "Stupid" to a couple of boys, but his comment was ignored. I am really impressed with his improved ability to take care of himself. I would talk to him and ask him how things were going. Sometimes he would speak, at other times he would just shrug and smile. He did wander around, but usually within the class or nearby. If I wanted him to do something, I would ask him to join us and give him time to make up his own mind. Usually within a few minutes he would decide. It wasn't always what I wanted but most of the time it was acceptable behavior. I have found that talking softly and calmly could at times bring him back to the class and I also found that giving him a choice to make, a decision that he made, helped keep him on track and be more likely to cooperate.

This was like eating a piece of wonderful chocolate cream candy or skiing down a slope with perfect snow! Later Gloria wrote,

The class was reading literature books and he stayed with his group and read for over half the period. I did discover that when he wanted to read or show something to me, he wanted to do it right away. If I had to make him wait it could trigger a bad mood. But if I could explain fast enough that I would get to him as soon as I could, he would sometimes wait patiently nearby.

The third conference day was another story. A different substitute with different expectations informed me that "Tom has many problems, and was very difficult. Has he been tested?" The children overheard comments by the substitute and later informed me, "Mrs. K., that isn't true. Tom was good." They asked if they could write about their observations. Statements varied, but they were all in support of Tom. "Tom was taking pichers of people of their buts, but he wasn't hurting anybody." "I like Tom taking pitchrs of us." "Tom didn't do nothing. all he did was playing with the chamara. he was using the film. but he did a little work."

The last day before our break, Joe and Tom discovered the chickens and ducks in our strand's chicken yard needed attention. They wrote a note to Mr. A.: "ChicKS' – NoWatER NoFood x Hungry Tom + Joe." They took care of the water situation, obtained the necessary feed, and saved the barnyard! Their encounter with a problem and a solution was a success.

An awards ceremony was held during the afternoon. All children received two awards—one their choice and one a teacher or parent choice. Tom's smiles were very broad as he received his awards. After the awards ceremony, Tom retreated inside the classroom because "my grandma didn't come to see me get my awards."

Thus ended the second trimester. Did we have questions regarding our experiences with Tom? We had plenty, but they had to wait.

April

Once again, we wondered what our lives with Tom would be like when school started again on April 10. Tom arrived early with big smiles and hugs for all of us. He held the door for children to go to their classrooms and joined the morning circle. We were witnessing a small feeling of belonging. Toward the end of the day, Tom's name was drawn to be the secretary for the next day.

He was very excited the next morning and took his job very seriously for awhile. He carried out the bells and song list for our strand opening (all six classrooms), did his self-designated door opening, and even stood just *outside* the door instead of inside. He got the roll sheet to begin the secretary duties, but looked at the floor and shook his head no. He whispered in my ear, "I'll do it another time." He chose Sam to take his place and observed everything she did. A later conversation shed light on his inability to cope with a new job at that particular time. "Did you know I saw my dad and my brother? That's why I won't take my jacket off. My brother gave it to me." I asked, "Did you see them over vacation?" "Yes. I went to visit my brother. My dad was in jail because he beat up my mother a long time ago. It's sort of like a traffic ticket that he didn't see about." How little we really know about our children and the incidents that fill their thoughts!

The next day, Tom took charge as if he were a seasoned leader. He designated jobs to different children, sent the bankers to collect daily pocket money, and called on Chris to read a story. He came up with a creative way to help him identify the names on the roll sheet. He refused Suzi's offered help and went to the posted class picture, looked for the likeness, matched the name, and checked it. More evidence that he could do a lot more than he was willing to do.

Another surprise accompanied a rehearsal for our soon-to-be-produced musical, *The Elephant's Child*.[12] During lunch recess, Tom informed me that he knew all the songs even though he had not once been an active participant. "Do you want me to sing the Limpopo River song?" He didn't wait for a yes or no; the song flowed from his mouth in the most beautiful bell-like tones. For six months we had all thought music was distasteful to him! Here was another proof that literacy is obtained in many ways. Tom was confirming Beth Berghoff's contention:

> Every experience with a sign is an opportunity to consolidate and to add to an existing understanding of the world. Learning amounts to building an ever more complex picture of the world and how it works. The larger our collection of related knowledge, the more we can grasp or understand.[13]

Toward the end of April, an unfortunate incident took place quite unexpectedly. Tom's sister, Cassie, was SARBed (School Attendance Review Board), meaning that numerous persons, from psychologists to parents to teachers to administrators to police officers, reviewed her school attendance and attitude. The legally binding meeting only applied to Cassie, but when the board learned she had a brother in school, it issued directives regarding him as well. Tom's school attendance had always been very regular, but now each absence had to be verified by a physician or a designated school official, the family had to attend family counseling, and Tom needed to participate in a school counseling program. The board issued all these mandates without looking at Tom's school records, without talking to Tom, and without discussing his school world with his teachers. The requirements were legally binding, but Mark, who attended the SARB, felt we already had an acceptable counseling program in the biographic literacy profile workup, which by now included evidence of a willingness and a desire to collect some writing and reading work for his portfolio, and Maria's proactive advocacy support plan, which provided guidelines to help Tom negotiate mediation when confronted with problems. This experience made each of us more aware of the serious, unfair, and degrading actions that can and do take place. It also confirmed that our advocacy for Tom was appropriate!

May

All teachers and substitutes have their own beliefs and philosophies with regard to learning and their own coping devices. When they have opposing beliefs and different expectations, it reflects on the children and *their* ability to cope. Tom's experiences with substitutes were painful or good, depending. Gloria understood and supported our beliefs and made an effort to continue the learning environment we were trying to create and to understand and negotiate the children's needs. We always made every effort to obtain a substitute whose views about children's learning were similar to our own. However, we were to be out of town for a few days to present our program at a conference, Gloria was not available, and the new substitute was of the I-teach-you-listen-and-do school.

"He said he didn't hear the bell and was on the playground after the other children had come in," was the message left on my desk. It continued, "Tom puts himself at great risk when he disappears and/or fails to return to his classroom." An informal suspension in the office was the result. The following day, the substitute had another complaint: "Tom was crowding in line, argued with a student, pushed him to the ground and proceeded to kick him." He was sent home, something that had not happened before. When I returned, the children expressed concern. "She just didn't understand. Tom and Mike weren't really fighting, they were just playing, and Tom wasn't really kicking. Why didn't they send Mike home, too?" Teachers need to walk a fine line. A little listening could have resolved these small offenses.

As a nudge to help Tom risk longer books to read, Denny suggested that an adult read a book to him daily and just talk with him. Heidi, our adopted class poodle, who belongs to one of our volunteers, Mrs. Hodge, frequently sits on a child's lap while the class is being read to. With Heidi on his lap, Tom responded very well. Mrs. Hodge also helped Tom read successfully from a no-longer-published *Frog Fun*[14] linguistic reader. He had lots of information about frogs and would ask Mrs. Hodge to "read that book so I can read more about frogs."

The children were busy creating dioramas about their favorite books and writing a summary. Tom decided to make a diorama story about Heidi. He dictated and copied, "Heidi is nice. Heidi is playful." Then he said to Mrs. Hodge, "You write the rest. This is too much to copy." "Heidi's coat is silver, but it is curly." Tom completed the diorama, and it was displayed with the others.

Just as there were many ups with Tom, so were there downs. The district testing program was scheduled, and Tom refused even to look at the reading test. He decided to "try" the math part, and successfully completed some of it, but stopped before completing the section. He had with him a book, *The Lion and the Little Red Bird*,[15] illustrated by a visiting author/illustrator. After the test materials were collected, he brought the book to me and said, "Look, Mrs. K., I can read the title." Not only did he read the title, but he asked to read more. With very little support, he read two pages of a real book.

May 19 held more surprises. During studio time, when children have the option to complete work they have started or choose a new challenge, Tom asked, "Can I paint a sign?" Picking up a large piece of white parchment, he copied a sign that said, "The Egypt Newspaper, by Tom," and hung it on the door. He informed me he would next write something on the computer for me, but when I asked to see it he said, "Somehow it didn't stay on the computer." However, other literacy events were evident. He read nine predicable books during the last two weeks of May and parts of two more short chapter books. Writing was becoming a little more interesting for him too. A culminating bus trip to a wild animal park was looming, and he copied a few words pertaining to the trip in his journal.

Another day, another happening! Joe asked Mrs. Hodge to read with him. Tom informed them, "I can read with Joe. You don't have to." As Tom pointed to words, Joe read the book. The two approached me with a request. "Will you tell the kids I helped him read?" Joe and Tom listened, smiling, as I shared the experience.

So many small, yet big, literacy events had taken place. I decided that the next day would be the opportune time to present a special award—the Once in a Blue Moon Award[16]—honoring some action above and beyond the expected. Tom received the first Blue Moon Award, which hung around his neck on white yarn. He then suggested with a grin that "other kids need the award, too." Thus the award for especially good things was inaugurated. Before the end of the year all children had blue moons, silver moons, and gold moons.

June

Our annual class autobiography, an idea we borrowed from Gloria Kauffman in Tucson, needed to be completed. Tom entered into this activity energetically as he planned his page and then dictated, "I like playing and I go places. I don't live with my brother. I went to his house and I had fun on Easter there. I like playing cars with him. I play war with him and with the little toy guys. I have fun playing at home. When I was three, I played and jumped on my brother. The first time I got to kindergarten I made friends. I liked to climb the monkey bars best. When I was a baby, I lived in the middle of nowhere. I lived in the spook house. I want to be a pilot in a jet." Another success story for Tom!

Final products for the children's yearly showcase portfolios this time included a videocassette recording of each child reading a book of their choice and answering questions taken from Carolyn Burke's reading interview.[17] Tom was very excited about this opportunity to be "in the movies" and chose a new, never-before-read predicable book, with a respectable number of words on each page. He breezed through it without help, making one miscue, which he corrected, and skipping over a few words, but continuing to read. His answers for the Burke interview were most perceptive. He said when he didn't know words he skipped them and that he learned to read by "just sounding out the words." He chose Jeff as a good reader because "he always reads books to me and got it all right." He answered "What do you think he does when he comes to something he doesn't know?" by saying, "He skips it. I'd say, 'Skip it Jeff,' and he did." He said he could help a child by telling them the words, and indeed he had done this very seriously on several occasions. His self-concept of himself as a reader was very poor—"I'm not a good reader because I mess up on the words." Still, he read the never-before-seen book, and we discussed this progress. He left the video session with the cassette in hand to share with "anyone who wants to see me read." Major literacy evidence now included reading, writing, computer printouts, and a videocassette. They still were not plentiful, but this was true progress.

The year's culminating trip to a wild animal park was finally in sight, creating a sense of excitement. Tom still watched as other children read and created stories about Africa. A few children invited him to be a member of their research group. Tom's reaction was to cry and crawl under a table. I commented very strongly, "Tom, this is not an option any more." He came out, sat by himself, and quietly said, "All the kids hate me, everybody hates me," and continued crying. Another child approached him, but Tom again withdrew under the table. Eventually he stopped crying, picked up a book, began looking at it, and then wrote a note. He asked one of his friends to deliver it to me. It simply said, "Mrs. K., I hate you. Tom." Every word in the brief communication was spelled correctly. Was my response to be punitive or supportive? I didn't hesitate. "I am so happy you wrote to me. I love you. Your writing is great, Tom." After some reflective time, Tom voluntarily joined a research group. The nudging from all those with whom he came in contact was surely paying dividends.

The day was June 21, the wild animal park was our destination. My plan was for Tom to be my partner for the day, but Nick, of "Sticks and stones may break your bones, but words cannot harm you" fame, chose Tom for his group, which included Nick's mother and two other children. With much hope and more than a little apprehension, we boarded the bus. Once inside the wild animal park, we periodically observed Nick, Tom, Karla, and Melina having a wonderful time recording their observations in their sketchbooks. At the end of the day, Nick's mom volunteered that the day had been perfect. Tom grinned, "This has been a fun day." Then the bus arrived and a cloud quickly crossed over his face. He refused to get on the bus. It was necessary to pick him up kicking and screaming. Once in a seat, he sat quietly for a very short time, then fell fast asleep. Upon our return, Nick's mom, as perceptive as her first-grade son, said, "I think he's just dreading the end of a happy day."

The following day another literacy event occurred. "Can I write to Nick's mom, because she was so nice?" He dictated, then copied, "Mrs. Burns, I thanK You F taking me to the park! I am sorry for throwing my book. I had FuN with Nick. Tom." A few days later, Tom had a letter in the mail: "Dear Tom, I had fun, too, Tom. Mrs. Burns."

The school year was nearly over now, and end-of-the-year events superseded regular school activities. A portfolio party was planned at which the children would share their year's work with their families. Each child wrote a note inviting their family and friends to attend. No one came from Tom's home. A fifth-grade student offered to be Tom's surrogate parent. Tom accepted the offer and carefully shared his portfolio, but his face again was cloudy.

The last night before school is over each year, we hold our annual sleepover, which includes an awards ceremony. Those children and parents who can spend the night and join in fireside tales, games, and a morning breakfast. Tom received his awards with no family member present to share his successes, and he was not allowed to stay for the sleepover.

The last day of school, the children said their good-byes. His Once in a Blue Moon Awards seemed to mean a great deal to Tom. He informed me that he had all of his moons and would keep them forever. The "olders" (third graders) were excited about the coming year in their new multiage grouping (grades four through six), and the "middlers" and "youngers" (grades one and two) were eager for their vacation and a new year with old friends, new friends, and familiar teachers. Again we wondered—would we see Tom? He had been a living lesson in patience, understanding, and love for us all, and we were pleased with the results—results that would not have been so evident had we not utilized the biography literacy profile and shared stories throughout the year about all of the children. Tom's literacy events provided us all with a better view of the literacy events of all the children. He had proved to us that even the most difficult situations can be modified when all children are included in a community of learners, when each one's life story is shared. Still, we had the battle of labels to wage. What would next year bring?

Another School Year Begins

The new school year resumed in early August 1995 without Tom. After a few weeks, Donna, Maria, and I made a trip to his house; we found new people moving in and a landlady who said the whole family had just disappeared, owing her money. A school in a town thirty-five miles away sent a request for Tom's records, and the school's principal requested information on any special testing that may have been done, since Tom was acting in a "bizarre way." Mark replied that Tom had been in a situation where six teachers collaborated to support him and that he had made miraculous progress; Mark also sent a follow-up anecdotal description of Tom's year.

Tom had come to us without an on-paper label but with an unending list of possibilities—AD(H)D, abandonment, truancy, dyslexia, special education, lack of societal expectations, poor academic achievement, and "in-the-head" problems from a fall. If any young person could be labeled, Tom was a prime candidate. We had to be constantly on guard in order to support Tom's search for identity and his efforts at making sense of his world. Although we had ended our year with him with many lingering questions, we also ended it *with hope*; we felt that his own sense of self had been greatly enhanced through his experiences with us and through his social learning experiences with and acceptance by the children.

The new school year began with a void. When I mentioned this to Denny, she said, "We will never know when or where in his life he will remember his positive experiences with you, and they will support him. Somewhere along the line, the way you worked with him will make a difference." But now he was gone.

The children continued to ask, "Where is Tom? We miss him." They wrote and sent letters to him, but they were all returned. The family had moved again and left no forwarding address. When we called the school later in the year, we learned that he was now "somewhere in the East." Disappointment in his absence was shared by teachers, volunteers, parents, and children alike. We missed being part of his efforts to feed his "satiable curtiosity."

We hope Tom knows that he has many friends at our school and that we all miss him. We also remember his smile. Each time we reflect on our time with Tom or see a picture that includes Tom in our learning community, we can't help but smile. The smile is remembrance.

Endnotes

1. We are six teachers building curriculum on a similar theoretical base. Multiage, whole language, and all children second-language learners in a family strand are viewed as components for providing learning experiences through social interaction, inquiry, and life experiences. **2.** "The Elephant's Child" in *Just So Stories* (New York: Weathervane Books, 1988), a tale by Rudyard Kipling, was read throughout the year as part of an overall theme—Africa. **3.** Eve Merriam so eloquently exemplifies the value of "think" and "discovery" time in order to gain wisdom in her story, *The Wise Woman and Her Secret* (New York: Simon & Schuster, 1990). **4.** Maria Almanzo is the Spanish language arts member of our primary multiage strand. Her advocacy model for negotiation provides strategies and options to use in negotiating problem solving. **5.** Denny Taylor's comments on page 16 of *From the Child's Point of View* (Portsmouth, NH: Heinemann, 1993) became quite clear after observing and learning from Tom for just a short period of time. She says that "the child's 'problems' are school defined. Thus, it is necessary to examine our interpretation of school . . ." This text became the "road map" for all six teachers' experiences with Tom and a way of thinking about each child in our classrooms. **6.** On page 12 of the same text (*From the Child's Point of View*, Portsmouth, NH: Heinemann, 1993) Denny speaks of "situated practical accomplishments" that are "internal to the situation at hand." We witnessed monumental changes in Tom when we and the children accommodated his social construction of behavior within situated points in time. **7.** A book that appealed to Tom would become his constant companion. *The Red Rose* by J. Cowley (San Diego, CA: The Wright Group, 1985) was read over and over for a period of over two months. **8.** Three-way conferences held twice a year have been very successful. Don Graves (*Portfolio Portraits*, Portsmouth, NH: Heinemann, 1992, p. 6) supported our belief that teacher-parent-student conferences could be beneficial when the child was the facilitator of the conference. **9.** Anne Haas Dyson (*Social Worlds of Children Learning to Write in an Urban Primary School*, New York: Teachers College Press, 1993, p. 12) helped expand our understanding of the different worlds children must control. As we gained more "knowing" of Tom, we realized how much each of his worlds (home and school) connected and intertwined. **10.** Frank Smith succinctly presented strong support for the necessity of belonging to a literacy club (talk given at the California Association for Bilingual Education, San Jose, 1994). **11.** Tom's coping with two very distinct worlds—the school and home—as Anne Haas Dyson presents, is a continual building of relationships, understandings, and a sense of place (*Social Worlds of Children Learning to Write in an Urban Primary School*, New York: Teachers College Press, 1993, pp. 2–3). **12.** Tom sang the intricate songs and music from "The Elephant's Child" perfectly. This truly was an unbelievable experience.

13. Toward the end of the year it was evident that Tom had expanded his "existing under-standing of the world" (B. Berghoff talk presented at the National Council of Teachers of English conference in San Diego, 1995). He had moved from almost total class membership to an almost full member of this world. **14.** Mrs. Hodge and her dog Heidi were able to create a bond for reading with Tom. She encouraged reading short, predictable books, but his favorite book was *Frog Fun* by C. T. Stratemeyer and H. L. Smith (Beverly Hills: Benziger Press, 1971). **15.** Elisa Kleven, a visiting author and illustrator at our school, apparently made a huge impression on Tom. Her book, *The Lion and the Little Red Bird* (New Jersey: Warne, Puffin and Kestrel, 1992), became Tom's first "real" book to read. **16.** The Once in a Blue Moon Award was an idea borrowed from a newspaper story (C. Andreae, "Is There a Blue Moon in the Sky Today?" *The Christian Science Monitor,* February, 1989). **17.** Tom's reading interview at the end of school showed a deep understanding of reading process. Carolyn Burke's Reading Interview in *Reading Miscue Inventory: Alternative Procedures* (New York: Richard C. Owen, 1987) is used with each child in the strand.

This interview was conducted by telephone while Marge was in California.

Denny: Marge, whenever we talk, you are advocating for a kid in your classroom or you're going to a meeting to advocate for children. What makes you so passionate?

MARGE: Well, I think it's that I see so much injustice with kids. I always have. Part of this injustice is that we are always pressuring kids. As an instance, a long time ago a child's mother came into my classroom and said, "I really appreciate that you haven't made Kevin's life unbearable over writing." His first-grade teacher had pressured him over neat writing, and he despised writing. The year I had him I took the pressure off, and he became a writer. And I just think its so neat to watch children think and watch them learn.

Denny: What did you mean when you wrote "when the time is right and the child is ready"?

MARGE: Children are different from one another. Each one has a different time clock. And I think when they are ready, they learn. As teachers it is our major responsibility to recognize that time. Today at school we had a horrible, horrible faculty meeting where they reviewed the spelling program in the district. They promised they would never compare teachers and schools, but they have. We got the results of the tests today. The teachers who work with me didn't follow the test-retest pattern. What we did was look at our students' writing and we picked out the words that our kids could spell. They spelled many, many words in standard spelling, but not specifically the words on the district test. We (six teachers) prepared a detailed, written document explaining our assessment and the growth of each student. And the kids in the school as a whole didn't do well. So now, according to the principal, we will be told how to teach spelling and not be given the opportunity to use our knowledge of the spelling process. We just felt, If they, the administrators, are going to make decisions about children's learning, what are we, the teachers, doing here? If you believe the research of people like Sandra Wilde and Donald Graves, when kids learn how to spell they need to learn strategies. Spelling strategies. That's the way we try to teach. Not all children are ready for the same spelling strategy at the same time. It's a long answer to your question but I think it is relevant.

Denny: So if your spelling is below the district's expectations . . .

MARGE: What's going to happen is that we will be given a spelling book, which all the research shows is not the best way for children to learn. I have children in the classroom who did a hundred percent on the list and some who didn't spell any of the words. Some of them are bilingual and just beginning to learn to read in

English. I just think all kids need time to develop the strategies and some of these six-year-old kids are not there. And we are trying to make them all the same.

Denny: I know you gave Tom a lot of space, but you also provided a lot of structure in his life. You didn't just sit back and wait for things to happen.

MARGE: Actually, almost everyone in the school appeared to be waiting for Tom to fall flat. We didn't just sit back and wait for him to fail. We tried to observe and be ready to nudge him a little bit. We tried to create situations where he would feel that he could do things. We were always anticipating the moment when he was ready. It's like that with every child. You do provide the environment. You do talk to them. You do everything you can to ensure that every child is able to have that moment when they are ready to do something else.

Denny: Let me play devil's advocate for a moment. How do you answer critics who say waiting for the child may be warm and fuzzy but it's not going to help the child learn?

MARGE: In that waiting period you are constantly providing experiences for the child. The critics seem to think that you can just teach the child and they will absorb it. But this is not the fact of the matter. You never know how much a child is absorbing in his or her own way from the learning environment. It is very important to provide the opportunity for learning.

Denny: What do you think would have happened to Tom if you had been forced— as California teachers are probably going to be—to teach Tom phonics for, what is it? ninety minutes a day?

MARGE: He has already been smothered in phonics. The only evidence of work in his folder was Zoo Phonics. It's a program where children learn little rhymes to teach them the sounds of each letter. [*Laughs*] They say they are filling the hole left by whole language. That was the only thing Tom had had in his life—that, and criticism of his behavior.

Denny: What effect did all this phonics have?

MARGE: Well, when we got him he was a total nonreader.

Denny: It seems to me your article is a wonderful response to anyone who thinks that phonics is the answer. It's much more complicated than that.

MARGE: He had all this backlog of phonics papers in his folder. As time went on, the more he watched what was going on, he began to participate. But you couldn't force him. When we said, Let's do something, he just ran away and hid. He'd homestead under the table. But later when he started to show interest in reading, he would start to use little strategies to come up with answers. When he started to read, it was not through phonics; he used many different strategies.

Denny: You weren't dealing with reading words or writing words, you were dealing with meaningful texts.

MARGE: His only success with reading, initially, did not come from knowing sounds. It came from a book that he really wanted to read. And if we helped him, he wouldn't want to bother with the sounds. He wanted to read the book. You know what they are saying in California is that at first you learn to read and then you read for meaning. I just can't believe what is happening. I just can't. About ten years ago in this district they were saying, Kids can decode words, but they can't read for meaning. We have to put more emphasis on meaning.

Denny: Now they are reversing themselves.

MARGE: That's a very short pendulum swing. That's a very short period of time. They are hollering balance, but in effect there is no balance. I saw so many kids turned off reading because they had to learn to decode. They just never became readers. And that is not to say that I can't improve in my teaching or that we can't all improve even if we don't throw out all we know. We have a very solid basis for what we are doing.

Denny: One of things that really impressed me when I read your article was the way in which you were able to reflect the importance of community in your classroom. The other kids tried to support Tom. They stuck up for him when he got into trouble with the substitute. They seemed to care. How do you manage to create such a climate in your classroom?

MARGE: We do a lot of talking. We do a lot of sharing of ideas. We talk about respect. We call it life skills. You need to have respect. You need to care for others. You need patience. Responsibility. We all talk about those every day. And if something occurs within the family—the strand—we all communicate to the children and tell them we are all there to listen and they can go to any one of us. They are all there in our care.

Denny: It's more than a family. You really are a community.

MARGE: I think this is one of the things that really helped Tom. He knew he had six people he could talk to, and I think, over time, that gave him a sense of security. His world kept expanding. As he got to know more kids and more teachers, all working together, he expanded his territory a little, and he would actually go in any of the six classrooms and walk around and talk to the kids and use the computers. In other words he had a tremendous amount of support, not just the help of one teacher.

Denny: Tell me about the documentation. First, of the official texts that were in Tom's file.

MARGE: That we got when he first came to the school? It had bunches of Zoo Phonics papers and a few pieces of attempted writing. There were comments by teachers about his lack of learning and his behavior problems. There were a couple of references that he should be tested. I think there were also signed papers that he should be tested, but they moved so much that no testing was ever carried out. I think school systems lose these kids. If a kid moves as much as Tom did, teachers tend to say, Oh he'll be gone soon.

Denny: One of the things you are saying is that the absence of documents told you as much as the documents that were there.

MARGE: That's absolutely true. There were no documents that provided any information except for the one perspective. It was very destitute. There was nothing there to guide us, and that may not be the teachers' fault. It's the situation.

Denny: What about your own documentation? Did you find it hard to keep notes?

MARGE: In the beginning. Remember how I kept telling you there was nothing to document because what I was trying to get was hard copy as well as observation? And there wasn't any hard copy. When you are observing a child doing whatever he does in the classroom, and he is not writing, and he is not reading, it's very hard to document that. He looked at tons and tons of books. And he hated writing, that was an absolute horror for him. I wish I knew the reason. I could never determine that.

Denny: So you wrote down your observations.

MARGE: Yes, but it really was very difficult. He would spend hours on the computer. He was a whiz at learning the mechanics, but he never saved what he was working on. He would promise, Oh yes! I'll save it! And the next second it was gone. It was as if he was absolutely determined not to have any hard-copy records of anything. He did some pretty major things on the computer. He learned all these things that I didn't know how to do. How to manipulate programs and how to transfer things. He knew a lot about the machine.

Denny: Eventually you were able to collect some documentation.

MARGE: When I went through it I was amazed to find how much I had. And the collaboration of the teachers really provided a lot of that. I would get something from Donna or from her mother, and they would say, Look what Tom did!

Denny: How did the documents that you were able to collect inform you about Tom?

MARGE: I think a lot of his work was very primitive, but he would explain. He would have a story. He would have something going on. He would connect things in his talking about things and that would inform us that he knew a lot more than his written work would indicate. And toward the end of the year I asked him to help other children read. And he would go over to the child and they would do something together, and the child would come to me and read. He would help kids with spelling. He didn't know how to spell the words, but he would locate them in different areas around the room. He really made leaps and bounds, from hiding under the table to helping other kids in his own way to going on that field trip with a totally unknown person. He came a long way from the kid who wouldn't communicate with anybody. But what would have happened to him if the state of California said that when he is in first grade he must be at one-point-five grade level and that he must be an independent reader by the third grade?

Denny: What do you think would have happened?

MARGE: Well I can only suppose. If we had made him sit? Made him join a group? Made him read? I think he would have withdrawn further into the behavior that was so unacceptable in school. I honestly don't think our educational system has any room for these children. How do you help these children? Where is their future if you don't let them learn like they should? I don't know. He would not have read at grade level. I couldn't force him. I couldn't force him, and he liked me! The promise was there. He was beginning to become a member of our literate learning community. And the kids liked him! You know, sometimes kids turn other kids off, but Tom didn't. They all worked hard to help him.

Denny: I'm obsessed by documentation. [*Laughs*] How were your texts that you produced different from the documents in his file?

MARGE: Well, I filled his file with documents of his choice. When he finally decided to read and finally decided to write, the things that I kept were the things he chose. As time went on we were able to negotiate with him a little bit. But there was nothing negotiable in his file when he arrived. Nothing that he chose to do. I assume that every child had done the same page at the same time. I also think that what was in the file was not appropriate for him. They were tracing and he was not tracing well at that time. They were coloring. There was a commercially produced kangaroo. First he had to trace it. Then color it. And to me that was not appropriate. He should have been asked to draw a kangaroo, and if it was a round ball, that was okay, that was his. The work in his folder did not reflect the things that he could do. None of it was his.

Denny: What about the documents that Tom produced by the end of the year?

MARGE: His drawings had progressed from nonintelligible objects to identifiable line drawings. He could draw something that he was trying to relate to you and tell you what it was. He was beginning to label things and beginning to talk a lot about them.

Denny: What advice would you give a teacher who wants to take notes in the classroom?

MARGE: I don't think you can document it all. By the time you start documenting, another child comes up and needs your attention. A very organized person could come up with a system that used a clipboard or Post-it notes, but my organization is not that great. [*Laughs*] I would tear off a scrap of paper. I would write on anything. I don't try to document everything. What I do is, every time I'm talking with a child, if they say something that gives me some insight into what's going on, I make a quick note. I do this every day. I try to write after school. I go back to my scraps of paper and write them out.

Denny: So you really have developed your own way of documenting. You've got your own system.

MARGE: Right. I've tried to follow other people's systems, and you really have to develop your own. It depends on your purpose. Why you're documenting.

Denny: Going back to the official texts. Do you have any advice for teachers on how to read them?

MARGE: I try not to look at those things until I have a chance to get to know the child. And then if there is a reason to look at them, I have a comparison. Then I have some basis for decision about what to do.

Denny: Can you talk a little bit about the relationships between close observation, note taking, and advocacy?

MARGE: Well they go together. What I did in this particular case study has made me a much better kidwatcher—for all the kids. You know, it's sort of like a beginning teacher has to have a lesson plan, and now I think I have a mind set for getting what is going on—

Denny: The complexity—

MARGE: Yes. I'm noticing many more things. And in that manner I think I have become a stronger advocate for children. For Tom. Because you have a deeper awareness. You go below the surface of what the child is doing and you see greater possibilities.

Denny: How would you use your knowledge to advocate for Tom?

MARGE: Once you gain insights, you also have better answers and you are stronger in your approach to other people. You have a little better understanding of how to negotiate, which is what happened when I was advocating for Tom. You have to say it like you mean it. You must believe in what you are doing. Then, once you believe in what you are doing and you have documentation to back you up, you are awfully hard to sway.

Denny: You visited Tom's grandmother. What would you tell teachers about home visits?

MARGE: Anytime you deal with a family, whether at school or at home, you have to be an equal. Not above them. You have to be able to communicate. It could have been a little hard to step over all the dogs and deal with the messy house, but it wasn't. You have to put yourself in her position—the grandmother. I think you have to accept her, as you would her child. I accepted him as a person who wanted to learn, and I believed he was a caring person, so if I have to deal with him that way, don't I also have to deal with his family that way? Then it's okay, because she has all of her worlds to deal with, and she was dealing with them.

Denny: You don't go in as the expert or the authority?

MARGE: [*Laughs*] You know you don't! I just think you have to deal with the person if you want that person to believe in you. And I think they have to deal with me on my level, too. I think it is a two-way street. It isn't one way. It's almost like if I tell the child, That's really great! then that child is going to try harder, and I think it's the same. And I'm not really good at this, but you have to try, too. Okay, let's use your words, you have to try to see from that person's point of view and go from there. I think that is why our home visit was so successful. And Grandma Jean had the same attitude. I am here because I want to learn, and I know you are doing the best you can.

Denny: There were certainly tensions between faculty members over the approach that you took in supporting Tom. How hard was that for you?

MARGE: There were tensions and there still are tensions. What we are doing is so different from the rest of the school and the rest of the district. I can't think of an instance when the tension does not exist. I guess I just think that they are where they are, and I am where I am, and that's fine. I think we need to get to a time when we can say, Hey! You believe in what you believe in and that's okay. It's better than believing that we will ever reach a point when we all believe the same. None of us would want that.

Who'll Take Care of My Baby? Advocating for Serena

JOANNA MARASCO

From the age of ten, Serena has lived in nearly a dozen foster homes. When we first met, she was fifteen, five months pregnant, and living in a home for unwed pregnant teenagers. Recently, she moved into what public assistance refers to as the "program for independent living." Serena will be eighteen on her next birthday. Her social worker has me listed officially on her case record as a "community liaison," but, thankfully, unofficially we have become good friends as well as coresearchers.

Serena and I live in a state with one of the highest teenage pregnancy rates in the nation, and her experiences have helped me understand the roles played by care providers (teachers, social workers, foster-care parents, and the administrators of bureaucratic organizations) and shown me what happens when assistance is decontextualized, provided without regard for the complexities of everyday life.

I am one of many teachers and advocates who have rejected reductionist, deficit models of education by working within a holistic perspective, and my purpose is to understand how Serena employs her literacies to make meaning. Our times together help us explore how her schooling does or does not build on her life experiences, including her views of learning. Her story and her literacies are a means to understand how conflicts caused by bureaucratic interpretations of her life impact her reading and writing and the sense she is trying to make of the world.

In documenting Serena's story, I spent a good deal of time with her. We went to restaurants, coffee shops, movies, and parks. Mercy Home, the residence for pregnant teenagers, is, conveniently, very close to where I lived while attending courses at the university, and I spent many afternoons and evenings there. Serena once came to one of my classes in the community college where I teach. She sat in the back of the room, smiling. She'd never seen me teach before; she enjoyed the experience immensely. We also drove around in my car, took long walks, and talked frequently on the phone. Many of our talks were tape-recorded and later transcribed. Serena became very comfortable with interviews, and she often checked to make sure the tape had not run out. I accompanied her to doctors' offices and made frequent visits to her foster homes. My association with her has now spanned three years. She tells me often that our friendship has helped her to talk about her hopes and concerns.

In addition to my direct dealings with Serena, I interviewed the director and the house mothers at Mercy Home (all names are pseudonyms). I spoke often to her two caseworkers, Margaret and Renaldo. Margaret had been Serena's caseworker for most of her life, but when Serena reached the age of sixteen, her case was transferred to Renaldo. It was a difficult time for Serena, because Margaret had become her friend. Although Renaldo seemed reluctant to share information about formal court proceedings, Margaret and I talked about them quite a bit. Once when Margaret answered some of my rather pointed questions, I asked her why she felt comfortable sharing these confidences. She said that when she was Serena's age someone had helped her, stood by her, "so I can never forget that."

I attended several formal meetings with Serena. Where dialogue is re-created, it is based on my memory and notes and the memory of at least one other person who was there. Every time a meeting or brief talk took place, either on the phone or in person, I made detailed notes on the substance of the discussions. Later, Serena and I would go over what I had written; she gave me her perspective on what I had heard or witnessed. I contacted the high school she had attended before leaving to participate in the city's teenage parenting program; I went there and gathered information about the school's educational mission, and I photocopied Serena's lessons and homework. I interviewed one of her teachers at length, and spoke to administrators and fellow students on the telephone. Several students in the community college classes I teach had also attended the teenage parenting program, and Serena and I often compared their experiences with her own.

Pursuing the Paper Trail

My association with Serena began when I was invited to observe and interview residents of a group home funded by Catholic charities and welfare. The director, a nun, was concerned about the schoolwork of these young women. I was given access to Mercy Home, including official documents (mission statement, state licenses) and the contents of bulletin boards. I interviewed the director and house-mothers many times. Sometimes I drove the girls to their doctors appointments or took them shopping. I conducted formal and informal reading inventories and interviews, and I began to collect samples of their school lessons, practice exercises, tests, and homework. Serena, especially, was focused on her education. For her, a high school diploma held the key to fulfilling her wishes for a good future. As she explained, "No one is going to take care of me. I have to watch out for myself and my baby now." Initially, I focused on three of the residents, but the other two decided not to continue in foster care at Mercy Home.

Serena moved into Mercy Home because "I liked the idea that it was a home;

that's what it said to me, a home for unwed mothers. That's what I expected it to be: a place where everybody would be like sisters." When I met Serena, she faced the future with all the hope and excitement of a new life beginning. She believed attending the alternative school and becoming part of the "family" at the home would help her attain what she and her baby needed to survive. But that is not how it turned out.

Mercy Home and Its Perspectives

Mercy Home is situated on a quiet street. A one-story structure, it is landscaped with gravel, sand, and cactus and fronted by a small driveway. The living room, decorated in tones of brown, is small but comfortable. At the time of my visits, the residents, a maximum of twelve unmarried adolescents in various stages of pregnancy or motherhood, were permitted to entertain boyfriends or family members here. There was a bookcase stretching along one wall that held instructional books on pregnancy and prenatal and infant care. The books were meant for recreational reading; however, as a young resident explained, "I think someone must have left them here. I don't think they're for us; they're for adults. I never saw anybody taking and reading them."

After several months of trying to understand how several young women, including Serena, used reading and writing, I presented some initial findings to the director. I described the rich literacies displayed by these young women. One young girl had discovered a way to explain her pregnancy to her parents by going to the library and patiently sorting through young adult fiction until she found a story in which the young protagonist had told her parents about her pregnancy. After studying the fictional account, she went home and told her mother and father. Furthermore, I had often observed the girls reading at the supermarket. They thumbed through magazines they could not afford to buy and later discussed with me or with each other the articles that interested them. Serena had turned to reading at the most critical time of her life. She had told me that her favorite story was "Juliet." When I replied that I didn't know that one, she was nonplused. "You don't know 'Juliet'? It's about a young girl who died from an overdose, for love." I told the director that I hadn't realized at the time that Serena was speaking about *Romeo and Juliet*, which was her favorite story. I had been so focused on seeking out reading "problems" that I was missing apparent strengths.

The director is a kind, caring woman, and we spent a long time talking about the literacy strengths of the young women. I felt that the approach taken in the compensatory teen parenting program, which was offered as an alternative to high school, and the effects of being on public assistance might be contributing to their indifference to their self-regulated learning. We found areas of mutual agreement; however, she worried about the chances these young women would miss in life if they did not receive the "basic skills" they needed. I reported that although they received basic courses in their compensatory schooling program, its major emphasis was on the most menial of office skills. My concern was that focusing their instruction on preparing the young women to fill low-income jobs would do little to ameliorate the cycle of poverty that had so far devastated their opportunities.

That night I looked over my notes and recorded my thoughts in my journal. I wrote that the director probably believed she had little input into the compensatory educational program or the state or federal financial assistance or guidance that the young girls received. Like so many dedicated teachers and welfare workers, she was overwhelmed by the complex issues that seem to defeat an ethic of care. She was intent on maintaining a holding pattern, convinced that social agencies' provisions were sufficient. The assistance provided the young women with a place to live and an education. Basic office skills were their ticket to enter the work force. What she did not take into account was that this reductionist orientation frustrated the young mothers' learning even these linear skills. I knew this because I asked them. There was a big difference between engaging with real learning on their own and the drudgery of their present schooling. At least in their regular high schools, some genuine inquiry took place; constantly rehashing their pregnancies took up most of the instructional time in the teen parenting program.

Then Serena gave birth to Mikey, a beautiful boy with long eyelashes and a full head of soft, blue-black hair. Serena told me that Mikey's birth made her feel confident about the future. She said she knew that she was capable of doing whatever would be required to ensure his happiness. Nothing else took priority. She and her child were a family now, and Mikey's existence would help her stay fixed on gaining the best life had to offer.

I continued to document what I saw on my visits to the residency, focusing on the structured conditions that influenced these teenage girls' abilities as thinkers and doers. I looked at literacy development within the context of new young mothers' experiences and circumstances. I began to take careful notice of how print was used at Mercy Home.

The Mercy Home Literacy Dig

The largest collection of print was on the bulletin board in the hallway. I asked for and received permission to disassemble it and photocopy the items for later analysis. Several newspaper and magazine articles centered on the notion of danger, on childbirth as problem: "Never Shake a Baby"; "Soft Bedding Linked to Crib Death"; "Strangers' Hands Can Infect Baby"; "Fetal Alcohol Syndrome" (this article was accompanied by terrifying photographs). Other articles focused on the vulnerability of the young childbearers themselves: "What Substance Abuse Does to the Body"; "Rape Prevention for Young People"; "Why Start Life Under a Cloud" (about the danger of smoking). These messages were based on an assumption that adolescents needed constantly to be vigilant in correcting undesirable behavior. In "Unwed Mom Takes Girls to Task," several adults complained that poor girls do not take enough responsibility for their fertility but depended on others to supply their needs.

The Mercy Home "contract" was also prominently posted. Its twelve single-spaced pages listed the requirements for residency and expected behavior, from grievance procedures to specific chores (the one correct way to clean toilets, for example). Every time a resident left the home or used the phone or had an upcoming appointment or completed a chore, there was a form to sign. Penalties for infringements included not being allowed to use the telephone or not being permitted to leave the house for any reason.

Print generated by the residents was rarely in evidence. They were required to keep all schoolbooks and papers in their rooms. Generally, no personal cards or photographs were ever seen in communal areas. They didn't post phone numbers or drawings, and the only inspirational messages were those put up by the staff: on the refrigerator door, the photocopied statement "You are loved," on a kitchen cabinet door, a cartoon drawing of a shy teenager with the caption "Don't wait for others to be friendly, show them how."

My assumption that the print displayed in Mercy Home would reflect a family atmosphere had been premature. Does a family usually display print that predominantly shows its members as victims prone to danger? Does a setting that regulates activities with military-like precision foster self-empowerment? The absence of writings generated by the pregnant teenagers and new mothers offered the most telling evidence that Mercy Home could not be described as a family. It was instead a holding area. Until they could claim ownership or membership in some other living room, personal books and writings were to be stowed away, kept out of sight. The displayed print related to the lessons that were to be learned; these lessons stressed pervasive vulnerability.

Alternative Schooling

Despite Serena's admonition by her care providers to "attend to your education," schooling played no part in the decisions that affected her everyday survival. But taking the admonition at face value and looking at Serena's literacy education, I discovered that the tension between her literacy capabilities and the schooling that was imposed without regard for her interests or language experiences was steadily wearing her down. Serena's writings outside school and her perceptions about the writing requirements of the teen parenting program help illustrate her frustration.

Reading and Writing for Reality's Sake

Serena's writings were ways for her to explore her world and make her own sense of it. For example, in this letter, which was never meant to be mailed, she sorts out her feelings about her mother (Roberto and Renee are Serena's brothers; Maude is Serena's aunt):

Mom. I don't understand. There's a lot I want to tell you that hurts. See when Roberto told me that you were arrested that day, I drove with your car to Maude's house and I couldn't stop crying. Everybody said I was about fainting twice. But that's my situation. How I feel is left out in the family. Like as if they don't really care for me. And if I'm with you I feel as if I'm a scapegoat, that you always leave me behind for anybody. And like Renee would come around and you would ignore me. I feel like I don't have anybody. I've been wanting to get it off my chest with you. About you not feeling loved and abandoned yourself I knew that's why you had us kids. I don't know why you keep running. You hurt a lot of people, including yourself.

It is a form of journal writing, but more personalized. In order to better understand her feelings, Serena had to act as if the letter were real, going so far as to address the envelope and draw a stamp on it. She asked the questions she couldn't ask in person; she used the social convention of the letter in an inventive process of self-revelation and renewal. Did her mother's incarceration, an external event, prompt Serena's realization of the place she occupied in her mother's life? I don't think so. Serena did learn from experience, but that wasn't all she had. Serena's drive to learn took the form of a symbolic reconstruction (a letter not meant for mailing), a simultaneous, highly individual transaction between internal and external experience. She used her mother's being in jail to help her sort out her feeling of being abandoned. The letter represented a tacit knowledge she couldn't bring herself to express in any other way.

In Serena's notebooks, the sections containing bureaucratic text about her welfare benefits and provisions are in stark contrast to the collection of cards she received from family and friends when her son was born. She also carefully glued in small pieces of the paper that had been wrapped around presents and included personal notes on the baby's progress. Serena showed me all the notebooks she had collected, notebooks in which she had systematically and carefully organized copies of the documents sent to her by the welfare organizations that served her, beginning when she first entered foster care.

Reading and Writing in the Teen Parenting Program

The courses provided in the teen program included general math, English, social studies, and biology. In biology, for example, the workbook asked students to solve a genetics problem. This section was left undone, because the teacher said it was "too hard for the entire class." In English class, there were a great many learning tasks involving comma rules, but only one reading assignment: *The Diary of Anne Frank*. And rather than being encouraged to discuss the story, the students were given highly detailed questions to answer:

- When did Mr. Frank find Anne's diary?
- Why were the Van Daans sharing the hiding place with the Franks? Why does Dussel join the group?
- What was daily life like in the hiding place?
- Write two sentences about each, a description and an opinion: Peter, Margot, Mrs. Frank, Mr. Frank, Mr. Dussel, Mrs. Van Daan, Mr. Van Daan.

Serena had met with a counselor and been advised to chose Office Support as an elective. One of the lessons in this course had to do with "dispelling misspelling." The instructions began:

The fact is, if you have a spelling problem, you are probably not stupid. You probably are careless, though. (This is especially true if you spell a word correctly one time but incorrectly another.) What can be done?

The suggestions that followed included pronounce words correctly; master the standard spelling rules; memorize the most commonly misspelled words. In this class, the students were required to keep a "Weekly Learning Summary" and encouraged to keep journals. Serena told me they were "for the teacher." When we looked through her school journal entries, Serena pointed this one out: "Today in class I had my papers checked for it to be graded. On one chapter section I have done, [it] was redone about three times because I would mess up. But I finally done the chapter section right." Commenting about it, she said: "In a way it helps keep track of what you did. But it's hard because you don't know what to think—what [the teacher] wants you to do: is it enough for her? It is, or otherwise she would say so."

One learning activity, the Self-Interpretation Profile and Guide, had a disturbing effect on Serena. It was designed "to help you in planning your career." One of the first directives toward accomplishing this was to list the occupational titles that the student thinks sound interesting. Serena listed "photofinishing," and went on to find the occupational code and the subsequent pages that described this field. However, the next activity asked the student to list the factors that affect future employment trends, and all the students, who had listed a variety of career options, were told by the teacher to write the following:

> Limited training facilities, salary restrictions, and undesirable aspects of the work can cause shortages of applicants. Very attractive work as in the arts or communication, *or the prospect of high earnings* [italics mine] can cause long-term surpluses of jobs.

Serena's highest score was for "clerical." She did not agree, feeling she had been steered toward this score. She said: "Just because they say that doesn't make it so. I know they are not true. They can't say for sure, You're good at this." This is but one example of how Serena's pronouns shifted from *me* to *they* when she talked with me about her views of literacy.

Outside school, Serena's reading and writing and the way she articulated her experiences reflected her self-confidence: she had used language in rich, inventive ways to help her sustain personal development. However, while she was attending alternative schooling, Serena's writings mainly focused on demonstrating the conventions that others demanded she acquire and display. For example, directed to choose one specific job or career and write a brief summary, Serena wrote:

> Yes. There are many sites where a sandwich shop will do well in a community. For highest volume and profit, look for a site surrounded by as many people as possible at lunch time. Start as on a shoestring. Some people start by spending hundreds of thousands on elaborate schemes that are not necessary. You can start with as little as $8,000.

Or again, when Serena was asked to cut out advertisements for jobs from a newspaper, she thought she qualified for "Coco's restaurant; Wendy's; and Wal-Mart." When I asked her about her choices, she said, "I'm sixteen, that's all I can do now." It was a good point—the assignment asked about her present qualifications—but the presumption behind the assignment was that her status would remain fixed.

So at a time in her life when her natural development required that she strive for knowledge to help her realize autonomy, her focus was systematically being directed toward school lessons that had nothing to do with her experience. It is schooling that projects knowledge as power. In school, Serena was given very little opportunity to explore the natural process of her unfolding humanity.

Regular High School or an Alternative Program?

It is difficult to determine whether Serena's reading and writing in her regular high school was different from the reading and writing she exhibited in the alternative format. By the time we met, she was already enrolled in the separate program. It was at that point that I began to photocopy her schoolwork. She did not choose to include any schoolwork among her carefully catalogued notebooks, except for one notable lesson from an art class at her regular high school. It was a drawing of a common lock, the kind with a combination. She was quite proud of it; she said, "I loved doing this." But when I borrowed some dittos she had received at the teen program, she wondered why on earth I wanted "that stuff." Clearly, the items she chose to collect had to fulfill very exacting criteria related to the importance she placed on their meaning for her life. At least during her time at the regular high school, she had taken a few courses she enjoyed. And while there, she felt she was still part of the community she had known all her life. She had great affection for some of her teachers, and it was hard for her to leave them. She changed schools because she wanted to do whatever others had determined was best. The disaffection that the social-service bureaucracies evidenced toward her family and community no doubt contributed to this determination.

Serena had been academically successful during the time she spent in her regular high school: she hadn't failed anything. When she became pregnant, she turned to her care providers for advice; she decided to move out of her neighborhood, where she lived with an elderly foster parent, to the home for unwed mothers and to participate in the city's alternative parenting program for pregnant teens. Serena was told that the alternative program was "much easier" than regular high school. She soon found this to be quite true. In an early interview, she told me, "I haven't done it yet, but you can even ditch [skip class] if you want to." Another plus for Serena was that the building that housed the teen parenting program was all on one level. Her regular high school had lots of stairs, and she anticipated that in the last months of her pregnancy, heavy and exhausted, she would not be able to keep up with her classmates. The alternative school also had day care for the newborn babies; the regular high school did not. No one ever told her that she could petition to use the high school's elevator or that the alternative program would not have the range of courses or the extracurricular activities she so enjoyed in the past. She could have decided to stay at the high school; her caseworker would have arranged for her baby to be in day care while she went to classes. But Serena was determined to do what was best for herself and her unborn child, and the advice of well-meaning adults shaped her decision during this most difficult time of her life.

There were few exceptions to the rigid focus on office support at the alternative program. At some point each year one teacher did bring in a camera and give the girls a chance to take photographs. Serena was quite excited about it. But no attempt was made to integrate this "diversion" into the curriculum or to transfer the students' interest in it to other coursework. The underpaid teacher moved on before Serena had the chance to take pictures, which was truly a loss, since she loved anything artistic.

To say the teen parenting program was not intellectually challenging would be a gross understatement. Funding for it was tied to enrollment, and all one had to do was show up. The majority of the learning experiences she encountered there eroded Serena's affection for the program. Despite this, she maintained her grades and attendance; she focused on the all-powerful diploma, and she believed it would be "exactly the same" as the diploma she would have received had she graduated with the rest of her class at the regular high school.

To Serena's credit, the practical focus of the program did confirm her belief in the difference a literacy education could mean for her. Rather than focusing on grades determined by others as indications of academic success, Serena challenged herself intellectually. She had a dream: she wanted to go on to the community college. With the birth of her son, attending college became her priority.

Hearing with the Foster-Care Review Board

Holding Serena's three-week-old child, I accompanied her to the state's Supreme Court for a hearing with the foster-care review board. We entered to find three members seated at the very end of a long table. We were told to take our seats at the opposite end. Serena's smile and greeting were wiped away by the abruptness of the first question: "What provisions have you made to take care of your child?"

Serena hesitated; searching for words, she sounded intimidated as she began a mumbled reply. One of the board members cut her off by again repeating the question. "How do you intend to care for this child?"

"I want to graduate," Serena said, "and I want to continue with my education, you know, go on to college or something." She was currently in tenth grade.

"Yes, I see," replied the board member, "college or something."

"Yes," said Serena. "I'm doing pretty good at the teen parenting program, and—"

"How's it going there for you?" asked the one female board member.

"I'm doing okay."

"Have you discussed with your caseworker returning to your regular high school?" the board member continued.

"Well, we talked about it. But I want to stay at the teen parenting program and graduate and go on to college and—"

A board member interrupted. "How do you expect to manage to continue your education and care for the baby at the same time; that's what we are asking you."

Serena began to fidget in her chair. When we talked before the meeting, she had said how excited she was to show them her baby. But not one of them responded to her new son; nor did they ask me who I was or what I was doing there. Serena said, "I want to do what's best for me and my baby. I know we'll be better off if I can get a good job. And an education is—"

Again she was interrupted. "And how would you do this? You have no job now, do you?" Her participation in the teen parenting program was a requirement for receiving funds from welfare; and her residency at Mercy precluded any possibility of employment during this time. We were both becoming confused by their questions; did they have the wrong file?

Serena's reply was almost inaudible. "I'll need some help. If I keep doing good I can get into the program for young adult living. I could finish up the teen parenting program, and then go on to the community college." Serena had done her homework. She had questioned other young mothers in the young adult living program for their opinions and views about it. She knew she would eligible in a few months when she graduated from the teen parenting program. Serena also knew that there was one vacancy in independent-living housing. Residents lived in their own apartments under the supervision of a housemother, who lived in a separate apartment. She entertained high hopes of being admitted early.

"We'll have your caseworker explain Job Core to you. That's a good program," said one of the men. It should have been clear from what Serena had said that the kind of training supplied by Job Core was not what she wanted. The other man pointed out something written on the file in front of him to the other two board members. They nodded their heads. Grim-faced throughout the proceedings, they had had little eye contact with Serena. For a few more minutes they continued, silently, to draw one another's attention to what was written on the pages before them, information to which we were not privy. Serena looked at me. I gave her an I-don't-know-either shrug. I had hoped to be supportive when Serena told them of her hopes, plans, and efforts. But she wasn't being given the opportunity to describe how she intended to achieve them.

One of the women asked, "Have you seen your mother lately?"

"No, I won't have anything more to do with her."

"That's good. You don't write to her or telephone her?"

"No. She doesn't care what happens to me," Serena said. "If I need to talk to somebody I go to my therapists; I have two counselors, one of them at La Vista, and they help me. They said I could make it in college if—"

"What about your brothers? Do you see them?"

"If I could get into the young adult program early, then I could see them more. It's hard for them to get to Mercy Home." Serena had three younger brothers, each in separate foster care. Quite suddenly, one of the board members began shuffling his papers noisily, and then the others did the same: the hearing was drawing to a close.

"We will recommend that you continue for the time being in the teen parenting program," he said, "and we will inform your caseworker about any future decisions."

At this point I introduced myself. I told them I had been investigating Serena's literacies. I had a thick folder; I had documented Serena's skills by analyzing her reading and writing in and out of school. I talked about how she used her literacy to problem-solve, and I described her considerable strengths as a learner.

The board members listened politely. One of them wrote down my name on Serena's file; I was listed as an advocate. They read back the minutes of the meeting; only one part addressed Serena's primary concern: ". . . and we will support her desire to continue her education." However, just what kind of support might be extended was never clarified.

Having had to rely for so many years on other people's help with the details of daily living, Serena thought the hearing had gone well. But at Mercy Home, tensions between Serena and the staff and other residents had begun to accelerate. Serena argued with other residents and counselors. The housemothers and director either ignored her or found fault with her. Serena was also becoming annoyed because the housemothers peeked in at her during the night to see whether she was disobeying them and bringing her infant son into her bed. In Mexican American households, this is a common practice, but the staff at Mercy House got quite annoyed about it. Finally, Serena telephoned me to announce that she had been granted permission to move in with Lupita, the same foster-care provider she had been with before moving to Mercy Home. Her stay with Lupita would last only a few months; then she would be able to enter the state's program for independent living. She sounded overjoyed, and I felt that this arrangement would be much better than the strain that Mercy Home had become.

At Lupita's

"I'm in Another World"

My phone rang one morning at seven. Serena's voice sounded shaky and scared. She asked if I could pick her up; something had happened and she didn't want to talk on the phone. I followed her directions to another section of the city. Lupita's house was surrounded by a sturdy gate. The yard was bright with flowers and a well-cared-for vegetable garden. The shaded porch was crowded with hanging plants. I do not speak Spanish, and neither Lupita nor Serena's new roommate spoke English, so Serena translated our greetings. She wanted to talk to me alone, so we went into her small bedroom and shut the door. It was immediately obvious that Serena's one-year-old son was not there. The crib stood empty; toys were neatly displayed on a small bookshelf.

Serena told about her final days at Mercy Home. She had heard gossip about plans to take her son from her care. She talked to Renaldo: "I was very scared, and he was telling me it wasn't true, that he was not going to take the baby away."

Later that night, she heard the same gossip again. The following day Serena brought Mikey to the day-care center and returned to Mercy Home to resume packing and cleaning. Renaldo, the caseworker, dropped by in the afternoon.

"And I go to him, 'Why am I hearing this from everybody?' And he goes, 'Oh, well, I am going to have to tell you the truth now. I am going to take the baby away from you.' So I said, 'Oh God, oh God, what did I do?' I went all paranoiac. I didn't want to live. I go, 'Please don't take him away from me, I'll do anything. I love my baby. He's the only person in my life. I don't have a mom and I don't have a dad; I don't have no family. He's the only person I have and you're going to take the one person that I have away from me?' I started calling to everyone: 'He's going to take my baby!' I was crying. I was asking everyone, 'Please help me.' I asked Sister Agnes. She said, 'I'm sorry, I can't do anything.' So then, I didn't want anything to do with anybody anymore."

Serena told me this story in a monotone; she seemed so detached, so unlike the lively teenager she had been just a few weeks ago. She continued, "It was a setup. They lied to me." She was never offered a reason for these draconian measures. The only account she had, which she took out of her pocket, unfolded, and displayed to me, was her thin copy of the paper that she had to sign; it awarded short-term custody of her son to foster parents.

Because Serena had said she wanted to kill herself, Renaldo brought her to his office, where a psychiatrist awaited them. She was proscribed the tranquilizer Prozac.

Serena subsequently found out that the baby was taken from her for "safety reasons," a decision based on two complaints: she had brought her baby to sleep with her during the night when she had been told not to; and several times she had left his seat belt unfastened on the floor-level baby chair. Serena thought it might also have something to do with the fact that she had begun to date a boy. Renaldo and the director did not approve.

Serena broke off her relationship with the boy. She also dropped out of the teen parenting program. Renaldo told her that if she participated in two intervention programs, Parents Anonymous and Life Skills, her baby could be returned to her in ninety days, depending on her "evaluations" and whether or not he interpreted these reports to mean she was "doing right."

Parents Anonymous

The instructional goal of Parents Anonymous was to get Serena to grasp one concept: don't spank your child. The final multiple choice test was preceded by a printed handout meant to integrate this erroneous assumption into the learner's conceptual system:

> What do virtually all juvenile delinquents have in common? What was a common feature of the childhoods of Hitler, Stalin, Saddam Hussein, and Charlie Manson? What do rapists, arsonists, torturers, serial killers, mass murderers, and product tamperers have in common? If you want to turn a friendly puppy into a dangerous attack dog, what must you do to train it?

The program was based on well-intentioned motives: why should Serena have to learn for herself what we can teach her? But the concepts were oversimplified and distorted, and the reflective thinking necessary to bring about any real adaptation was repressed. Instead of being allowed to discover the perimeters of convention, Serena was faced with narrowly interpreted conventions transmitted by "experts." Moreover, Serena had a very real strength that had it not been ignored, could have brought her in contact with a full range of social conventions as they naturally occur. Serena had never spanked her one-year-old son. Instead, she had invented a way of coping with frustration that avoided the abruptness with which she herself was often treated; she provided her child structure in a loving, nurturing manner. On her own, she had made the social convention of loving care a personal concept. As she struggled to accommodate these arbitrary concepts within her own ethic of caring, she began to distrust her own inventive capabilities.

Life Skills

When Serena described this program, she called it silly. But she never protested; she said, "I just don't say I've been taking care of my younger brothers since I was ten. Maybe they'll come back and say, That's why they're in foster care now, because you didn't do a good job. So I keep my mouth shut and do what I have to do."

Life Skills is intended to provide students with skills needed for daily living (it includes segments on responsible pet care, time management, toxins in the home, etc.). But Serena is more than aware of dysfunctional environments, has become adept at avoiding the dangers inherent to growing up poor. She had long ago recognized the need to provide a caring environment for her young brothers. She remembered birthdays, did the food shopping, sewed the ripped clothing, and above all, really listened. Everyday life taught her how to be responsive and caring to others and taught her resiliency. This resiliency derived partly from her own inventiveness, because her social experiences imposed a different view of the world. When confronted with learning relevant to the reality she faced, Serena was consistently enthusiastic, focused, and creative.

Inventing Ways to Cope

According to her social worker, if she "did right," her child could come to live with her full time. However, the state continued to assume custody of the baby. In a few months she would be seventeen, and, over the course of two years, I had seen her physical, social, and intellectual capacities expand dramatically. Her rapid and profound growth signaled a reconfiguration of the sense that she makes of her world. However, Serena was an unwed teenage mother in foster care, and this difference was treated as a deficiency despite evidence of the competence she continuously displayed in conforming healthily to social conventions. In fact, her inventiveness was looked on with suspicion. She understood this only too well, and learned to accommodate this false view of her capacities by dampening her own inventive strength and performing as expected.

Writing for Compensatory Schooling

Serena asked me to review an assignment due the following day. She said, "It's got to sound right, no mistakes. They are evaluating me." (Always, at the forefront of her concern was the eventual return of her infant son.) The assignment was her homework for the Life Skills program:

> Dear Foster Parent,
> I'm feeling confident, excited. I like to spend time with my baby when I get out of this program. I hope I am well educated on the skills to learn to understand my child as well as for myself. My goal as a parent is to be better than my own parents.

In reality, the relationship with her foster parent, Lupita, had become strained. She told me that she felt she was blamed for feeling depressed, and she wanted Lupita to understand how much the separation from her child affected her moods. If we look at what Serena's letter says against the background of what she could have said but did not, we see that Serena chooses language meant to initiate herself into the dominant social processes.

My concern is that in attending to these lessons (i.e., "doing right"), Serena is assimilating the belief that knowledge is detached and separate from self. Scripted exercises in cultural rigidity teach people to surrender to frustration, not develop self-reliance. What are the consequences of these lessons? Serena was learning that as a mother and young adult, her real opportunities to affect her life were as limited as when she was 'Rena, a little child.

Infantilizing 'Rena

The school-based intervention programs that were to determine Serena's suitability for regaining custody of her child gave the illusion of using real objects, real problems, and real materials in addressing adolescents' role as caregivers, because they centered instruction around three goals: to help young mothers continue their education, to help them learn to control their fertility, and to help them become parents. However the programs' educational practices, which centered on the acquisition of discrete language skills in isolation and disregarded students' interests or self-learning, reflected a reductive, linear, fundamentally behaviorist model of learning as a series of skills hierarchically acquired.

Proponents for the programs explained that continued school enrollment was the highest priority for teenage mothers, both because of the value of an education for living and parenting and because certificates of completion are required for further education. If this threat is the assumption underlying such educational interventions, it is little wonder that an adolescent's developing ability to actualize self-reliance and autonomy is inhibited. It is dangerous to promote the untested assumption that simply by being a warm body in a program, future social and economic advantages are forwarded.

Even if we take as a given that Serena needed the skills, she had to be prepared to see herself in a different light if these skills were to make a difference. In effect, Serena was given permission to give up. Serena's drive to become an empowered participant in the world was smothered by forces that steered her ever toward a childlike dependency and acquiescence. Her inventiveness, interests, and aspirations required more effective learning tasks that reflected the fact that she was seeking, on her own, knowledge that would help her solve everyday problems.

Care providers positioning themselves as survivalists stand rigidly behind the notion that the only priority is day-to-day subsistence, and even that undergoes constant threat. For the bureaucracies that served her, academic success was viewed as a measure of Serena's independence, but the substance of what was being taught was secondary. In all of her classrooms, including the regular high school, the teen parenting program, and the intervention programs, a transmission-oriented pedagogy discouraged real engagement. There was no opportunity for the kinds of collaborative learning activities that foster a sense of community and individual self-confidence. The message that life would be lived under inevitable threat because she was female, Mexican American, and an early childbearer was meant to persuade Serena that living independently meant living in continual self-denial.

During her pregnancy and afterward, educators appeared to assume that being part of a community of learners in this context meant mere contact with other pregnant girls. The opportunity for the girls to develop a sense of community was discouraged. Serena was encouraged to leave her regular high school to attend the teen parenting program, a program with a lot fewer academic resources. And even in Serena's regular schooling there were no opportunities to address young women's sexual selves in caring, risk-free environments that valued open-ended discussion. Instead, sexuality was seen as a pervasive danger to be addressed in lectures about sexually transmitted diseases. When the alternative school's unchallenging program began to become a factor in her disengagement with school learning, Serena was directed to attend two alternative educational programs that did little more than require her attendance.

For educators, Serena's experiences and circumstances in school contain a number of themes, some of which are by now familiar in literature that addresses girl-friendly environments: learning activities involved little cooperative group work, were seldom self-paced, discouraged interaction with teachers and classmates, and worked directly against a classroom climate that was relaxed, fun, and purposeful. Rather than encouraging Serena to consider herself a valued member of the community, they taught the lesson of isolation: take what is offered for your basic survival and remain suspicious, solitary, and ever-vigilant to your own propensity to self-destruct; you are in a war zone; trust no one; you have made yourself vulnerable.

Serena's disaffection for school learning became the basis for care providers to adopt a blame-the-victim philosophy and to offer learning alternatives that assumed Serena was unable to achieve academically, an assumption that had no basis in fact. Serena and I produced a number of well-documented accounts of her literacy strengths. I offered evidence that often it is not the student's inability to learn but her lack of desire to learn that widens the gap between academic success and failure. The assumption that cognition must always be externally motivated results in transmission-oriented pedagogy. The primary obstacle to Serena's learning was not that she could not learn; it was that she could not learn in programs perpetuated by people who were intent on coercing her to change her attitude. Schooling was not the issue; convincing Serena to accept the directives of those in authority was the issue. In this context, academic success must be seen as a cloak for perpetuating structured power arrangements. Serena was coming to know the game of school, to participate unquestioningly in procedural displays that made her appear to be engaged in real adaptation of new knowledge. For education to be the real motive, Serena needed a penalty-free environment in which to take the risks that learning requires. Eventually, the battle became too exhausting. Working against the reductionist philosophy of compensatory programs exhausts even the most well intentioned teachers and care providers. There are good ways and bad ways to coerce children. A key implication when working with disenfranchised adolescents is that fear is the inseparable companion of coercion and also its inescapable consequence. Making Serena afraid of what will happen to her if she does not do what figures in authority want her to do causes her to learn that the only protection from life's dangers is the goodwill of adults, which is perishable. We need to understand how feelings of being unable to cope are influenced by various external pressures and the ways in which these pressures impact the lives of those who are poor and marginalized. Serena's circumstances highlight ways in which experiences shape a knower and doer's self-image into one of insecurity, low self-esteem, and overreliance on others for approval.

Hearing with the Caseworker and Psychologist

A meeting was held to determine whether or not Renaldo, Serena's caseworker, and Betsy, Serena's counselor, would recommend that Mikey be returned to her. Betsy's confidential report of her therapeutic counseling sessions with Serena was included in the documents providing evidence of Serena's suitability to regain custody of her child.

I learned two things right away. Serena would need to continue taking Prozac and Deproprevera (birth control pills) in order to go on receiving welfare benefits and cash allotments. Renaldo asserted that she would continue to take this medication "even after you are released from foster care." And the tacit reason that she would follow these orders carefully was that if she didn't the state would regain custody of her son.

Serena was much more relaxed here than she was at the earlier state hearing. It was quite a serious procedure, regaining custody, but she knew she had done what she'd been directed to do. Renaldo asked her about her concerns and fears about where her life was going. Serena replied, "Money. I'm afraid I'll never have enough, or that something might happen to me. Who'd take care of the baby?" Renaldo answered, "I'd take him." It was a joke, a comment on what a charmer the child had become, and everyone laughed, but it seemed particularly insensitive under the circumstances. The language became very formal at times: "out of home placement issues," "continued commitment to educational goals," and "adoption severance specialist." But the atmosphere was friendly. There was no conflict here. Serena had demonstrated "exemplary skills at following directions."

At this point, Serena was once again being steered toward entering the Job Core. It would not get her a GED, but it would provide "job skills." She had progressed from "life skills" to "job skills." Obviously, the assumption here is that whatever literacy skills she had already displayed were inadequate, despite evidence to the contrary. Renaldo confirmed that on the weekend she would be able to enjoy a three-day visit with her child. He said, "I want you to list for me every activity, every person and place you go to, because I may or may not drop in. You are not to leave the baby with anyone. You are not to go to your mom's home. Get a plan to me by Thursday. Every one of the next three visits with your child, a parent aide will come by the house. Show her what you are capable of doing." I found myself wondering if Serena would be able to show her what it had been like trying to raise three younger brothers when she had been only ten years old. Renaldo apologized for having "had" to lie to Serena that day months ago at Mercy Home. Serena later wondered if his apology might have had something to do with my being present, but she received a great deal of satisfaction from it anyway.

The meeting ended with this warning by Renaldo, who pointed his finger at Serena and said, "The consequences of you messing up in any way with the child, or at either instructional program, will be him living with someone else for a very long time. The barrier to getting your baby back? You, yourself, will create it. This treatment plan will be reviewed every six months." At the close, Renaldo asked me to "sign in." He explained that with my name in her file, I might be able, one day, to get a look at it. He was pleased that recently I had brought Serena over to the community college to talk to the financial aid director about funding from the Urban League. But this acknowledgment did not translate into any action on welfare's part. We didn't talk much about Serena's life goals. This hearing was about the possibility of Serena's regaining custody of her child. It took two hours and resulted in Renaldo's and Betsy's evaluation of Serena as a "fitting caregiver."

Deficit Perspectives

Serena's victimization was not the fault of any one agency: the teen parenting program, Mercy Home, welfare, or foster care. But at no time was any serious effort made to assess or credit the multiple strengths of Serena's literacies. What the agencies shared in common was that they were ever alert for signs of weakness. If weaknesses did not exist, the circumstances imposed on Serena would certainly have caused them to surface. The agencies' purpose was to devise strategies that prepared Serena to anticipate crisis. In the end their combined efforts resulted in self-doubt rather than self-regulation.

Advocacy for Teenage Mothers and Their Children

The most effective thing I can do for those who seek to advocate for young mothers like Serena is to sum up the things I think a teacher/advocate can do now, today. Let's assume that you do not know where to start (as I most definitely did not).

1. Guard against the prevailing assumption that low income levels mean low literacy levels; such a blatant misconception masks the strength of people's literacies. Help single mothers use the resources already available in their homes. Reject any notion of academic, linguistic, cultural, or intellectual inferiority based on their being pregnant or early childbearers. Promote the genuine involvement of family members through a process of mutual respect. Help improve what already exists. Examine information about existing models of parental involvement that are available in the community.

2. In your capacity as teacher, advocate, or care provider, ask the teenager what she wants, rather than provide only those services that are immediately at your disposal. Encourage administrators to run interference with societal forces that would seek to maintain the status quo.

3. Industriously collect and document the way the teenager uses print to make sense of her life. Focus on categorizing this documentation, because you may be called on to present it as an argument at any time. The rationale for steering marginalized adolescents into untenable educational interventions is often based on unexamined interpretations of their grades or normed test scores.

4. Help single parents form support networks to better articulate the greater requirements or needs of single mothers. Make knowledge available to them and help them find out for themselves what is available from federal or local resources and where to go to petition for it. Use role-playing, visualization, or rehearsal strategies to accomplish your purposes when confronting seemingly immovable institutional bureaucracies.

5. Discuss ways to use teacher assistance more effectively. Understand all the facts about leaving high school and about alternative schooling: visit, read mission statements, talk to people. Know all you can about these different environments and their effects.

6. Accompany the teen to bureaucratic meetings; often these times are so intimidating that young women are unable to articulate their needs and goals. This is a high priority for advocacy because the documents you have compiled can indicate abilities that are not generally part of school assessments: for example, Serena's care of younger siblings; her sophisticated organizational skills; the kinds of reading and writing that she turns to for self-enhancement; the natural development of a growing articulacy regarding the effect of structured arrangements.

7. Encourage knowledge-driven curriculum that relates academic content to the teenager's own environment and experience. The best programs require high degrees of student interaction in small heterogeneous peer groups; skills are not a fundamental target of teaching, but are tools for acquiring knowledge.

8. Ask yourself why *affect*—discussions about feelings and emotions—appears to be missing from the indexes of most literature about cognitive development and teaching. Go the index of books that deal with the needs of students who are gifted and talented; the word is there, and the instructional strategies that are offered will help teachers create lessons that include students' affective domains by promoting intellectually stimulating and challenging learning projects.

9. Understand that isolating contexts in order to describe the teen as a thinker and doer does very little to improve the situation, no matter how negative or positive. See literacies within the complexity of life circumstance and personal experience. Help the teen learn what is happening and what to do about it.
10. Be there, be a friend, listen when she is overwhelmed by having little money and little support from family and friends. Talk about your own concerns. Rely on each other's strengths. Celebrate small victories and anticipate the reality and promise of teenage moms who have the right to position themselves for self-empowerment.

The traditional emphasis in secondary education for pregnant teens has been remediation. There are too few opportunities for individual response, reading whole literature, or student choice in writing. Yet, the lives of these young women provide a wonderful opportunity for the kinds of thematic approaches to instruction that make learning more purposeful. Skills are acquired when they are seamlessly woven into teachable moments. Unexamined linear directives are aimed more toward power arrangements and less toward self-liberation. Setting up environments and opportunities for user-friendly classrooms requires a paradigm shift to a philosophy that promotes literacy as a way to develop thinking, problem posing and problem solving, and self-assessment. The change begins by believing in and listening to students; neither was a priority in Serena's education. Education for early childbearers does not appear to take into account the cultural perspectives of adolescent mothers and the framework within which they make sense of themselves. Indeed, Serena's academic performance was often used as the reason for draconian measures meant to demonstrate others' concern. But her competence was systematically ignored. In particular, we need to explore the learning mechanisms involved in the construction of literacy in order to understand how they can be most effectively triggered. Many young voices like Serena's continue to be silenced by the rhetoric that heralds perceived defects. For teenage mothers to be empowered, their intellects must be engaged within the context of their evident and developing literacies.

Recently, I accompanied Serena and waited while she took a reading test she needed to pass in order to be able to enroll for courses at the community college and be tutored for her GED at the same time. After the test, Serena kept saying, "I'm stupid. I'm stupid." The secretary told us she had failed the test. When I asked when Serena could be retested, she said in two months. That meant Serena could not enroll for the spring semester but had to take a job at the nearest burger joint. The secretary added: "That's too bad, because if she'd waited she could have taken it in September and it would have been a better test." I asked why Serena hadn't been offered this "better test." The secretary replied, "It will be a new test because of questions about the validity of this one; it doesn't measure what its supposed to."

I wondered how many other young mothers had taken this same test, failed to meet it's dubious criteria, and had doubted themselves as severely as Serena had. It is a lens through which to view the social construction of Serena's internalization of failure; the unrelenting circumstances that wear her down.

Denny: When you first met Serena and the other young women who were at Mercy Home, what were your expectations?

JOANNA: My expectation was that I was going there to conduct an informal reading inventory of some kind or take a look at their schoolwork and conduct some kind of criterion-based tests and be able to say things like they needed more help on finding the main idea or that they—

Denny: Is that true? Is this where you were?

JOANNA: Yes, because the director said to me that they were having problems with their reading, and so if someone would diagnose their difficulties and propose some strategies they'd do much better at school.

Denny: Was that part of the reasoning you had in the beginning? This isn't a research project?

JOANNA: Right. Mercy Home is only a few blocks away, and I wanted to be involved in the community in some kind of volunteer effort. What played a big part in it was that I had just arrived here from getting my master's degree, back East, and there I was very much involved with these kinds of diagnostic tests.

Denny: You were trained in developing diagnostic tests?

JOANNA: Yes, that's how it started, that's why I was invited into Mercy. But before long I realized how uncritically I had accepted the director's explanations about their reading habits. I'd bought into a view that they all had difficulties with reading.

Denny: What were your preconceptions of the home? What did you expect?

JOANNA: I guess I thought they were lucky to have a place where they could be like a family, where they were being protected and safe. They could all be like sisters, you know, and that was really nice. And the director impressed me as being a very gentle person. So, I believed that being there offered the teenagers a much broader range of social services during their pregnancies.

Denny: So your impression was that this was a wonderful place for these young girls to be?

JOANNA: Yes. And also it was an opportunity for me because I had come with questions about what happens to their literacies when young women are involved in a process of reinventing themselves as mothers; what happens in the process of people changing when they've decided they need to.

Denny: Then your interest in literacy was already there?

JOANNA: Yes it was, and I intended to do what the Director wanted me to do, but I also wanted to investigate how they all were using their literacies to get information they wanted or needed. I was taking the course with you on family, community, and bureaucratic literacies, so it also became a research project for that class.

Denny: And what did you find?

JOANNA: Well, right off I found I didn't share the director's belief that there was something flawed here. But I thought I could ignore it, just work within it, and that turned out to be a false assumption on my part, because you can't pretend that this perspective doesn't exist. When you acquiesce to it, you are in essence going along with it, because it'll pervade everything you'll try to do. The first thing that I found, for instance, was from a Native American girl who told me that she didn't know how to tell her parents she was pregnant. So she went to the library and she leafed through books. She went back and back and back again, until finally she found a young adult novel in which the girl tells her parents she is pregnant. So she simply memorized and rehearsed what this character had done and then went and told her own parents in the same way. She'd used her literacies in a very inventive way. I was seeing some real strengths here.

Denny: So your first hunch that the young women's personal literacies were important was really proved; whether it's Serena writing letters that she doesn't send or writing in journals, but their literacies were important to them.

JOANNA: Yes. And I think one thing that startled me was realizing that when they dipped into their literacies, they went much deeper.

Denny: I like that: "dipping into their own literacies."

JOANNA: Yes. They immersed themselves much deeper in reading for themselves than they did with the lessons or homework from the school.

Denny: So you felt . . . ?

JOANNA: That they were really using their emotions in a good way to support their literacy development. It was an asset. But emotions were targeted to be overcome, to be fixed so they wouldn't be a problem. I think that was because their pregnancies were viewed as a problem to their reading and writing progress. That notion seemed to be accepted without question.

Denny: So they didn't need help with the main idea [*Laughing*].

JOANNA: [*Laughing*] They didn't need help with the main idea, certainly not. But I needed help with my main idea—that was more like it.

Denny: When did you begin to find that your role was changing? The first focus was on developing some kind of tutorial program for these young women, and then you really, I think, began to shift gears. Was that after you started working with Serena?

JOANNA: Well, circumstance played a part, because at first I was focusing on three young women: an Afro-American, a Native American and Serena, who is Mexican American. The other two left; Serena was the one who remained. And we became friends. She seemed to be excited about the interviews. And the more time passed, the more I came to appreciate the part she was playing as an inventor of her own literacies.

Denny: When did you become disturbed about what was happening to Serena?

JOANNA: When I went with her to the foster-care review board meeting after the baby was born. It didn't seem to me that the board was trying to support her. The tone of the meeting was very accusatory, sort of like, You let us down because you had this baby. Serena was so proud of the baby. She was expecting them all to admire him, she expected such kindness and caring, and these things didn't seem to be there. Their attention was solely focused on the official report they were making.

Denny: And the disturbing things were in texts? They were written down?

JOANNA: They were written down. Yes. And it was there also in the tone of these people's voices. They wouldn't look into our eyes, or even speak directly to us, or tell us what they were reading that was so disturbing to them.

Denny: So it would be the beginning of official behavior . . . the kinds of things that were being written down became the problem.

JOANNA: Yes. Also even before we went to that meeting, when I started looking through Serena's notebooks, which she'd been keeping for so long. She'd kept carbon copies of documents, letters, and so on. And I would say, What does this mean? And she would say, This happened on that day. So that's what this paper means to her. She was making inferences and predictions about some very real issues and supporting them with the texts. I mean, there were so many documents—all written in legalese—and she had no problem reading and interpreting them. She told me if it concerned her baby or herself she wanted to make sure she read and understood every page.

Denny: So she could look at these official documents that had been written about her.

JOANNA: She had a great depth of understanding about them, too. Not only what was written there but what it could mean. She gave me very complete details about what she thought it meant for her life. And so, to think that I had wondered about her understanding thesis statements and all [*Laughing*], you know, it was so . . . it pushed that idea right out of my mind. And I told the director about all this. That all three of these girls, including Serena, had great powers of comprehension and concentration. But to me it was as if she dismissed these facts; maybe she thought, That's fine, but that's not what I wanted you to do here.

Denny: She wasn't . . . she couldn't or didn't respond to it.

JOANNA: You know, she was very kind. But I think she was really looking for me to say to each young woman things like, If you'll spend an hour and a half practicing punctuation, then everything will be fine. She was really tied into the notion that the best thing I could be doing there was to discover an area of reading or writing weakness and work out a strategy to minimize it.

Denny: When do you think you became an advocate for Serena? Because it's very clear that you did. I mean, I remember when you went through that review board for foster care, you were very concerned about what was happening.

JOANNA: I began to look at how she was being forced to devise strategies that made her consent to her own subordination.

Denny: What would have happened if she hadn't been compliant?

JOANNA: If she hadn't been compliant she would have been labeled as a delinquent, a troublemaker.

Denny: Even though you were concerned about her being co-opted, the alternatives were unpalatable; pretty grim.

JOANNA: Oh yeah, definitely. I think she understood that better than I did.

Denny: So there was a role that she had to play if she was going to survive. And what was your role there, Joanna? I mean, I'm not putting you on the spot, but I'm thinking about other teachers who find themselves in the same situation. You must have been between a rock and a hard place.

JOANNA: I think in the beginning I believed that my role was going to be simply to shut up and just document what I saw. And then pretty soon . . .

Denny: Because?

JOANNA: I guess at first I believed that my job was simply to gather "objective" evidence. But it wasn't ever only objective evidence. At every turn it called for judgment, concern, opinion—and all of this was based on what I knew about the way students develop as readers and writers. So I think there was a trade-off, in that I began to find out more about my role as a teacher and as an advocate. It didn't stop with the idea that I wanted to do this research. Instead, it became, as an advocate for Serena, how do I support her literacies? What was the next best thing that could be done, and how did it fit within a holistic framework? Because real issues were the things that engaged her. Like a magnet, she just honed in on what was relevant—no matter how difficult or complicated that kind of learning might have seemed to someone else. And it was done on her own because that wasn't what she was offered in the alternative education program.

Denny: If you didn't support her in being compliant, would you have jeopardized . . . I mean, did you feel you might have jeopardized her situation and made it worse for her?

JOANNA: Yes. I did feel that.

Denny: Were you made voiceless at times?

JOANNA: I was. And I recognized that her parents were also made voiceless. When I met her mother at the baby's baptism, what became obvious to me was she and Serena both understood a lot more than I did about the repercussions that could occur from my standing up and being chesty.

Denny: Being chesty?

JOANNA: Being impudent—that's how it would have been considered by social agencies. They both understood what could happen because they both have a long history of dealing with it.

Denny: Did you ever feel like you had pariah status with the organizations?

JOANNA: Oh, yes. I recently tried to mend bridges at the Home, and I was always walking on eggs with Serena's caseworkers. I gave the director an earlier paper describing what these teen moms were reading and writing. There was no need for me to construct lessons and tests for these girls. They used their literacies to hook up to information quite extensively on their own. They just were pragmatic about the issue—they knew they had to keep their interests to themselves. Maybe, yes, they didn't read the books on the bookshelf, but if they could pick books that interested them . . . but the director didn't want any young adult romance novels around.

Denny: [*Laughing*] There's been enough romance?

JOANNA: Yes. Yes. [*Laughing*] And then with the social agencies, it seems almost that the hardest job I had was not taking things at face value. I had to take a walk and say to myself, Wait a minute. This is not what I am being told. Because it was always presented so logically, This is the best thing for her. You have to take a deep breath and go off and talk to yourself and say, No, this isn't right, now let's see what exactly was said here. I really had to rehearse the way I'd say something, because if they'd get defensive the conversation was over.

Denny: There are always multiple stories, the dominant story being the story that is in official texts. In that first hearing the documentation mentioned her beating her baby when she'd never done so; that became part of the official text. And then there are Serena's interpretations of those texts and her own writing, and her own life and her story. And what you were doing was moving back and forth between these two stories trying to work out . . .

JOANNA: It always seemed to me that whomever I was talking to about Serena was holding in their hands some metaphorical snapshot. And this snapshot, this photo, now represents reality instead of the actual person.

Denny: And usually it was from an official document.

JOANNA: Yes, and it was taken on a certain day at a certain time, and this was all there was to it, no thought about what happened before or what happened after. First these official texts just pictured her reality, then they became her reality.

Denny: It seems very clear to me that you helped Serena in ways that will probably always be intangible. That you weren't always able to challenge a lot of the official texts even if you disagreed with them, because if you had, there would always be the fact that it might be dangerous for Serena; she might not get the baby back. In conversations we had at the time, there was always the fear you had that in speaking out you might make it worse. You were really walking a fine line, and yet quietly, and certainly not with official sanction or with the officials realizing, you were able to help her and you continue to help her in ways that are intangible.

JOANNA: Yes. You know when Serena would complain about the office support program, we'd talk about the fact that she didn't have to take an office job—be a receptionist, let's say—if she didn't want to. She could go on to college. I told her not to doubt that she could do it. She's very bright.

Denny: So you believed in her. And not only did you help her with her literacies, but also in friendship and in believing in her.

JOANNA: Yes. We are honest with each other. Our friendship was—is—important. She also understood that I couldn't understand some of what she's been through. She knew she was helping me learn, too.

Denny: That to me is one of the biggest revelations that come out of all of these studies and certainly from your work—that we have tremendous sophistication, and we all have advanced degrees, and whether we're working on doctorates or we've got our doctorates, we've got years and years—hundreds of years—of schooling among us. And yet I certainly had no idea what it meant to try and work within a bureaucratic, official organization. How it is you deal with those texts. I had no idea how they worked. And I think you're the same. We have a sophistication, but then we are completely naive about some official forms of literacy.

JOANNA: And about these forms—these texts combine to reproduce subordination and vulnerability. We can see the part they played, also, in her mother's life. It reveals what being officially labeled means to a family. The way Serena's caseworker defined things made it possible to punish her by taking the baby away. He held her responsible for his personal definition of what it meant for a young woman to "do right."

Denny: And once it's written down that she was abusive, even though she had not been abusive . . . I can't remember why that was written there.

JOANNA: It was a form. The form that was used to take away her baby was the same form that's used for endangering a minor, which usually means abuse. But it had nothing to do with abuse, it had to do with Serena not following orders. I mean, no one hit the baby. They just used that same form. What was that about? What? Were they economizing on paper or something? And now it's become part of the historical record.

Denny: Which is going to always be in the official record. And it's the same for all of us. We don't understand the significance of the official texts in our lives and how these stories determine what happens to us.

JOANNA: Yes, like Serena being prescribed Prozac. So now she's been labeled as having severe depression. How will that medical record . . . suppose the time comes when she's paying for her own medical insurance?

Denny: Right. So we take away her baby and she's depressed so we give her Prozac for depression. I cannot think of anything more ludicrous . . .

JOANNA: She was seventeen when that happened. It really seems to me that a lot of these texts are set up so a bureaucrat can say, You know, I'm not being subjective about this interpretation, this is simply objective truth, and we're just people who are expected to work within these particular guidelines. But the guidelines are meant to deal with deficiencies, so the evidence they're looking for is evidence of weakness—of pathology. So there are assumptions being made all over the place that have very little to do with who she really is or her competence and strengths. For example, We're not going to give you assistance unless you're taking birth control pills and a tranquilizer. I was there when Serena was told that. And that is just a power move—complete control over her body and her mind. It's horrendous. So now each day when she has to make these extremely strategic decisions about her own and her son's survival, she's medicated. She didn't come up with that "strategy" on her own. That's part of the reductionist perspective that engineers her dependence.

Denny: When you talk with her, is she aware how disturbed you are by these things?

JOANNA: She knows I'm on her side. But I don't think anybody is really aware of how disturbed I am by it—my sisters, my family—I don't even think I communicated it that strongly in my writing. Sometimes I am absolutely horrified by what she faces. I feel scared and mad at the same time.

Denny: This is an interesting point for someone who is working as an advocate, because you could be almost militant. I mean, you could get very angry about this, and try to deal with the agencies, and you've chosen not to—I'm sure after lots of very deep contemplation of the situation—and tell me if I'm wrong, but my interpretation is that Serena's well-being is always at the center of whatever it is you're doing. Am I right?

JOANNA: Yes, right. What would it mean for her if I called up, say, a supervisor in the welfare organization and said, I saw this happen at an official hearing, or, Your policies are steering her into defeat? That could be a scary thing to do. This is her reality. This is her life here. I've seen that a lot of their decisions play havoc with her day-to-day life.

Denny: If she said, Joanna, I want you to do this for me. I can't do this on my own. I really want to fight them on this, it would be a different situation?

JOANNA: Oh, yes. Absolutely different.

Denny: But that's not where she is, and so that's not where you are. It's a tremendously important point, because we're not advocating as individuals. Advocacy can take so many different roles. And advocacy within this situation is in trying to understand what is happening to Serena within these different organizations. And to support her in ways that make sense to Serena, and we hope she's going to come through it and she will have her opportunities to go to college. And a lot of it will be because of your friendship. But it isn't using Serena to change the system. I mean, you really are not using her, which is important—this is not your cause. This is her cause, and you're doing what makes sense. It really is standing side by side. Let's shift gears. Here I am, I'm a teacher and I'm teaching fourteen- or fifteen-year-olds and there are several young women who are pregnant in my classroom. How would I advocate for them? What advice would you give me?

JOANNA: I would petition the school to arrange for day care within the regular school if that's where the girls want to be. We'd need to investigate who each girl is an individual learner and then to arrange for curriculum that offers the support she needs. Also, Serena was in foster care, so we need to take a look at how a girl in the same situation may be being defined by this status. Is she being given any kind of medication? And if so, why? Has she been labeled as having some kind of a problem, and does that have anything to do with her being poor and pregnant? Labeled as a delinquent? We'd want to know about the circumstances that caused that determination. We'd need each other's support to brainstorm about the possible effects these circumstances are having on developing literacy. Is she being victimized simply because of a proximity to other situations, like a family history of drugs or low socioeconomic level or whatever, and therefore she's been judged to be "at risk" and certain things are done to her because of it?

Denny: Does that happen?

JOANNA: Sure it does. She was moved out of her "dangerous" community, and she was discouraged from contact with her mom, dad, friends. Being labeled "at risk" means lots of things can be done to her. She gets pushed and pulled from one intervention to another. Remediation because she's "at risk." It becomes a self-fulfilling prophesy. For Serena, intervention aimed at "at risk" meant interfering in her intellectual development.

Denny: So for a teacher to understand the home circumstances of the young women and then to understand it from a young person's perspective and then to look at how they are being defined within particular official circles, whether it's through the foster-care system or some agency that is dealing with them at this point because of their pregnancy, and to question that?

JOANNA: Yes.

Denny: You'd set up day care?

JOANNA: If their literacy development is to be furthered by schooling, they need to know their kids are safe and close by. Most important, I'd take a look at the kinds of programs that are being mandated by official care providers for the young women themselves. The kind of control they assume over the children of these young mothers—these decisions seldom include mom, except as a passive recipient. I wonder what part being forced into compensatory programs plays in their interest and affection for learning? It was certainly no help for Serena's literacy progress. We've surely got to know by now that the majority of these programs are failing for single mothers who are young and poor. When we investigate, it's all about power and control under the guise of guidance. And at the heart of it, whenever Serena does manage to open a door for herself, it's slammed shut, quote, for her own good, unquote.

Tagging: A Way to Make Meaning

DEBBIE SMITH

My presentation on my students' tagging [a kind of graffiti] has gone well. I have met several people who are willing to work with my students. I am feeling good as I open the door to my apartment. Like a beacon, the light on my message machine is blinking. "Debbie it's Barb, Kenny and Danny's mom. I've something I need to tell you." My heart sinks. Her voice sounds tense and concerned.

"Barb, I got your message, what's up"

"I wanted you to know Jesse Torres was shot and killed last night."

"My Jesse!?"

"Yes!"

The newspaper headline—"Teen Slain Last Night." Next to the article is a picture of Victor (one of Jesse's homies) covered with blood—crying. "The city's 55th homicide."

No! He's not a number. He was a young boy who loved playing in the caves, on the water slide, and with Nintendo. He was my student.

I have taught high school for twelve years. No day is the same as another. I can enter my classroom and find two big "tuff" boys arguing for the chair next to my spot, hungry for and at times demanding my complete attention and help, dare I say love. But on the very next day the same boys will be pushing me away, letting me know that they can do what is required, that they don't need—don't want—my help. I have watched my students act and think like children, and I have watched them deal with adult problems. They no longer want to be the little kid at home, but they are not yet ready or willing to buy into being an adult. They don't belong to either world. For many teenagers, it is a struggle they may not survive. On October 26, 1995, when Jesse lost that struggle, this became real for me.

In February 1995 I started teaching at an alternative high school. My students were eight boys, who ranged in age from fifteen to eighteen. Six of them were members of a west side gang known as the Crips. Two were members of a tagging crew. Seven were Mexican Americans, one was Euro-American. They had a community. They had all grown up together. In their own words, they were "down" for each other, meaning they had proved worthy of one another's loyalty. I was an outsider, and the first thing I had to do was earn their loyalty as well.

We talked about loyalty, and I tried to explain that I was there for them. I was their teacher, yes, but I was also there to help them whenever they needed it—jobs, transportation, court hearings. SadBoy said, "Do you want us to jump you in [initiate you into the gang]?" We all laughed.

My students dressed in what has become known as the gang look (see Figure 1): oversize clothes, pants riding on the hips or lower ("sagging"). For my gang kids, blue was their color. They would "sport" this color in everything they wore.

On average, these kids had spent less than a year in a traditional high school. They were considered trouble, nonlearners, by the school. In reality, they had been marginalized and forced out of the school system. Once, soon after I became their teacher, my students started talking about their memories of school. I recorded what they said in my field notes:

> Plucy tells how on the first day of school the vice-principal comes up to him and says, "If you are like your brother, you might as well go home now."

> Smurf shares how he is constantly called into the office and "padded down."

> The boys had nothing good to say about school. The school tells them they can't wear blue. For these kids it would be a whole new wardrobe—a new way to think.

> School officials would take their belts and/or belt buckles, shoes, everything that "school" associates with gangs.

For these students, school was a place where they were harassed. School was a place that didn't accept them. School was a place that was part of the struggle.

One of the first things I noticed was that these students did little writing and what writing they did was filling out worksheets. The program was designed around what I call individualized, outcome-based, mastery-learning worksheets. I naively plunged in, assuming that if I provided free writing time, the kids would write.

Figure 1
The "gang look"

First I had them generate a list of topics they could write about. Then I asked them to choose any topic from their list and write for ten minutes. Not only didn't they write, they didn't *want* to write. They sat, at first quietly, later just talking. Finally one of them said, "Can we tag?" I replied, "Sure." I wasn't really sure what was going to happen.

Another time I asked the students to sign their name on a big piece of paper I had placed on the table. In my own graduate class on writing development, we had talked about how teenagers play with their signature. I wanted to see what my students would do when asked to sign their name. They seemed not to know what I was asking. I instinctively said, "Tag on the paper like you do on the walls," and the students went wild. They tagged, and they invited anyone who came into the room to do the same. The more my students tagged, the more curious I became. The kids tagged all the time. When they were sitting around talking, they would get paper and a writing implement and tag. Tagging became a part of my classroom, and I began to form questions:

• What function/purpose does tagging serve?
• What can we as teachers learn from our students' tagging?
• What would happen if tagging was accepted in the classroom?

I started to put big giant sheets of paper on the walls and doors and regular typing paper on the tables. My kids would get excited when I put new paper up.

Tagging was part of who they were, and for the first time they had permission to tag in school. They didn't have to worry about being sent to the principal and in some cases being suspended and their names given to the police.

Their fear of getting in trouble was apparent when I entered the classroom one day, and fifteen-year-old Smurf said, "Miss [this is what they called me] my PO [probation officer] saw me tagging." I wasn't sure what to say. I didn't see the problem. "I'm on gang condition," Smurf explained. I learned that the courts had placed Smurf on a strict probation which included "gang condition."—Smurf wasn't allowed to do anything considered gang-related (dressing, talking, tagging).

"Smurf, tell your PO to call me. I will explain that I allow my students to tag in my classroom, that it is part of a study. Don't worry."

Milkweed piped in, "Miss you are the only teacher who lets us tag."

Some Definitions

Brewer[1] has developed three categories of what he refers to as *hip hop graffiti*. The first category, *tags* (see Figure 2), are the simplest and most elemental form. The most prevalent manifestations are stylized signatures written in markers, spray paint, grease pencil, paint sticks, shoe polish; they proclaim the writer's self-fashioned street name. *Throw-ups* (the second category), or *bombs* (see Figure 3) as my students call them, present the writer's name formed in bubble, block, or similarly expansive letters. The third group, *pieces* (see Figure 4), are multicolored murals depicting a word or words (often the writer's street name) in connection with backgrounds, designs, characters, messages, or comments.

Tags are made by *taggers* or *gangsters*. Taggers are crews made up of kids who all come from different parts of town and who write tags anywhere in town. Gangs form in neighborhoods and claim the hood as their turf. As I examined the tags in my classroom, I thought I noticed some differences between tagger and gangster

Figure 2

This tag includes the street name and the name of the gang

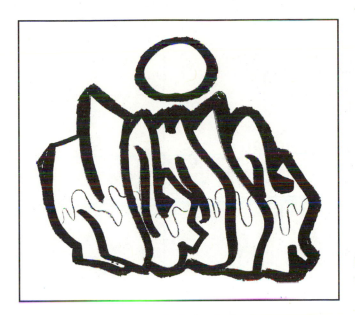

Figure 3
Throw up or bomb tagging

Figure 4 Piece tagging depicts words in connection with backgrounds, designs, messages, or comments

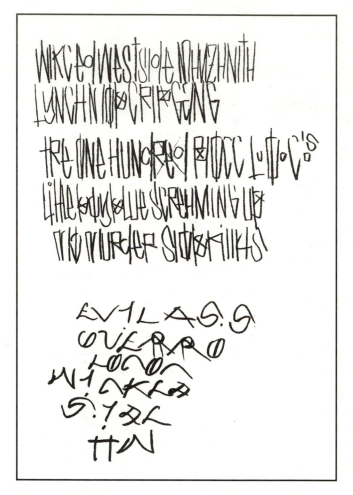

Figure 5

Tagger and gangster tags have a different appearance

tags. In the examples in Figure 5, the tagger tag (bottom) has a more artistic look. The letters are softer. The gangster tag (top) has sharper-edged letters. Both tagger and gangster tags contain nonconventional spelling. I asked one of my taggers if he saw a difference between what gangsters do and his tags. He said no, that taggers come from all over town and that gangsters are from a neighborhood, but that tags are just tags.

Watching my students tag, I noticed apparent thinking and planning. My field notes for April 5 record Smurf writing a rap and tagging:

> Smurf is working on a rap. He stops and rereads, looks into space. Gets out a second sheet of paper and starts to tag. He moves the paper around looking for a spot. He tags. Looks for a new spot. It isn't random, put wherever, it is clear. It is like he has a plan—a place for everything.

Not only does there seem to be a form of prewriting to tagging, but how a tag looks is very important. Many writers view their tag as having an aesthetic appeal.

A good tag helps the writer gain fame and respect within the gang and the tagging community. He may even change the spelling from one tag to another, depending on how it looks. In other words, the writer will manipulate the spelling and the print to get the look he desires. Some of the tagging I observed in the classroom also included revision. The writer has a certain meaning he wants to get across, and he will revise his work until the meaning is achieved.

Function and Purpose

Research has revealed several reasons why adolescents have turned to tagging. One reason is to stake a personal claim to the surface written upon or to claim "ownership" of an area of the city. Since I use portfolios in my classroom, I provided each of these students a gray notebook in which to keep his work. Their first reaction was, "Miss, you got the right kind. Can we tag on them?"

"They are your notebooks to keep your work in. You can do what you want on them." With new felt-tip pens (blue and black), they spent the next thirty minutes marking their property. They shared their tags and commented on them.

At the end of that initial semester, I decided to paint the classroom. I wanted to make the room brighter and friendlier. The boys took all the pictures off the wall and plastered the nail holes. To celebrate the hard work, we decided to have pizza for lunch. Coming back from picking up the pizza, as I reentered the room, my chin dropped. The kids had tagged the room. I recorded the incident in my field notes:

> The boys looked like they had just got caught with their hand in the cookie jar. Yet they seemed to have a big smile. I started to talk and Smurf pops in, Miss we are going to paint over it. According to Smurf they were going to do just a little tag, but realizing we were going to paint the room anyway, they then tagged all over the room. The two boys who went with me to get the pizza felt left out. Before they could eat, they grabbed color crayons and left their tags.

It was obvious that they had enjoyed themselves and were proud of their work. While we were eating the pizza, they said, "The classroom looks better. Miss, don't you think it looks better?" To me it looked like little kids had gotten hold of some crayons, but I could tell for them it was much more. They truly owned the classroom. It was now theirs and everyone who went into the room knew who spent time there. Without argument, three boys volunteered to come in the next day to help paint the walls.

Proclaiming one's identity is another function of tagging. A tag consists mainly of the street name of the writer, the name of his gang, and the address of their hood. Tagging identifies the teenager to the world of the teenager and provides a way for the writer to gain fame and respect. It becomes an expression of power for the individual writer and his gang. The tag lets people know who the writer is, where he is from, and a little about his experience. Some tags also identify an enemy, or rival.

As children, our world is developed by the adults with whom we interact. As

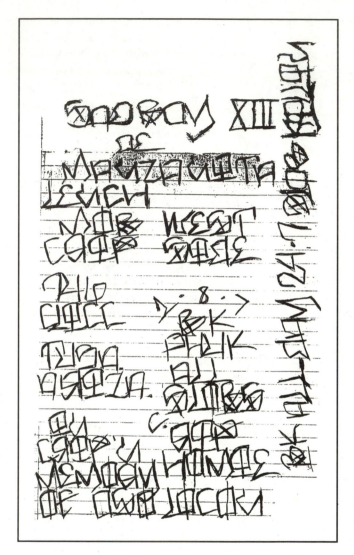

Figure 6
SadBoy's tag

we grow up, our environment changes. Language, spoken and written, becomes a tool for representing the experiences we have. Language is a way to create meaning in our world. Therefore, tagging is not only a way to establish ownership and identity, it is also a way to structure community, to give meaning.

Let's look closely at SadBoy's tag shown in Figure 6. SadBoy tells us where he is from and the name of his gang ("Manzanita Lench Mob, Crip West Side") written at the top of the page. Looking down the left side we also learn SadBoy's zip code and town, "746" and "Tusa, Ariza" (Tucson, Arizona). He emphasizes he is Crip by playing with the words. In the bottom left corner SadBoy writes "Crippen memory" and in the right corner he reveals who his enemies are and how he feels about them. In the very center he has written "1 8 7/BK/PHUK/ALL/SLOBS". 187 is the law's code for homicide; BK stands for Blood Killer. Bloods are a rival gang. The word slob is used by Crips in the place of Blood. Written up the right side of the tag is "BK ALL DAY 24–7 SLOB KILL IN," self-evident, except that 24–7 is shorthand for twenty-four hours a day seven days a week (think of stopping at the 7–11 on your way home from work and this etymology seems a lot less bizarre suddenly).

The crossing out of letters and the spelling of words also reveals who the writer is and who the enemy is. In SadBoy's tag the letters B, P, S, and R are crossed out: B because of Blood, S because of Slobs, R because red is the Bloods' gang color, and P because of Police, with whom my students associate harassment. Also, in the Crips' world CK signifies "Crip Killer"; therefore they always spell the *ck* combination *cc*. Notice this in the word "Clicc" written under 746.

SadBoy is writing about his anger and trying to make sense of his hurt. He covers up his vulnerability by writing openly and powerfully. He also pays tribute to his dead homie, making his memory live. His is not to be forgotten.

During the last year and a half, I have discovered that when my students are upset about what's going on in their world, more tagging goes on in the room. Tagging helps them deal with it. This was one way they dealt with the death of their homie, Plucy (Jesse). Death is a hard concept; but the violent death of a friend is even harder. During the first week after Jesse's death, I observed students sitting for hours, tagging and sharing stories and memories, or tagging in silence. Smurf looked at an empty wall and asked if he could write. I turned to him ready to say no, but the look in his eye made me say yes. His tag (see Figure 7) was a tribute to all his lost friends.

Cecil Day-Lewis states, "We do not write in order to be understood, we write in order to understand."[2] This is true for teenagers who tag. Tagging helps them understand their world. In many cases, it would be easier for them to cut off their arm than to quit tagging. They must tag. It is a real need. It may seem foreign to those of us who do not feel the compulsion to write, but it is familiar to authors. Somerset Maugham confides, "We do not write because we want to; we write because we must."[3] Many adolescents tag because they must.

Advocating for the Disenfranchised

Adults tend to look at adolescence as a transitional time between childhood and adulthood, ignoring the fact that teenagers are creators of their own culture. Even though it may be a short period of time, adolescence isn't a subculture of adulthood. Adolescents have their own culture, and language is one way they create and transfer it. Tagging is language. In their tags, teenagers deal with issues in their world. They announce who they are. They struggle to make meaning. It is so much a part of them that my students had a hard time understanding why I was unaware of their conventions. An incident I recorded in my field notes illustrates this point:

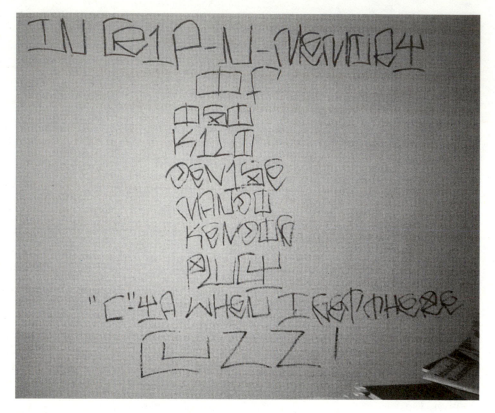

Figure 7 Smurf's tribute to all his lost friends

While I was asking Danny about his tagging, he made an interesting statement. He said, "Miss, it's strange that you don't know this. We grew up with it." Another student stated, "We have always done it." I am realizing that this is an important part of them and I need to understand and accept it.

Teachers need to acknowledge the experience and knowledge students bring to the classroom. The curriculum should be built on this knowledge and experience. Before a teacher can accept the whole student for who he or she is, that teacher needs to understand the student's culture. Part of accepting my students—and many other teenagers—is to acknowledge their tagging. Accepting the whole student turns a classroom once filled with disenfranchised students who were not willing to risk and learn into one filled with students with the courage to take the risk and learn. Because they know they are accepted and valued in my classroom, my students who once refused to write are now writing on their own time. SadBoy and Smurf sat down at the computer and wrote a story, for example (see the appendix). This wasn't an assignment. It was something they wanted to do. They wrote the story and then shared what they had written with the other students. The story is in their language and style. The subject is from their world.

As I incorporate my students' culture into my classroom, I now find myself dealing with the ethical issues associated with them and their culture. Tagging in the eyes of society is simply the destruction of property and a manifestation of violence. But tagging is also a tool—a valuable tool—many teenagers use to work through the struggles associated with adolescent culture.

I deal with the destruction-of-property issue in my classroom by providing a place for tagging. My students and I discuss what they may or may not tag on. They know I disapprove of the destruction of property. As members of the classroom community, we negotiate. We talk about appropriate places they are free to tag on and surfaces they are not allowed to tag on. When they tag in an inappropriate area, they must clean the tag off. This is our agreement. However, tables, chairs, any surface in my classroom, can be marked for a tag. Early on I didn't get it. I said, Guys I provide paper for you to tag on, so why do you still tag the tables, chairs, and cabinets? Their response? "Miss, the paper isn't permanent." Cleaning the tag off and providing paper are not solutions. They are strategies I employ. When students tag where they are not supposed to, I get upset and they know I disapprove. We discuss the right others have to unmarred, protected property, and the tags are cleaned off.

However, for me there are greater issues we as teachers need to deal with. We need to help our students survive; we need to provide an environment in which they are acknowledged as a whole person. Providing a learning environment is more important. Why make tagging in the classroom such a big issue? You can clean it off. I keep a can of graffiti remover around.

The violence communicated in their tags comes and goes. My kids are very much aware of my feelings about violence. Jesse's death has made this a real issue for all members of my classroom. By allowing my students to write/tag about the violence they have experienced and felt in their lives, I am giving them a safe place to express their hurt, a place where they will not be harmed. And by writing they may eliminate the need to act it out.

I don't have any set tagging "rules." Every day brings new situations with new complications and needs. My goal is to acknowledge the whole student and to offer an atmosphere that will provide safety and acceptance for everyone. In my classroom today, my students aren't tagging *on* the furniture as much; instead, they are showing me that they are willing to take the risk to learn. Acknowledging the whole student is my only rule. Should students be allowed to tag in school? is not the question. The question is, *Can we teach those whom we do not acknowledge or value completely?*

Postscript

On August 16, 1996 another student from my class died. George worked hard to finish high school. He was working as an electrician and he had an apprenticeship at a community college. On the night of August 16 he shot himself in front of four of his friends.

Appendix: SadBoy and Smurf's Story

Although this text is disturbing it represents the first writing produced by my students. As they gained confidence they wrote poems and essays about their families, their friends, and about themselves. They also wrote critiques of movies and books, such as Always Running[4] *and* A Boy Without A Flag.[5] *Their other writings included letters to two judges to advocate for friends and a letter to the mayor to ask if the city would provide a new building for our school.*

It was a dark blue night kiccin cacc on the 31 bloc, with some 40's of O'E, weed, and some homegirls that night was going well until a strange car full of slob's roll up. Smurf and I had two Desert Eagle's so you know we wern't slippin. The Lbb crew had two Sawed off Guage's with Shaggy on the side strappin a 45. The sound of screeching tires are coming on both sides of us. At least five heads in each car, slowing down as they pulled up slowly towards us. All of a sudden they stop, silence was all through the bloc, not a word said for atleast 10 seconds it seemed like the longest 10 seconds any one could ever go through. "Let's do this" was the words heard from the two cars as they opened there car doors slowly creepin out. Silent for another long 10 seconds exept for the clicc clacc of the cold steel hammer cliccing bacc. Eyes wide awake thouhgts of death are going through our heads hoping we do die, but voices are telling us that every thing is gonna c alright. Different thoughts went through each one of our heads, about our kids, our parents, and thinking what a wonderfull future we would have had with our beautiful "ladies". But knowing if those triggers get pulled we'll never get to give our ladies a child or to have there hand in marriage. The first time that we ever cared and loved for a person were gonna loose it for our pride, and what we believe in. It's trippy how so much things go through your mind in such little time. I wish we could c our hynas once again "Till Times Ends". As we pull out our cuates were praying to god asking for forgiveness and asking if Mauricio to c with us the whole way, and to c waiting for us in that "GANGSTER LEAN". Should have been an "L O C" yelled out Shaggy as he started going cycso on the solo rampage. "Watch your cacc Cuzz" screamed out Bad Boy Pumping his guage like there was no tomorrow. Clicc clicc bang bang Lynch Mob Crip Gang yelled Boy Blue dumping on fools like he was suposed to. I ran up to the car with plenty of fear in my heart "ah phuk" im hit said Shaggy. I turned around grabbed a slob by his throat with an evil mind "got any last words" I asked, well phuk your life bang, bang I started unloading my clip on his face. After I dumped my whole clip on his face I popped a new clip in, then I looked cacc and saw little SMURFY LOC pistol whippen some slop to death then I saw the slob fall to the ground and lil SMURF took to three to the chess but he was till shootin cacc. those lil PEE-WEEZ SMURF and SHAGGY went our like some real soldgers, at the age of 15. The sound of hot bullets go through our bodies but not giving a phuk cuzz Mauricio gots my cacc so we kept gunning yelling out "Crip for Life". all the girls are dead six slobz are down four are still fightin for thier lives SMURF and SHAGGY are cacc on thier feet poppin in some new clippz the Lbb crew are still bustin on foolz when all of a sudden lil BAD BOY was hit in the necc but hez still gunnin, Lil BOY BLUE took a gage to the leg. then all of a sudden everybodys down silence is in the night once again flood and smoke is everywhere. All you can hear is an helicopter and the sirens of police cars. Before we continue my name is MR.SMURF LOC and ill -C- tellin the rest of the story. The only ones still livin is those insane locstaz SAD LOC , SHAGGY , Lbb crew , and me. were all struglin half way dead runnin from one time. Hoping we dont get caught just RUNNIN , RUNNIN ,and STRUGLIN. We -C- a house with no lights on so we think nobodys home so we brake in to that mothafuccer but what we didnt know is that there was a mother of two in there havin thier good night sleep. So we had to hold them hostage one of the motherz children was a 16 year old boy that tried to get brave so I hit him with my gun and knocced him out and SHAGGY started to kicc him Lbb tide them all up when all of a sudden the hoota surrounded the house CUZZ they knew were we had gone. Then next thing you know the pigs shooting the shit tellin us to give our selfs up they know were injured so they broke the doors down and tried to rush us but we started to blast at those pigs we took down four of them fools but they taccled us LOCSTAZ and locced us the fucc up.

Two weeks in jail and we already run the joint. But we got to watch our cacc's CUZZ there is a mob of slob's tring to shank us, all. They were good friend's of the fools that we bucced on. But we aren't going out like a bunch of pussiez so we stay strapped with anything we could find. Ice piccs, sharp sticcs, or whatever tha phuk. But Phuk this shit I can't take it anymore so I got up went to the spot where the slob's chill and started going cyscho, shanking fool's left and right all you could C was fool's dropping loosing there lives Cuzz I lost my mind, brain gone already Locced to the fullest hoping I die through all this drama. As the guard's rush me off to solitary. I think of how we used to get into all kinds shit and get rushed off to PCJCC. But this is the real deal doing two life sentences each, in FLORENCE there goes the rest of our lives but phuk it that's the way we choose to live. Three young killers ready to die point blank downer then phuk for one another. Solitary time is slower then slow it seems your never gonna C the light of day. All you can do is think of how you could change your life when you get out but with two life sentences all I can think of is how to make my life worse or maybe even taking my life by sucide.

Endnotes

1. Devon Brewer and Marc L. Miller, "Bombing and Burning: The Social Organization and Values of Hip Hop Graffiti Writers and Implications for Policy," *Deviant Behavior* 11: 345–69 (1990). **2.** Donald Murray, *Shoptalk: Learning to Write with Writers* (Portsmouth, NH: Boynton/Cook, 1990). **3.** Ibid. **4.** Luis Rodriguez, *Always Running* (Willimantic, CT: Curbstone Press, 1993). **5.** Abraham Rodriguez, *A Boy Without a Flag: Tales from the South Bronx* (Minneapolis, MN: Milkweed Editions, 1993).

DEBBIE: At one of the presentations I gave on this topic, I started out by telling the audience that they had to remember about the confidentiality of what I shared, because the kids could get . . . into trouble. One of the people in the audience asked me, that being true, how my kids felt about me sharing it. So I had to think about that one, and one of the things I've noticed with them is that they seem to take a kind of pride in it, even though it's kind of secretive and they worry about it. They seem to have their own sense of wanting to share it, to let other people understand they're not the hoodlums people see them as.

Denny: Have they seen this article?

DEBBIE: Yes. They've read almost all the versions.

Denny: You actually get into quite an in-depth description of tagging. The thing that impressed me was the realization that I can drive or walk along Fourth Avenue or into the center of Tucson, and what I see is this mass of graffiti. I can make out some words, but it has no meaning for me other than the knowledge that a young person has been there with a spray can and has put this stuff up. Even on the legal tagging walls, I wouldn't know the significance of what was there. While reading your article I began to understand the complexity of the message. So one of the ways you're advocating for these kids—and you haven't said this—is in making that information available to teachers.

DEBBIE: That's the whole reason for the essay.

Denny: So by implication are you saying that if you're going to teach adolescents who might tag, you have to—or you should—make an effort to understand the language of tagging?

DEBBIE: Yes. I think if you can read the tag or if you can understand why he or she tags, then you understand the kid.

Denny: You understand the kid and it's not as threatening.

DEBBIE: It's not as threatening for me because I know what . . . I know more of his life now. I understand when he says BK, which is Blood killer. Even though my first reaction might be how violent this is, I know that there are things that have happened in his life that would lead him to write that. And that is the priority. The frame of mind that led up to that. And, I'm not a "Blood" so it's not intimidating to me [*Laughing*].

Denny: So what you are also saying is that tagging is another language and that it would be a bit like teachers working with children whose first language is Spanish and not being bilingual?

DEBBIE: I don't know if I would say that it's another language—

Denny: Another form of language.

DEBBIE: Yes. And as you accept that child, yes, it is like accepting someone who speaks a foreign language. What happened in my classroom was that as I accepted their tagging, it could come into their schoolwork because they knew that I was their audience. And as I came to understand it, they did other assignments. It was part of their other assignments and a part of our dialogue—our oral language—it became a part of . . .

Denny: It changed the language of the classroom. Fascinating.

DEBBIE: I asked one of the students if I could use one of his raps for the yearbook, and his first statement to me was, "Will I get it cacc?" For them the letter B means blood, so they try to avoid it in their written and oral language. Instead of *back*, they say *cacc*. And because I understand their language now, there was no meaning lost. I knew he was just asking for it back. It is part of our language in the classroom.

Denny: And the more you know of it the less threatening it becomes.

DEBBIE: For me that's true. I don't feel threatened by it at all, but the more you accept your students the more you are a part of their lives. As you said earlier, a teacher might wake up and find graffiti on her door. The only way I would find graffiti on anything I own would be because it was done by a rival gang. It would never be any of them that would do that to me because of the respect we mutually share. And, I don't think a rival gang would do it either, unless I had done something to them.

Denny: Several questions come to mind. Obviously, I'm an illiterate tag reader, but once you get to the point where you can read tags, where you can communicate with the students in your class who are taggers, and you have accepted that it's okay to use tagging in the classroom, how do you help them reach a point where—just as a dialect speaker would learn to shift the dialect—they can shift into traditional texts?

DEBBIE: They know that when they write and speak publicly—at their presentation at the graduate colloquy, for example—they have to use language that an audience can understand . . .

Denny: So they're code switching.

DEBBIE: Yes. Even when they were doing the yearbook project, every once in awhile I would have to stop them and say, Now remember who your audience is. If you're limiting your audience to your friends, then this is okay. But if you want to branch out then you're going to have to deal with people not understanding what you're writing.

Denny: So in advocating for these kids, one of the things you are saying is that it's important to accept the students' language, culture, the way they communicate—to accept them unconditionally as they are. But it is also important to share with them that there are other audiences, other ways of writing, other ways of communicating, and that they need to be able to master those.

DEBBIE: Eventually they have to be in the world of society, I guess you'd call it. I mean, they switch all the time. They've written letters to a mayor, they've written letters to a judge on behalf of their friends. And they tell each other, No, don't put the gang stuff in it, because they know that it turns people off. When we did the presentation, we talked about what type of language they'd use with the people at the college.

Denny: It becomes a personal and a shared genre. Recently at AERA someone questioned a teacher allowing kids to write violent stories, and when I was in Salt Lake City, teachers made the important distinction between violent stories that are there for violence's sake and stories that deal with the violence in students' lives. And there is at least an argument to be made that students who experience extreme violence in their lives—as these young people have with one of their friends being killed—then they need an avenue to be able to work through it. Do you make those distinctions sometimes?

DEBBIE: That's a conscious decision I made when Plucy was killed, because at that time more of their tags contained violence. They were tagging such things as "everybody killer," with their own spelling—24–7, which means twenty-four hours a day seven days a week. And I was really concerned. I went and asked a counselor in the psychology department at the university about it. She claimed that the more they write about it and work through the process in their writing, the less likely they will probably be to go out and do it. And that's what I'd hoped: if I provide an avenue for them to express this feeling, for whatever reason they have to want to express it, then it is being expressed. It's out of their system, it's not a part of them anymore.

Denny: They're working through events that have taken place in their lives. As opposed to a fantasy story based on some movie they have seen, or some book they've read, or some cartoon.

DEBBIE: Every bit of their tagging deals with something in their lives. They don't write it arbitrarily. A lot of times their anger goes out against the whole world, and that's when you get the "everybody." I guess you never really know, but I hope . . . I mean, writing is supposed to be an avenue to make meaning and to express feelings—to bring them to the surface so you can deal with them. And I believe tagging is writing.

Denny: That's something that comes through very clearly. For many of us, tagging is a very threatening form of communication that we have been taught to believe is done only by gang members and has everything to do with turf wars. Some of that is true, but there are lots of other kinds of taggers, and you can be a tagger and not be a gang member.

DEBBIE: Taggers have competitions, too, that go on, and they can turn violent. But even with the gangsters, a lot of the time they go after the coup instead of the violence. If they can get into a neighborhood and leave their mark and get out, that makes that neighborhood look bad.

Denny: So in many situations it's an alternative to a violent act?

DEBBIE: Yes.

Denny: I didn't know that either. There have to have been tremendous ethical conflicts for you as you've been working through this. You articulate the importance of tagging in the lives of kids, and why we should be more aware of the importance of tagging to taggers because it's one form of language. Those are things they have that work for them. But the fact that they want to tag inside the classroom looks like a small problem in comparison with the problem of trying to help these kids when one of them has been killed. Or other things, like what is my role here with the probation officer?

DEBBIE: It's true that in my classroom tagging is often a very small issue. Because I believe it's what helps them structure their lives and their worlds. The bigger issue is the everyday things that they deal with.

Denny: How they exist.

DEBBIE: Yes, and that's what I need to help them with. When I will or won't have time to clean off the tag, or when they do or don't, that's a minor issue next to helping them understand the death of a friend, that this was a violent death, that they have to live with this and make sense of it in their world, and that they can't have revenge. That's not an option—violence isn't a choice they need to be making.

Denny: So, basically the other thing that you have done is that you've created a context in which you can discuss the issue.

DEBBIE: Yes—I try to in my classroom. I hope it's a safe place for them to talk about their issues—where they don't have to be sent to the principal's office, or they don't have to be put on a gang list, or they're not being arrested, but they can talk about the issues that they deal with in their lives every day.

Denny: You have a couple of kids who have gone on to college.

DEBBIE: Three kids who are graduating are going on to college. One is in college right now, taking seven credits and getting As and Bs. The other two are all planning to attend community college.

Denny: Do you know if that's the norm for the kids coming into this alternative high school?

DEBBIE: No, it's not. They're the only ones who have done it.

Denny: That's quite an affirmation of the way you have been working with them and really supports what you have been doing.

DEBBIE: I think it's because I have accepted them for who they are. They accept themselves more and realize they can have their dreams back and go for them. Then it's a reality for them. It's been like society doesn't accept them, school doesn't accept them, and they are judged purely on their appearances. The question is, How or where do they get validation for being—for simply being? In my class they are accepted for who they are. Don't get me wrong, I disapprove of some of their behavior, like drinking, using weed, and some others, but who they are, good or bad, they are. And that's acceptable in my classroom. I think this makes it possible for them to believe in themselves. That's what it's all about. By accepting the kids, culture and all—the whole kid—then you can help them realize their dreams, to dream again. In talking with the kids I learned that like all little kids they had their dreams, but as they got older they learned that the dreams could never come true. As they believe in themselves, their dreams live again. They take a risk.

Denny: Really, it's extraordinary stuff, Debbie.

DEBBIE: None of those kids when I first met them thought of college.

Denny: What happens to the other teachers when they see the tagging going on in your room?

DEBBIE: I still get in a lot of trouble [*Laughing*], except for the moment we don't have as much of it on the furniture. They know it's okay to tag on my stuff but not on Frank's stuff. But we do have a tag on the wall they tagged when Plucy died that I keep covered right now—the other teachers are totally against it. They think I am totally wrong in what I am doing.

Denny: And yet you have a track record for getting these kids into mainstream school and also into college.

DEBBIE: Yes. But I don't know what they attribute it to. I know I attribute it to the fact that I accept the kids for who they are so that they can then accept themselves.

Denny: What would you tell an administration?

DEBBIE: If I sat down with another teacher or an administrator, I would tell them first that tagging is language and that I don't advocate for destruction of property, I don't advocate for violence, but I do advocate for the student as a whole student. That it is part of their language. That it is part of who they are in everyday life, and if it is part of them then it has to be part of my classroom. Because they can only learn if they are accepted as a whole person in my room. I believe if I eliminate their language I eliminate their learning potential.

Denny: That's pretty profound.

DEBBIE: Well, if you silence them how can they learn? And by taking away their language and their tagging, you are silencing them. You can't learn when you're silent.

Early Biliteracy: Ty's Story

NAN JIANG

Ty and his mother came from China to join his father in the United States when Ty was four years old. His father is studying for a Ph.D., and his mother has a part-time job. The family live in an apartment complex where most of the residents are Chinese. Ty, the only child in the family, is eight years old now and has just finished second grade. As a neighbor and close friend of the family, I witnessed, over the past three years, how Ty changed from speaking only Chinese to being bilingual to using English as his dominant language.

I was particularly impressed by Ty's early biliteracy. About a year ego, I decided to do a project on his English literacy development for a literacy development course I was taking. I hoped to find out what contributed to Ty's high level of literacy development in English, his second language, within a relatively short period of time. I conducted several interviews with Ty's parents, primarily his mother, during which we reviewed Ty's work in the past three years and discussed questions we had about his biliteracy, also the topic of many of our informal conversations.

I went to Ty's home for the first interview on a Sunday afternoon. Ty's mother had put three large paper bags on the floor in the sitting room and was removing things from them when I arrived. They were work Ty had done at school and at home in the past three years, arranged chronologically. We sat down on the floor. In front of us were piles of paper and books. Ty was studying in his room.

"We started to teach him Chinese characters and reading when he was about three years old. I designed the character cards myself and helped him recognize and copy them one after another," Ty's mother began. After their arrival in the United States, they continued this home literacy education. "What we did was learn three to five new characters before going to bed each day. The next evening we could review the characters previously learned and learn the new ones."

Recognizing and reading characters, copying the characters, and doing math problems were daily activities for Ty. His mother prepared the Chinese and math

143

homework, and "after he came back from school, we would ask him to finish the homework before he could go and play."

"This is what he did in kindergarten." Ty's mother handed me a book of drawings and writings Ty and his classmates had done at school. On the reverse side of each page, there were numerous Chinese characters and mathematics exercises (see Figure 1 for an example). Each page was divided into two parts by a vertical line. On the left side, straight horizontal lines were drawn; above each of them, at the leftmost side, there was a model Chinese character. There were numbers around some of these model characters indicating the sequences in which the strokes should be written. These characters were followed by ten or eleven copied versions. On the right side of each page there are math exercises—addition and subtraction of five or six digits, and three digit multiplications. These math exercises were all checked and graded. There were dates on the pages—12/29, 12/30, 12/31, 1/2, and so on. Each day of that winter break, part of Ty's homework, done in this book to save paper, was to copy four to six characters ten or eleven times and do five to eight math problems.

"Here is something he did in the second semester of kindergarten," Ty's mother said, showing me a copy book specially designed to include both Chinese and English words. In each of the five rows on a page, there were ten rectangles for copying Chinese characters, below which were solid and dotted lines for copying English words. "I got a blank page from a friend and made copies of it and made this book," Ty's mother explained. I looked through the book. Each of the thirty pages was covered with Chinese and English words (see Figure 2 for an example).

There were several other exercise or copy books on the floor, all made of recycled pages. On one face of each page was work Ty had done at school or a draft version of one of his father's graduate papers; the other face was covered with Chinese characters and math exercises. There were many loose papers covered with Chinese characters and math exercises in the piles as well. When I asked how much time she and Ty spent on this kind of homework, his mother told me that Ty usually spent fifteen to thirty minutes a day on it before and while he was in kindergarten; in addition, she had to prepare the homework, demonstrate how the character should be written (particularly the sequence of strokes), and explain how to do a math problem, then review what Ty had done to make sure he had learned or done it properly.

Mother and son also spent much time reading the Chinese books they had brought with them from China or that had been sent by Ty's grandparents. "We would read the stories in the books to him and show him the Chinese texts in them at the same time. He enjoyed listening to stories. To motivate him to learn Chinese, we told him if he could read, he would be able to know all those stories in the books by himself."

Ty was eager to learn, and his parents were determined that their son should be able to read and write in Chinese and succeed in his future schoolwork. They persisted in their efforts, and Ty made steady progress.

When Ty was in the kindergarten, he was able to recognize more than five hundred Chinese characters and use more than one hundred and fifty of them productively, by his mother's estimation. He was able to read the Chinese popular

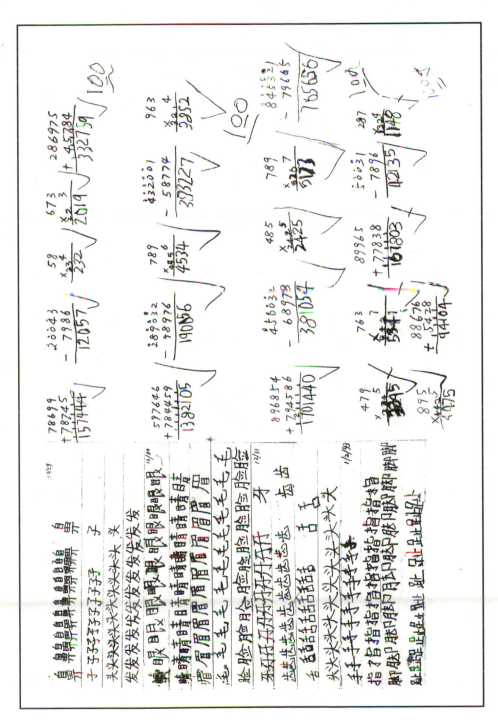

Figure 1 Part of Ty's homework (age 6)

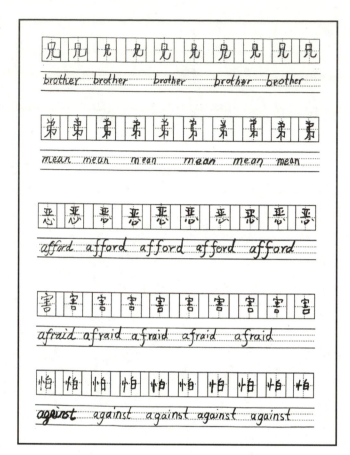

Figure 2

A page from Ty's copy book

science series *A Hundred Thousand Whys for Preschool Children* and some other books independently. He was also doing well with the Chinese textbook for first graders. He would write his own letters to his grandparents.

When Ty entered first grade, his active Chinese vocabulary had so increased that, at his father's suggestion, he began keeping a diary in Chinese. Figure 3 shows one of his entries. It clearly demonstrates his well-developed writing skill. "Misspelled" characters are rare, both in this example and in his diary as a whole. Where they do occur, they are often minor errors that do not affect understanding. The words, including some difficult conjunctions, are used properly; the grammar and punctuation are all correct. Each entry of the diary is a coherent and complete piece of writing.

More important, his Chinese literacy experience helped him develop a great interest in books and reading and a positive attitude toward study in general; he became an able learner. Reading and copying characters, monotonous as the latter may be, became something he enjoyed doing, rather than something he was forced to do. All of these traits were reflected and reinforced in his later English literacy development. Early on "he would show us the words he could recognize in the

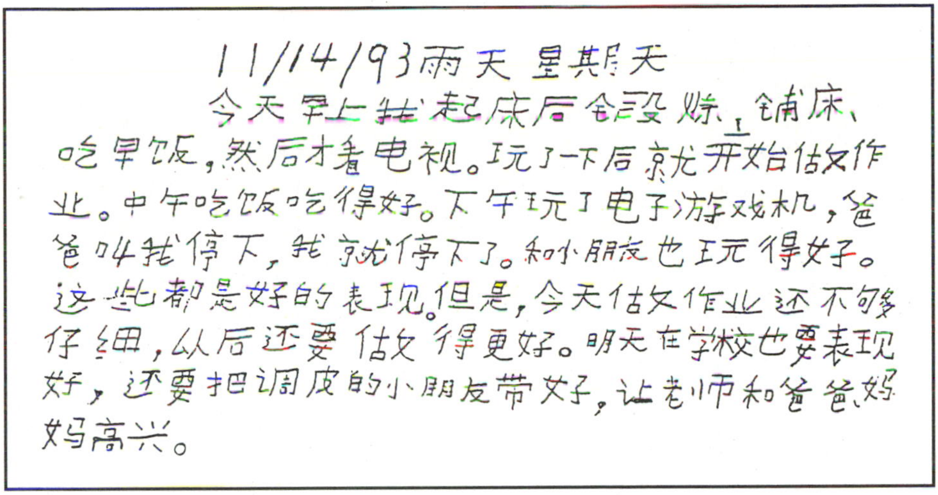

11/14/93 雨天 星期天
　　今天早上我起床后全没烧、铺床、
吃早饭，然后才看电视。玩了一下后就开始做作
业。中午吃饭吃得好。下午玩了电子游戏机，爸
爸叫我停下，我就停下了。和小朋友也玩得好。
这些都是好的表现。但是，今天做作业还不够
仔细，从后还要做得更好。明天在学校也要表现
好，还要把调皮的小朋友带好，让老师和爸爸妈
妈高兴。

Figure 3 An entry in Ty's diary

books and newspapers around home. He was excited to find that he could recognize those words" his mother recalled. Later, he would ask for a book as a birthday present.

We focused on Ty's English work in another interview. His parents have kept most of the work Ty brought back from school or did at home. Reviewing that work and listening to his parents' explanations and comments gave me a fascinating and colorful picture of Ty's literacy development in English and helped me see what lay behind this development.

We started with the more recent work. Ty's mother showed me a bunch of loose papers, Ty's weekly spelling tests throughout his entire second grade. There were about thirty of them, twenty words on each. Ty had made only two errors, *I'm* written as *i'm* and *October* written as *Octomber*. They were both careless errors Ty could have corrected by himself if he had noticed them.

Next his mother handed me a folder containing Ty's contribution to a Famous Women project that had been part of the gifted-and-talented program during the second semester of second grade. Ty had chosen Beverly Cleary, an American writer, because he had read some of her books and enjoyed them very much. He read several more while doing the project. There was artwork on the folder cover, followed by a My Favorite Woman page, a Famous Woman page, a letter to the postmaster general requesting that a Beverly Cleary stamp be issued, and a suggested design for the stamp. Ty begins the letter (see Figure 4) by requesting that Beverly Cleary be on a stamp. He then explains why she should be on a stamp, telling the postmaster general that Ty and other children have enjoyed and learned things from reading her books, and then lists her achievements. His request is restated towards the end of the letter. However one looks at it, this is a well-developed piece of writing by a second grader.

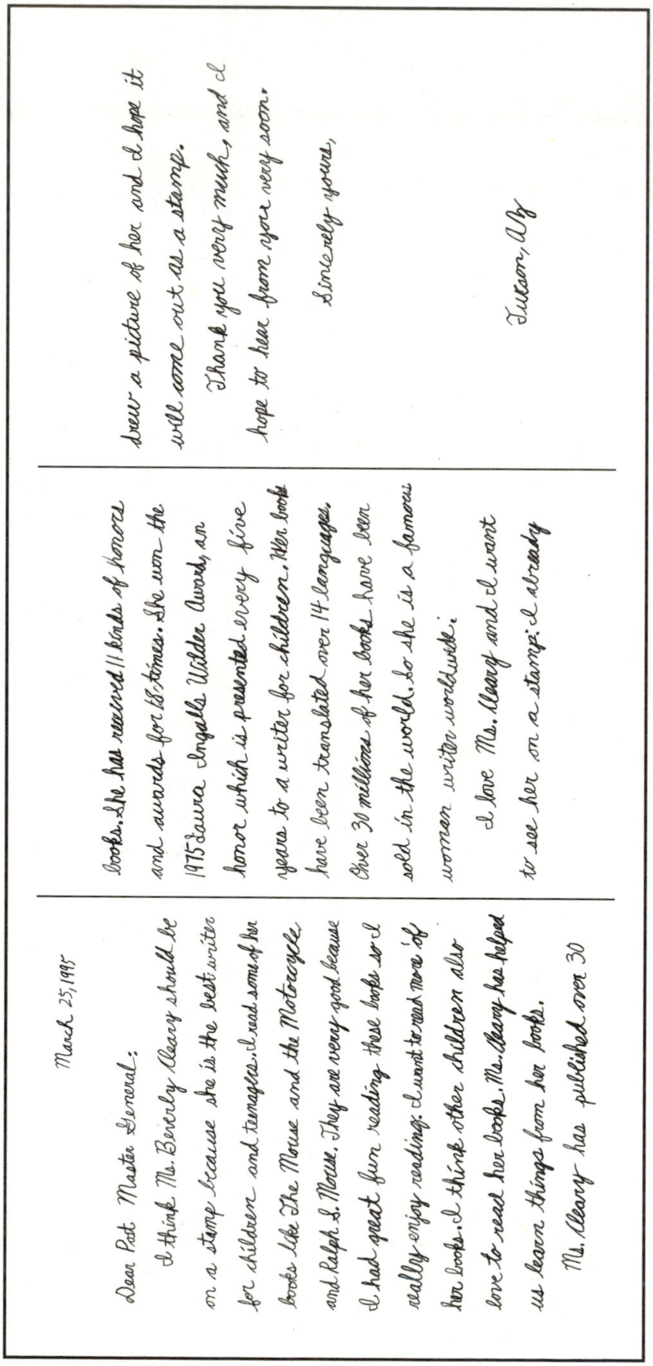

March 25, 1995

Dear Post Master General:

I think Ms. Beverly Cleary should be on a stamp because she is the best writer for children and teenagers. I read some of her books like The Mouse and the Motorcycle and Ralph S. Mouse. They are very good because I had great fun reading those books so I really enjoy reading. I want to read more of her books. I think other children also love to read her books. Ms. Cleary has helped us learn things from her books.

Ms. Cleary has published over 30 books. She has received 11 kinds of honors and awards for 65 times. She won the 1975 Laura Ingalls Wilder Award, an honor which is presented every five years to a writer for children. Her books have been translated over 14 languages. Over 30 millions of her books have been sold in the world, so she is a famous woman writer worldwide.

I love Ms. Cleary and I want to see her on a stamp. I already draw a picture of her and I hope it will come out as a stamp.

Thank you very much, and I hope to hear from you very soon.

Sincerely yours,

Tucson, AZ

Figure 4

Letter to postmaster general

February 1, 1995

Dear Jack,

How are you? I received your letter and enjoyed reading it.

Now I am going to tell you things about our school. We learned many things in our class. We learned how to write cursive writing. I love to write cursive and make loops. We had a spell-a-thon test last Friday. You get money if you spell words right. The hardest word is "encyclopedia." We had a five dot crayon project. We made five dots and colored around them to make them a circle. We also worked on solids and liquids. Solids are things like sands and rocks, and liquids are things like water and oil. We also learned that oxygen plus hydrogen equals water. We are going to have a Science Fair. A science fair is when you do a science project and show it to other people. It will be very exciting.

Last time I told you that I like to play chess very much. I play chess every Thursday after school at our Lineweaver Chess Club. I also told you that I got a medal last time, but this time I won a trophy. It was the Arizona State School Grade Championship. I won three games out of four, and took the ninth place of the Second Grade Section. I was so happy.

I have many favorite things. My favorite video game is Mortal Kombat II. My favorite TV shows are The Simpsons and Carmen Sandiego. My favorite movie is The Lion King, because it is pretty sad in the middle but it has a very happy ending. I like Simba in the movie. My favorite books are Scary Stories to tell in the dark and Goosebumps. I like science books about planets and dinosaurs, too. I don't have any pets right now, but I might get a dog. I have four hobbies. They are roller-blading, swimming, playing soccer and Chinese painting. Roller-blading, swimming and playing soccer are all good sports. Every Saturday morning I take Chinese painting class. We usually draw plants, animals and rocks. We had a Chinese painting exhibition last November. We will have another Chinese painting exhibition this weekend for Chinese New Year. When I grow up, I am going to be a scientist or a doctor.

Have you seen any movies recently? Do you play guitar and piano everyday? It was Chinese New Year Day yesterday. Happy Chinese New Year!

Your friend,

Ty

Figure 5 Ty's letter to his pen pal

Ty's highly developed writing skill was also demonstrated in his letters to his pen pal, one of which is included as Figure 5.

Ty's reading proficiency was also way ahead of many of his contemporaries, and the books he read were often on the fourth or fifth graders' reading lists. I once asked Ty to show me some of the books he had read recently. They included *The Return of the Indian*, by Lynne Reid Banks, *Gentle Ben*, by Walt Morey, *Brave Dog*

Blizzard, by Sharon Salisbury O'Toole, and *Keep Out, Claudia*, by Ann M. Martin (the Baby-Sitters Club series). He told me that he had read twenty Baby-Sitters Club books, almost all the Goosebumps books, and some of the books in the Teenage Mutant Ninja Turtles series.

I asked Ty's mother whether they had taught Ty English at home. She said that in the beginning they had been concerned about whether Ty would have difficulty at school because of his Chinese background. So for a time they did ask Ty to copy English translations when he copied Chinese characters. They also tried to answer Ty's occasional questions. But they had never tried to teach Ty English as they had taught him Chinese.

The most important factor in Ty's English literacy development seems to be his profound interest in and enthusiasm for reading, qualities first developed when he was learning Chinese. This interest and enthusiasm were transferred to English after he went to kindergarten. When he was in kindergarten, he would check out two books from the school library every week and take great interest in reading them and the books his parents bought him.

The effect this self-motivated reading had on his English literacy development first manifested itself when Ty took an exam for the gifted-and-talented program at the beginning of first grade. His parents' intention was to see what the exam was like and what Ty needed to do to pass the exam if he took it a second time. They were pretty sure Ty would have no problems with math, but they didn't really expect him to do well in English, since he had been in this country for only two years. However, Ty got all the available points for all the test subjects, including English. "This came as a real surprise to us," his mother commented.

Soon, the school library could not satisfy Ty's growing thirst for reading. His mother recalled:

We found it necessary to go to public libraries and the university library. In grades one and two, he read about sixty to seventy books each semester, with great increase in number in summer and winter breaks. He has finished reading more than fifty books in the first two months of this summer. This summer, he spends about an average of two hours a day reading. Sometimes it can be three to four hours.

He also participated in the "Rocket Readers" summer reading program sponsored by a local public library. The program invites school children to read fifteen minutes a day. If they are able to do fifty hours of reading from May 18 through July 29, they receive a certificate and have their names published in a local newspaper. Ty learned about and participated in the program in late June, but still did enough reading to get the certificate and have his name published.

Reading has become an important part of Ty's life. It is his pastime. He watches less TV and plays a lot fewer video games than many other kids his age in the neighborhood. Going to the public library on Saturday afternoon has become a family ritual. "We once checked out eighteen books," his mother told me.

Ty's literacy development, however, is not an entirely happy story. While his English literacy skyrocketed, he was struggling to maintain his Chinese literacy.

I started this project when Ty was beginning second grade. I talked with him and his parents about the project and asked him to show me some of his work. One of the things he brought me was his diary. He had started keeping his diary, in Chinese, at the beginning of first grade; as his English literacy developed, he made entries in English as well. For a while, he wrote one entry in Chinese, the next entry in English. I read some of the entries and became very interested in how the language a child uses influences what he writes about and how he writes it, though I failed to notice that the more recent entries were all in English. Thinking to take advantage of such rare naturalistic data for a project, I bought Ty a diary as a birthday present and asked him to continue keeping the bilingual diary. Ty agreed.

A few weeks later, I asked his mother how Ty was doing with the bilingual diary. She told me, to both of our surprise and disappointment, that Ty could no longer write in Chinese. He had forgotten many of the characters he used to be able to write. He did try at first, but had to ask his parents for words so frequently that it didn't make sense to continue.

To test how many Chinese characters he still remembered, I chose fifteen bisyllabic Chinese words (thirty characters in total), all from his earlier diary entries, and asked him to take dictation. He was able to write both characters for four words, one of the characters for six words, and neither of the characters for the remaining five. He even wrote down the English translation for one of the words.

As for the diary, it was now exclusively in English. Ty's father's feelings of hopelessness and frustration were obvious: "He was able to write to his grandparents in summer. That was only a few months ago. It is hard to believe that he should have forgotten everything so fast."

Several factors seem to have been at work in the loss of Ty's Chinese literacy. First, since there is no correspondence between the spoken and written forms of the Chinese language, he first had to learn a few hundred characters, often through imitation and memorization, before he could practice reading and writing for authentic purposes. A literacy based on several hundred memorized, out-of-context characters can be very fragile when there is no continued exposure to and practice in the language. Unfortunately, at the critical time when Ty's early literacy in Chinese needed to be developed with more characters and more practice, less time was available for him to learn Chinese. At the beginning of second grade, Ty joined the gifted-and-talented program, available only in a school far away from his home. It took him an hour and a half to get to school, not the ten minutes it used to, and another hour and a half to get back home. Joining the gifted-and-talented program also meant more schoolwork, which was of course all in English. He also joined the chess team of the school and became very enthusiastic about it. And beginning the summer after first grade, Ty started going to a Chinese painting class every weekend. In a word, Ty was too busy to continue devoting the same amount of time to learning Chinese as he used to.

Perhaps more important, as his English proficiency grew, Chinese began to appear less important in his life. Over time English gradually replaced Chinese in Ty's daily life. Though there was no obvious sign of attrition in his oral Chinese,

English became his preferred language for daily communication. Unless someone spoke and continued to speak Chinese to him he tended to use English. This was true even at home, where speaking English was intentionally discouraged by his parents. In addition, as a student who had been continually rewarded, in one way or another, for good academic performance and as a child from a culture that emphasizes schoolwork above anything else, Ty seemed to have developed different attitudes toward what he was asked to learn or do, depending on whether it was school related or not. He made every effort to accomplish school-related work, even such nonacademic work as practicing chess. On the other hand, he was much less motivated to do what he perceived to be irrelevant to his academic life, not "real schoolwork"—in this case, learning Chinese.

In retrospect, there is a fairly clear pattern in Ty's biliteracy development. Before he entered first grade, his literacy level in Chinese was way ahead of that in English. First grade witnessed a rapid development of his literacy in both Chinese and English, the former the result of three years of persistent training at home, the latter boosted by his increasing exposure to the written language at school and at home. At this point Ty's biliteracy reached its highest level. Though his literacy in the two languages seemed balanced for most of this period, a transition was taking place: the two languages began to reverse their roles as the preferred language, not only for reading but also for daily communication, and Ty formed different attitudes toward them. By the end of first grade, his English literacy had definitely caught up with his Chinese literacy. Already he was doing much more reading in English than in Chinese. His English literacy continued to grow fast in second grade, and he began to lose his Chinese literacy.

What Ty has done and gone through is very informative about early biliteracy development. First, it shows that children have the potential to become biliterate. With the help of his parents, Ty had become a competent reader and writer in both Chinese and English by the end of first grade. Turning this potential into reality requires that children experience each language in an organized and persistent way. Furthermore, research suggests that early biliteracy is an attainable goal not only for gifted children or children from high socioeconomic families, but also for children of average intelligence and those from lower socioeconomic families.[1]

Second, early development of literacy in the native language can facilitate the development of second-language literacy in many ways,[2] one of them being the transfer of literacy-related skills from the native language to the second language.[3] This transfer can be found in many aspects of Ty's English literacy development. His accuracy in English spelling, for example, can be attributed, at least in part, to his experience copying Chinese characters, which required and trained him to be accurate about the written form of the language. The diary he started writing in Chinese provided him with one of the earliest opportunities to practice his written English in meaningful context. Some strategies he developed for reading Chinese (e.g., guessing the meaning of unknown words from the context or skipping new words where necessary) may have helped him become a more flexible, tolerant, and thus more competent reader in English.

Ty's second-language facility may also come from what his mother called a "good learning habit"—that is, he was able to plan his time for study and play and to stop playing and get down to work at designated times at an early age. And the most important positive impacts on his English literacy development seem to be his profound interest in and enthusiasm for reading and his positive attitude toward learning in general, qualities that were first formed and developed in the course of becoming literate in Chinese. It is not hard to imagine that without such a strong interest and positive attitude, Ty might not have taken the initiative to do more than was required of him at school, let alone to persist in his effort over the years in spite of the difficulties a nonnative speaker may have in learning English.

Ty's biliteracy development also tells us that successful early biliteracy can be best achieved through collaboration between the family and the school. Both Ty's biliteracy development and the literacy development literature[4] show that the family can play a very important role in early literacy development. Ty learned to read and write Chinese exclusively at home, because of a huge investment of his parents' time and effort. Ty's parents understand that their son's future lies in a good education and that learning the first language is part of it. Thus, over the years, they have been very supportive and encouraging, and they have been strict and persistent as well. They always reviewed the work Ty brought home from school or did at home, whether it was English or Chinese, and made sure that what was taught was also learned and errors were corrected. They listened with interest when Ty told them what a book he was reading was about and make sure that he always had books to read.

However, the disruption in Ty's Chinese literacy development also tells us early biliteracy development can be very fragile, particularly when the family is alone in their effort. It took only a summer for Ty to lose much of what was learned through so much effort, something Ty's parents and I never expected when I asked Ty to continue the bilingual diary. The regression in Ty's Chinese literacy tells us that there are certain limitations on what a family can do. As the child becomes more involved in schoolwork and his English more proficient or dominant, the school and the teachers are often in a better position to exert influence on his study. Both Ty's parents and I feel the speedy loss of Chinese literacy could have been avoided if support had been available from the school and the teachers. For example, a thoughtful teacher could have helped Ty change his perception that Chinese was irrelevant by creating situations in which Chinese literacy became uniquely meaningful and valuable.

Biliteracy has been found to be positively associated with educational achievement, family income, employment, and political participation,[5] and the consequence of losing the first language can be far reaching.[6] Ty's experience shows that literacy in the first language has a positive impact on second-language literacy development.

As teachers, we need to become more aware of and responsive to language-minority children's unique linguistic and cultural background and needs, and to understand that we can also play an important role in maintaining and developing the first language of these children. What we teachers do influences the attitude of the children and their parents. If the parents know they are able to obtain support from the school, they are more likely to start or continue the effort and seek support from the teachers. If the children realize that their first languages are highly relevant to schoolwork, they are more likely to learn them.

In many cases, the parents don't expect teachers to help their children study their first language, so it is important that we take the initiative, telling the parents that we are willing to help and discussing how we may be able to do so. Although the kinds of help we can offer may vary, the message should always be that their first languages and their efforts in learning them are appreciated.

Endnotes

1. See, for example, Robert Lado et al., "Biliteracy in Preschool—The SED Center Experience," *Agenda* 11: 7–9, 41 (1981). **2.** See, for example, K. Escamilla's *The Relationship of Native Language Reading Achievement and Oral English Proficiency to Future Achievement in Reading English as a Second Language*, unpublished doctoral dissertation, University of California, Los Angeles, 1987. **3.** For a theoretical account, see J. Cummins's works such as "Language and Literacy Acquisition in Bilingual Contexts," *Journal of Multilingual and Multicultural Development* 10: 17–31 (1989). **4.** See, for example, Denny Taylor's *Family Literacy: Young Children Learning to Read and Write* (Portsmouth, NH: Heinemann, 1983), and E. Quintero and A. Huerta-Macias's "All in the Family: Bilingualism and Biliteracy," *The Reading Teacher* 44: 306–12 (1990). **5.** See, for example, a study by T. G. Wiley, "Literacy, Biliteracy and Educational Achievement Among the Mexican-Origin Population in the United States," *NABE Journal* 14: 109–25 (1991). **6.** See L. Wong Fillmore's "When Learning a Second Language Means Losing the First," *Early Childhood Research Quarterly* 6: 323–46 (1991).

Denny: My first impression of you in class, you'd said you had been "working at the word level," and I thought that this was a different experience for you.

NAN: It was very different from my other classes. At the beginning of the semester, you asked me to find a child, and that was easy for me because I had a very good friend who had a child learning English. So I went to that family. I asked the boy to give me a general idea of what he was reading, and one of the things he brought me was a diary. The mother had made the diary by cutting sheets of paper in half. The child would write in Chinese and then in English. The diary he brought me was about twenty pages, and about ten or eleven were in Chinese, the rest in English. It was basically about his daily life: what he did in the morning, afternoon, and evening; his New Year's resolution; and so on. So I had a chance to get an idea of what differences the language may make. The working hypothesis was that language affects content. In November it was his birthday and I bought him a new diary. I said, "What I'd like you to do is keep on writing in the diary in both languages." He promised he would do that. A few weeks later I asked his mother how he was doing. She said, "Well, he just can't write in Chinese anymore, and the diary is all English."

Denny: This was a change that took place quite rapidly?

NAN: Yes, and the mother, who is primarily responsible for Ty's study, didn't realize this until I brought the diary to Ty. His parents thought he could still write in Chinese. The father told me during the summer that Ty wrote a letter to his grandparents, and it was pretty good. So when I asked Ty to write what I dictated and I showed the parents the results, they were really surprised. They were frustrated because they had put so much time into his study of Chinese.

Denny: You were saying that the mother's English is . . . ?

NAN: She doesn't speak much English. Since she's been here nearly five years, she can speak a little English, but she would really prefer Chinese.

Denny: So the little boy is still speaking Chinese. Was this affecting his oral language, too?

NAN: No, the kids were speaking English and the parents would speak Chinese. That's the way we are. [*Nan nods his head at his daughter, who is drawing while we talk*] She basically speaks English to me about 80 percent of the time. Last night we talked a little before she went to bed, and when I insisted she speak Chinese to me, she did so, but after a few sentences she went back to English. They had gone to the wildlife museum yesterday, and I asked her to tell me what happened. She could tell me the names of things in English, but it becomes a problem.

Denny: So the irony is that you now find yourself in the same situation as the family of the child you were studying.

NAN: I'm not trying that hard, but I'm still trying to teach her Chinese. Last year my parents came to visit. They brought a lot of Chinese stuff, Chinese books for the first two years of school and character cards. But we didn't really spend a lot of time teaching her. My wife is not that interested, either, she says as long as my daughter can speak Chinese, then that is all right.

Denny: Can you talk a bit about first-language loss? For many teachers, I think, especially third- and fourth-generation Americans, it's very difficult for them to understand what happens to a family when the children begin to use the dominant language of the country—in this case English.

NAN: For many Chinese families living here, there is an emphasis on learning English to have success in school. There are about thirty families living in the area where we are, and I'm not aware of any families whose kids are having a problem learning English. Some kids are even considered better in English than other American kids. When Ty was taking exams, he got better grades than some of his American classmates. The problem is that in the beginning—say during the first two years after their arrival—the parents are really anxious about their kids' ability to learn English. As a result, the parents often neglect the maintenance and development of the first language.

Denny: So there is not much emphasis at that point in their home language, on Chinese?

NAN: Right. Well, in this case Ty's parents would be kind of an exception. Then, many problems occur. His mother told me how embarrassed they were when Ty was in second grade and when they were making phone calls to their parents, Ty was speaking so much in English that his grandparents had to ask him, What are you talking about? All of his grandparents are college teachers, and they were very concerned about his Chinese.

Denny: How does it affect the language of the child if the child is speaking only English to the parents and the parents are speaking Chinese to the child?

NAN: It can be a problem. You can't expect to communicate only in Chinese or only in English. For instance, my daughter knows the names of many animals in English, and I don't. She knows the names of lots of dinosaurs.

Denny: [*Smiling at Nan's daughter*] Like brontosaurus?

NAN: Yes, or rhinoceros. It can be a problem because if she tried to say that in English, I wouldn't understand. So the communication breaks down. Sometimes I can't really help, even though I am insisting she speak Chinese. It's a problem. When she was three years old, just after she moved here, she was a very articulate person in Chinese. She had a smart way of using the language. But she's no longer like that anymore in Chinese. She can still keep the language. She can use it for purposes of communication, but her Chinese language is no longer that good.

Denny: You were talking earlier about your language and the options you have, about how it's impacting the decisions you make about your future.

NAN: Yes. My daughter's Chinese will affect our decision to stay here or return to China. And I think that is true for many Chinese families. If my daughter lost much of the language, then I'd have to stay here. Even the elementary school in China is very competitive. Whenever her cousins write to her here, they always talk about how much time they have to spend studying the language. And it's true if you go to a typical Chinese town, what you can see at four o'clock is the kids sitting at a small table doing their homework. It is usually the first thing they do when they come home. After they've finished, then they can go to play. If she returned to China after the second grade, there would be no way she could catch up. If she were to go back to China in the second grade, then we could find a tutor for her, and probably she could catch up. We would have to spend a lot of time helping her. If she didn't go to the elementary school, then she couldn't go on to high school or on to college. If you don't go to college, then there are a lot of problems. We're not talking about gangs in China, but if the kids can't use their energies in study, then it might lead to something else.

Denny: When you were talking about the child in this study, it seemed to me that a real shift had taken place in your thinking once you'd realized that this child was losing the Chinese that he and his family had worked so hard to gain. We got to talking about school and the roles that schools play both in promoting his English and also almost in silencing him in Chinese because there is no recognition of his home language. If you were talking to a group of teachers, what would you suggest that they do? Did your study help?

NAN: I'd want to say that it's important to make Chinese relevant to school, especially for these children who have a certain prior attitude about language learning and who come from a culture that really emphasizes schoolwork. They consider that what's related to school is important and what is not related to school is unimportant.

Denny: So you'd ask teachers to advocate for their students whose first language is Chinese by trying to bring that language into the classroom?

NAN: Yes, by making this inclusion more specific in some way. For example, when Ty was working on a school project, I am sure there was some way to bring the Chinese language into the project. If teachers are really aware of the importance of a Chinese student's first language, they can ask that student to read some Chinese material or to do a project that is basically about the Chinese language, the Chinese culture, or even the local Chinese community.

Denny: And generally the Chinese community speaks English because they are third- and fourth-generation Americans?

NAN: Basically there are two groups. First, there are the ABCs, that's American-born Chinese, whose primary language is often English, and second, Chinese who came here from China for study in recent years. Ty's family is one of them. A high percentage of them have green cards under President Bush's executive order after the 1989 democratic movement in China. So if the teacher is aware of this large population, a student project is quite possible even in Tucson.

Denny: And they could invite parents in to work alongside the teacher while the child is writing in both languages. Parents could translate for the teacher and other students and talk about the Chinese culture.

NAN: Some teachers may complain that Chinese parents are reluctant to help. That sometimes seems to be true; I have never volunteered any time at school. For many reasons many Chinese parents are not that active in community work.

Denny: So it would be difficult for a Chinese parent to volunteer?

NAN: They would feel a little bit scared to be in a situation where they felt inadequate. One reason is that they don't speak English that well. And also they feel they don't know much about this culture. They may feel, because they don't know the culture well, that they appear or act strangely and put themselves on the spot. So the teachers might think, Well, Chinese parents are not that active or responsive to a situation in school. But that's not true. If a teacher is more outgoing to the parents, the parents will respond, particularly when it concerns their kids' education. The problem is who will make the first move. Generally, Chinese parents will not take the initiative. They are modest, humble people, and they don't want to appear aggressive or too active.

Denny: So in Ty's case, the school didn't know and probably doesn't know even today that there is a very serious problem of first-language loss for the family.

NAN: Yes.

Denny: When you were taking the class, I began to see you becoming more and more aware of the implications of this child's first-language loss. You became an advocate for his parents in trying to explain to us the difficulties. It seemed to have an impact on you, and I think it came out of looking at his work and seeing the death of one of his languages and seeing how the other became dominant. It's tremendously difficult for many of us to understand the effects of this situation on the family.

NAN: One thing I learned from doing this project is how fast a kid can lose the first language. Before I did this project, all I was concerned about was my daughter's English, not Chinese. I thought once her English is good enough, I could teach her several hundred Chinese characters. Then that's it. Her Chinese would take care of itself. Now I know that is not the case. I think there is a strong feeling of helplessness and frustration on the part of many Chinese parents. They want their kids to learn Chinese. They are in the middle of many communication problems because of their kid's loss of Chinese. And I have seen many parents simply give up. I have even heard one parent call it a waste of time. It is not that they don't want their kids to learn Chinese, but I think many parents stop trying because they feel they can't handle the problem single-handedly, all by themselves. I think most Chinese parents would agree that it is tragic that we can't communicate with our children in our own language. We can all anticipate the questioning looks and blames from our folks and friends for not teaching our kids Chinese.

Denny: And from the teacher's perspective?

NAN: One thing that can help teachers to see and understand the problem is to visit these kids' families. In China, many schools require that teachers visit the family of every student at least once a year. It's a very good practice.

Denny: I couldn't agree more. I think visiting a student's family should be a prerequisite for classroom teachers. We need to be in the communities, and we need to visit more children in their homes with their families.

NAN: Is it because my daughter is in kindergarten that nobody has visited us, or because we really don't have this system here?

Denny: There are very few teachers who actually visit families. Often there are excuses made. But I know teachers who do visit families at least once a year. But it's interesting to hear that this practice takes place in China. How big are the classes?

NAN: Forty-five to fifty.

Denny: Forty-five to fifty, and the teacher visits every family?

NAN: Sometimes twice. When I was doing my teaching practice in 1984, in that particular school the principal required that teachers visit the family of each student at least twice a year. That was a significant experience for me. There was one student who was almost abandoned by his parents. He was so naughty that the parents didn't really want him anymore. He was making all kinds of trouble and stealing things as well. That is a big disgrace in China. So the child was spending a lot of time with his uncle. When I visited his family, they were so grateful to see a teacher coming to the family and to know the teacher really cared for their kid. That was very important for me to see. I think it's so necessary for teachers to do that.

Denny: It's tremendously important.

Vale La Pena: Advocacy Along the Borderlands

MELANIE UTTECH

As I head south on the interstate, my taste buds come to life thinking of the sumptuous meals I have had at a charming restaurant carved out of the side of a cliff in Sonora. I park my car in Arizona, a stone's throw from the border, and wind my way along the dusty, desert sidewalks to Mexico. I am allowed in without incident, without question. I enter the country through one-way revolving steel bars. (Why am I allowed in without incident, without question? The doors do not continue to revolve so that others may enter the United States as easily. What is the implicit message here?)

After my meal, I saunter back to the newly constructed, monolithic building I must pass through in order to return to my native land. I proceed through customs.

"U.S. citizen," I report.

"Are you bringing anything back?"

"Just a full stomach," I joke.

The paunchy uniformed officer chuckles and waves me through. The dark-skinned mother behind me, carrying her newborn close to her breast, does not approach so confidently. Not that she does not have the proper documentation. She does. But she knows she will be examined suspiciously and not warmly welcomed.

This vignette portrays a slice of the attitude that saturates the air we all breathe along the border. The division between Mexico and the United States, a man-made line reinforced by steel partitions, is insignificant to the variegated pigeons flying from one courtyard to another. It is not, however, insignificant to the community members living on either side. The political, social, and economic implications, though rarely explicitly stated, are nonetheless deeply embedded. This community is formally considered *Ambos Nogales,* an endearing term signifying the union, the togetherness, of Nogales, Arizona, and Nogales, Sonora. In the streets, however, where political realities hit home, Mexico is referred to as *el otro lado*—the other side.

Though I have painted a disturbing picture, my intent is not to induce a feeling of hopelessness for the inhabitants of this border community where I live and work. On the contrary, we embrace life eagerly, with joy and optimism. My images simply illustrate the social and political contexts defining the status of Latinos and endeavor to expose the mythical concept of equal opportunity for all.

In an era of increasing anti-immigrant sentiment toward Mexicans, clearly evident in the passing of California's Proposition 187, the implications for Mexicans and Mexican Americans living in the United States must be addressed socially as well as pedagogically. The tacit, unspoken insinuations as to who possesses cultural capital and whose knowledge is valued are ever present. They exist in our stratified society and they are often amplified, rather than modified, in our schools. As teachers, however, we have the power and the obligation to confront the many issues rooted in social injustice that affect the lives of our students, and to strive to make positive changes. We have the ability to assess and modify the learning environments we create to best suit our students' needs. The curriculum we present is of great importance within that environment, and we become advocates for our students when we develop curricula that value and expand on, rather than degrade or ignore, their diverse experiences, their knowledge, and their heritage.

The question of how we can best develop curricula to serve the needs of Latino students is not limited to border communities. But the question was one I asked myself time and again when I accepted my first teaching job, in an elementary school located three miles north of Mexico. As a white middle-class female raised in the Midwest, I had a lot to learn about my students and their families, 98 percent of whom were Mexican or of Mexican ancestry. I knew nothing of my new community's norms and mores. Not willing to accept the defeatist attitude that I could not learn, nor the elitist attitude that my students were now in the United States and needed to adapt to me, I decided to search for the answers to some lingering questions: What strengths and resources are these children bringing into my classroom? What are their cultural and linguistic backgrounds? How can I make learning meaningful to my students? In short, I needed to know what my students' prior knowledge was in order to build on it.

Throughout my first two years of teaching I became increasingly incensed at the repeated labels the students in my school were given. They were "limited English speakers" and "low achievers" because they did not do well on standardized tests. As their teacher, I was in the best position to recognize the inconsistencies between what I knew my students knew and what was generally reported about their knowledge. Their rich backgrounds and budding bilingual skills were not "standard." Therefore, their knowledge was never fully illuminated for the world to see; it was instead hidden behind low standardized scores and undervalued.

If I was to achieve my goals of learning about the lives of my students and adapting curricular materials to meet their unique circumstances, I was going to have to take a closer look at the social conditions inherent to their families and their home lives. I tried listening to my students' words, to their stories, their experiences, but this was not enough. It was obvious I had only scratched the surface; I needed to probe much deeper.

The First Step (or One Giant Leap)

Maritza, whose long, dark lashes frame her intensely penetrating and beautiful charcoal-colored eyes, is an energetic eleven-year-old Mexican girl. I had the pleasure of teaching Maritza in the fifth grade, as well as her equally enthusiastic mother, Lydia, and two aunts in evening English classes for adults. Maritza wrote and spoke both English and Spanish with ease after living in the United States for only four years. Lydia knew some English vocabulary, but I believed that a lack of confidence kept her from using the language at home. The complex implications of learning to be bilingual in this environment intrigued me, since most of my other students had parents who were monolingual in Spanish.

Because of the growing relationship I was establishing with various family members, I pursued the idea of learning more about Maritza's home environment. I approached Lydia with my curiosity and timidly asked if I could make a home visit to learn more about Maritza and discover the multiple uses of language and text within the household.[1] Lydia smiled patiently as I stammered through the self-invitation, and without hesitation, she asked when I would like to come. And so the path was cleared for my visit. The myth that families are reluctant to have teachers in their homes had been exposed in a matter of seconds. I later discovered that the ease of access should not have been such a surprise nor such a frightening experience for me. Generally parents are eager to participate in their children's learning by sharing the knowledge only they can supply, and they are grateful and honored to be asked to do it.

The following week I drove to Maritza Silva's house. After turning off from the main road, I drove down a short, dead-end alley and parked my car. Nervous about overstepping my bounds into someone else's private sphere, I slowly collected my notebooks and headed toward the Silva home. I approached a metal gate, opened it, and apprehensively walked up a set of well-worn wooden stairs leading to the front door. I knocked with trepidation on the wrought iron decorating the screen door, but my fears immediately subsided when I was warmly greeted and welcomed inside. My plan was to make systematic observations of each room, detailing the extent of Spanish and English print used throughout. These observations, combined with a few questions addressed to family members for clarification, would let me better understand the literacy environment in which Maritza lived. What I learned, however, surpassed my expectations.

My notes describe the setting:

Maritza lives in a home with her extended family. In addition to her mother, Maritza lives with Marcos [her mother's boyfriend who has served as a father figure for the last nine years], her grandmother, her nine-year-old sister, and three aunts ranging in age from sixteen to twenty-three. Soon another member will be added as one of the aunts is now seven months pregnant. I first entered into the family's living room. In the corner sat a new TV. When asked if they watch programs in Spanish or English I was told, "Los dos" [both]. The living room walls displayed a sampling of schoolwork created by the two young girls. A typed paper titled "What I Like Best about [My] School," written by

Maritza's younger sister, was taped in a prominent position.[2] On the same wall one could admire examples of the children's artwork posted on the otherwise bare wall.

Toy boxes were stacked up in the corner with their English names and directions printed on them. A business card, electric bill, vehicle renewal form, and tax information, all in English, could be seen on the living room table. The English correspondence prompted me to ask how the family dealt with such items if they could not understand them. Lydia explained the importance of the children's bilingual abilities in deciphering much of the mail. Their role as translator was vital to the entire family. A *TV Stars* magazine, in Spanish, sat alongside the English items.

After exploring just one room of the house, I had gained insights into the family's interactions with print. I realized the children's ability to read and write in English was a valuable family commodity. The great pride the family had for the children's schoolwork was evident from its prominent position on the walls. But I had more rooms to explore:

I was invited to walk through the rest of the house. From the living room I proceeded into one of the two bedrooms. This small room housed Maritza, her sister, mother, father, and one aunt at night. A double bed and one single bed left only small pathways to walk. Clothes were hung or folded in piles throughout the room. On the solitary wooden dresser were many toiletry items—cotton swabs, cold cream, and deodorant—all with English names. A Spanish comic book shared the space on top of the dresser. Proudly displayed on the dresser's mirror was an honor roll certificate. A Shakey's Pizza bumper sticker adorned one of the bedroom walls. A backpack with school papers stored inside was brought out from under the bed and Maritza's younger sister eagerly showed me her work. Although I spotted a children's book order form, I did not see any books in the room. Maritza walked into the bedroom to show me a poster she colored for her mother for St. Patrick's day last year. It was in English.

Though I was truly amazed at the aggregation of Spanish and English print, other observations were important as well. The lack of adequate working space within the home made me realize the homework assignments I had been giving were probably difficult to complete, the more so because they were usually in English and Maritza's parents would not be able to help her. Perhaps the school needed to designate the library or a classroom as an afternoon homework area.

I knew from my research courses that during systematic observations it is just as important to note what is missing as it is to document what is visible. I had not seen any books in the house, though the family was surrounded with a variety of print. I surmised from the partially filled out book order form that a desire to read books was present even if the income to provide them was not. I silently vowed to make sure all my students had a public library card and knew how to use it. Normally this task falls to primary elementary teachers, but it dawned on me that many of my students had recently transferred in from Mexico and might not be aware of the community resources available.

My inquiry continued as I completed my tour:

A Spanish song on a cassette player and the smell of sweet batter were battling for air space in the kitchen. One of the aunts was busy baking a cake for dinner as I entered the third room. There was a Spanish notice taped above the sink that Maritza had made for others in the house reminding them to wash their own dishes. On the refrigerator was another reminder, in Spanish, of all the prenatal doctor appointments for the aunt. Food labels in both Spanish and English were evident; labels on the small bag of flour, the corn tortillas, and the hot cereal were in Spanish, while the garlic salt and black pepper labels were in English.

From the kitchen I could see one other bedroom, occupied by the aunts. I was not invited to enter this room and did not ask for permission. Perhaps it was not within the rights of Lydia or Maritza to allow me to enter.

We walked back into the living room, the original starting point, and I was told the grandmother sleeps on the couch, assuming the role of gatekeeper at night. Lydia pulled out a folder that was tucked in a special area on the bottom shelf of the end table and proudly showed me a collection of papers saved over the years. Report cards and other cherished papers had been carefully filed. I ended my visit, and my seemingly endless questions, shortly after the arrival of additional family members who lived nearby. Echoes of stories told and news shared, all in Spanish, were resounding in my head as I stepped outside the house.

I remember walking away in awe of the mixture of languages within Maritza's home. I glanced around, and from the top of the porch I could see the back parking area of a commercial building. The words painted on the wall read "Customer Parking ONLY Others Will Be Towed." Next to these words, just as prominently displayed, were words with the same meaning: "Estacionamiento para clientes unicamente. Otros serán remolcados." Inside and out, Maritza was being raised in a rich bilingual world.

Dazzled by the wide array of print I had always taken for granted and never really noticed, I made my way back down the steps, through the gate, and into my car. As I drove away I realized that I had answered many questions concerning Maritza's family and home life. I understood a little more of Maritza's bilingual literacy environment, yet the bilingual print revealed more than words. I had also learned about Maritza's culture. A plea for individual responsibility for the common good was evidenced in the dishwashing sign. Concern over the arrival of a new family member was indicated in the openly displayed prenatal doctor visits reminder. I thought about the eight people sharing the same house, the single bathroom, and I wondered if similar situations with other students would explain why children were often late for school—not for lack of motivation, but for lack of time and hot water. Three adults and two children shared a double and a single bed. Could this explain some sleepy yawns in the mornings?

Digging Deeper

I was left with more questions than I had answered. My observations were informative, yet I realized that when I combined them with in-depth interviews I could learn even more about family history, family members' daily routines, their attitudes, their philosophies, and the social dynamics of this family and their community.

The idea of conducting family interviews is not original. Research examining what has been called "funds of knowledge" informed and guided me.[3] Understanding students' social environments and personal cultural values in order to discover the skills and knowledge they use in their lives at home is at the heart of this research. The qualitative results can then be used in the classroom to build curriculum based on the children's experiences.

Several months after my initial visit to Maritza Silva's home I approached Lydia again, asking her if she would allow me to conduct a series of three interviews about her family. "Claro que sí" [Clearly yes], she answered once again, and our relationship was reestablished.

Though this endeavor may seem limited, much can be gained from learning the intricacies of just one family. Maritza's home life was similar to that of her classmates in countless ways: many of them lived on the same road, had monolingual Spanish-speaking parents, and lived with extended family members. The information I gleaned would therefore not be isolated and insignificant. It would be extremely helpful in the classroom.

The interviews I conducted were in Spanish, and Lydia gave me permission to tape-record each one. I asked primarily open-ended questions, with some structured content, so that family members could reconstruct their experiences in their own words. Each interview lasted from ninety to one hundred and twenty minutes and was later transcribed and translated. After analyzing the transcripts, I used the data to produce relevant units of instruction for classroom use.

Before the first interview, Lydia told me that her immediate family had moved (periodic moves were another common characteristic of students in the community). Presently, Lydia, Maritza, Carla (Maritza's younger sister), and Marcos lived in their new home less than a mile from the previous household.

The four family members appeared quite happy during the first interview. By the third interview, however, Marcos was in jail and was not expected to return home. However, since he had lived with the family for nine years, he is still included in this study. His work and attitudes helped influence the family during formative years and the girls continue to call him their father.

The Interviews

The interviews to discover and learn the history and social patterns of the Silva family were engaging. Lydia answered my many questions about her life, her family, and her philosophies with enthusiasm and ceaseless energy. Maritza and Carla were extremely attentive, their elbows on the table, chins in hands, their eyes following closely every lip movement. I asked questions about language use, networking, household activities, parental work history, attitudes, and aspirations. The information I learned is summarized below.

Language Use

Both Maritza and Carla are bilingual in English and Spanish. Lydia has taken a few English classes and nurtures a strong desire to speak the language fluently. Marcos speaks some English when necessary for work. Only Spanish is spoken in the home, however, much to Lydia's chagrin. She would like her daughters to help her learn English. "No me quieren hablar en inglés. No me quieren enseñar. Me da vergüenza" [They don't want me to speak English. They don't want to teach me. This embarrasses me], Lydia soulfully reports.

Lydia likes to try to speak English. She mixes the two languages sometimes (a typical practice for many who live along the border). She laughingly states that she may say, *No hay parking* [There is no parking], at which her daughters promptly correct her and say *estacionamiento* [parking]. She views this code switching as a step in learning English but thinks it is incorrect to use it all the time.

The girls speak Spanish and English to their teachers and friends at school. Lydia wants the girls to learn to speak both languages perfectly and even a third if they wish because "una persona bilingüe es más . . . es más facil platicar con la gente . . . es muy, muy, muy interesante una persona bilingüe, pues muy intelegente y si sabe aprender tres idiomas que bueno" [a bilingual person is . . . it is easier to converse with people . . . a bilingual person is very, very, very interesting, well, intelligent and if (her daughters) can learn three languages, all the better]. Maritza would like to learn French.

When I ask about the girls' Spanish ability, Lydia claims that it is good but they still need to be corrected from time to time. She says that the girls will often ask, "Como se dice en español?" [How do you say that in Spanish?] because "se confunden con el inglés" [they get confused with English].

There is no question that living along the border, where the dominant language is a mixture of Spanish and English (sometimes referred to as Spanglish), makes the art of perfecting one language difficult. Code switching is the norm in the community, yet students are discouraged from speaking this way in the schools since it is not standard English. Though the students may know the material, they do poorly on standardized tests that are presented in English only.

Maritza and Carla experience a social contradiction in their lives as their budding bilingual skills often work to their disadvantage in school yet are highly valued at home. They act as linguistic brokers for the parents in many situations. The girls translate in stores, they translate bills, and they translate medical information. They are the communication lifeline to the outside world. Even though the girls no longer live with the extended family, they often help their aunts and grandmother translate from English to Spanish too. This sharing of resources is but one of many in which the extended family engages.

Networking

Networking and sharing resources can serve a variety of functions. With the Silvas, the exchanges are primarily between extended-family households. Lydia's stepfather lives in Nogales, Sonora. Her mother and six sisters live in Nogales, Arizona. Family members visit with each other regularly. (When asked how often she visits her sisters and mother Lydia giggled and replied, "Todos los días" [Every day].) Lydia's family rarely comes to her house to visit; her mother's home serves as a central meeting place.

Additionally, the whole family goes to her stepfather's house in Sonora every Sunday. They travel in two cars because, in Lydia's words, "Somos muchos" [We are many]. While there, Lydia's mother makes *carne asada*. The adults talk and listen to music while the children all play together. Sometimes the whole family plays volleyball; Lydia always has a volleyball net in her car.

Sharing is generally social, but an exchange of skills is evident. Lydia's stepfather works on her car when it needs tuning. Lydia picks up her niece from school each day for her sister. The girls translate for their relatives. Child care is exchanged. According to Lydia, her sisters are always there to help her any time she needs anything.

Household Activities

Sharing responsibilities is the norm within the Silva home. Everyone helps with housecleaning. Every day the girls take care of the garbage, pick up their clothes, and make their beds. Marcos used to help clean the floors, wash the dishes, and wash the car. Lydia does the laundry, although the girls help iron, and she also does the cooking for the family. She is in the process of teaching Maritza to cook. Maritza can make a few soups, chile con carne, spaghetti, beans, and a few other dishes. Carla will learn to cook when she turns eleven or twelve but right now she is too young. When I ask whether Marcos ever cooked, the reply is, "Nunca" [Never].

After school the three females spend a lot of time together. Carla and her mother exercise together; they own an exercise bike but many exercises are simply done on the floor. Maritza does not enjoy working out with them. After exercising, the females watch TV, play games, and listen to music.

Music, in fact, is an important feature in the Silva home. Lydia reports that music is on at all times in their house, "todo el día, todo el día" [all day, all day]. (My visits verified this statement.) The radio plays songs in both Spanish and English. They all like romantic songs that make them cry. Lydia likes to listen to music when she is cleaning. She tells me that song has played a large role in her life. Lydia sang to the girls frequently when they were babies. They know the words to many songs she has taught them.

When the girls were younger, besides being sung to, they were also told stories. Lydia began talking to her girls when they were five days old. She says others used to ask who she was talking to. When she said her daughters, they would call her *loca* [crazy]. When the girls were a little older they used to ask her a lot of questions about her childhood. The girls always wanted to know more about mom. She says she never read to them, "puro hablar" [only talked].

Oral histories are one way to pass down memories and photos are another.

Photography is a hobby all enjoy. (During a couple of the visits I was shown pictures of vacations, family, and special events.) Maritza, Carla, and Lydia each have a camera and all enjoy taking pictures. Chores, exercise, music, storytelling, and photography are all activities family members engage in when they are not in school or at work.

Household Work History

Marcos is what Lydia calls a landscaper. He works independently cutting trees and grass, planting flowers, and doing other yard-related tasks. He gets his jobs by passing out cards to people and then he calls them or they call him. He has been doing this for eight months in Nogales, Arizona. Before that, he worked for a landscaping company in Phoenix. He lived alone in Phoenix for awhile while the rest of the family was living in Nogales. He learned his landscaping skills in Phoenix. Marcos owns a lawnmower, and is happy in his work because he likes the money and enjoys working in gardens.

Lydia was a cashier at one time. She likes to type, a skill she learned at the store. She worked at a clothing store two years ago but the pay was very low. (She was looking for work at the time of our first interview, but sadly stated, "No hay trabajo" [There is no work].) To fill her free time, she volunteers in her youngest daughter's classroom. She helps primarily by cutting paper for classroom activities or by putting things on bulletin boards. She is not asked to read or write with the children.

By the time of the second interview, Lydia has been hired to work as a cashier at a restaurant/bar. The restaurant is about to reopen after being closed by the health department. Lydia is not excited about it, because heavy drinking often takes place there. At the third interview, however, I learn that she has been offered another position as a clerk in a jeans store and so never had to work at the restaurant/bar. She is elated at the new opportunity because she desperately needs the employment; Marcos is no longer bringing money into the household.

The girls never helped Marcos with landscaping but listened to and took part in enough conversations about it so that they have a repertoire of work-related terms in both languages. They know the machinery and the labor involved.

The girls have not participated in any activities that would supplement the family's income, although they have had impressed upon them the importance of hard work and assuming responsibility. These are two of many values that Lydia nurtures in her children.

Attitudes and Aspirations

One of the most important values that Lydia tries to inculcate in her children is respect for friends, elders, and family. She believes that the best way to teach these virtues is through example. The work ethic has been stressed since the girls were four years old. At that age they were expected to carry their dishes to the sink and help with the garbage.

Contrary to research indicating that Hispanic parents have low aspirations for their children, Lydia's hopes for her children are high. Lydia would like for Maritza and Carla to be trilingual. She expects them to have good grades, work hard in school, and study all they can. These desires are explicit within the home because Lydia wants her daughters to have fulfilling and rewarding jobs when they become adults.

Lydia's definition of education is not just what is learned in school. She sees education as a shared responsibility and asserts that academic training is not the sole element to being educated. She believes good manners, knowing what is right and what is wrong, and the importance of family are all encompassed in education.[4]

Lydia's wants her children to understand the value of money too. The girls do not regularly receive an allowance. Lydia worries that like other young kids today, her daughters might begin to think that money is easy to get. To reward them for good grades, she buys them practical items. When Maritza and Carla do have money, they are encouraged to spend it on clothes, shoes, school materials, and other necessary supplies.

In addition to serving as a good example of the personal values and beliefs Lydia hopes her daughters will possess, she talks to them a lot about why these things are important. She knows the girls are being raised in a different time from when she was young. Lydia sees adolescent girls living a fast life and having babies when they are still babies themselves. She wants to protect Maritza and Carla from these and other dangers she perceives.

Pedagogical Implications

The real mystique of qualitative inquiry lies in the processes of using data rather than the processes of gathering data.

HARRY WOLCOTT[5]

A teacher/researcher discovering a family's funds of knowledge is in the perfect position to integrate students' experiences, linguistic practices, and histories into the learning process. To believe that all students benefit and learn equally from the same materials, teaching styles, and forms of evaluation is naive. Academic success is not a hopeless concept for minority children if teachers make appropriate connections and create a learning environment where backgrounds are given priority.

My limited attempt as an interested teacher to better understand my students' backgrounds and social environments proved to me that "family" is a rich resource that, when mined, provides the raw material for refinement and future use in the classroom. Observations and interviews in the home become the basis for action in school, and the teacher/researcher role changes to one of teacher/advocate. Situations that may at first seem negative become better understood, and we begin to focus on strengths rather than weaknesses.

Bilingual, bicultural activities and lessons designed from the information gathered can easily cover all subject areas. However, I am not suggesting that each community of learners, each class, be taught different concepts and skills. On the contrary, I believe we all need to master certain basics. My point is that we have the power to make those concepts come alive for our students and fuel their desire to learn by valuing who they are as humans in our multicultural society and valuing their prior knowledge and understanding in our classrooms. The students, in turn, find learning meaningful to their lives.

The depth of knowledge, skills, and values transmitted to Maritza and Carla within the Silva family is immense. This information can guide not only *what* is taught but also *how* the subject matter is taught. When the Silva family's history, social dynamics, and range of interests were tapped, multiple possibilities emerged to develop motivating, relevant units of instruction across the curriculum. To close the circle in the research process I brought my findings back into the classroom, from which I first emerged with my unending curiosity about my students. I did not do this alone, however. When I began this project, I was Maritza's fifth-grade teacher. Soon into the new school year I became a curriculum specialist for the district. I therefore had the opportunity to apply only a few of my ideas in my own classroom. Nevertheless, through my new position I was able to share the curricular possibilities with other teachers, adapting them to their unique needs and grade levels.

Curricular Possibilities

Music is an integral part of the Silva household. Lydia has been singing to her daughters since they were born. All of the girls enjoy listening to the radio, primarily in Spanish but also in English. When asked what songs they knew, Lydia gave several examples. She said she particularly liked romantic songs that are full of emotion and make her cry. Lydia could be invited into the classroom to teach and share the traditional Spanish songs that have been a part of her life. Because children enjoy singing, and since the majority of the community members are Spanish speakers, the class could learn a series of songs for a special evening program under Lydia's guidance. Lydia has much more to offer a classroom than paper-cutting skills. Her musical expertise with Spanish songs would serve to compliment my knowledge of English songs.

Additionally, several language arts activities could be created using the words to the songs. Interpretation and point of view are two key literary concepts that allow for the possibility of elaboration. Interpretation could be approached from two separate angles: What do you think the song is saying? What does it mean to you? or How would you translate this to English? Are certain emotions or feelings lost in the translation? Why or why not? After an extensive review of various lyrics, the students could write their own verses to known melodies.

Spanish songs often offer glimpses into Mexican history and culture, thus creating openings for social studies lessons. Music need not and should not remain a closed subject in and of itself.

Since Marcos has made a living as a landscaper for several years, first working with a company and then working independently doing yard work for others, a unit on indigenous plant species and local plant diversity would build on an already established foundation the girls presently possess. Though Maritza and Carla have not been directly involved in landscaping, they have been included in the conversations surrounding this type of work. Engaging the children in an outdoor gardening project presents myriad possibilities.

For example, in science, the growth cycle of plants could be explored; in language arts, keeping a garden journal and reading and writing nature poetry could be easily integrated; in math, the measuring of plots, depth of seed planting, and spacing between rows would lend themselves to unique lessons; and in social studies, traditional medicinal purposes of plants in ethnobotany could be examined.

Mothers and fathers with landscaping experience could be invited to help supervise this school gardening project, offering advice from past experience and perhaps even lending specific tools that would be required. A deeper level of community involvement strengthens the roots of an authentic bicultural curriculum.

Students could raise money to have a local artisan craft ceramic or wooden labels containing the names of the plants in Spanish, English, and Latin (the universal name). Local business within the community could also be involved. Within a plant unit, old flowers obtained from local flower shops or grocery stores could be dissected and their parts examined and identified under a microscope.

Several women in the community are well versed in the medicinal uses of various plants and herbs—a common practice in many homes. An invitation to one or several of these women to visit the classroom would take advantage of community expertise. The women can serve as models for the students, perpetuating an ethnic pride that is lost in prepackaged curriculum.

The rich tradition of passing on oral histories is a valuable asset laden with bountiful classroom potential. By researching and recording stories gathered from family members and combining these accounts with some creative photography, students could create treasured books depicting family history. Many basic skills are reinforced in the process of producing these books. The students must decide what kinds of questions interest them, what will be their focus. They must use their listening skills to record stories correctly with or without a tape recorder. They must take pieces of history and combine them into a coherent whole, thus exercising their writing skills. And their creativity will be tapped as they compose photographs and blend these images with written text.

I include photography since the love of photography is immediately noticeable in the Silva home. Photo albums abound and are brought out with pride. Pictures on the refrigerator show off family members and past events. Tiny frames with pictures are displayed throughout the living room. If using a camera is not a common experience for other students, Maritza and Carla are in perfect positions to assist or lead their classmates through the procedures.

Maritza and Carla's roles as the family's linguistic brokers cry out for elaboration. As we have seen, they often translate bills, miscellaneous mail, and conversations in stores. The girls have ample experience at helping run the household, as do most of the students with monolingual Spanish parents. With this in mind, a miniunit on practical life skills would help the girls hone their developing expertise. Creating a budget, writing checks, and following recipes are all mathematical lessons in the making. Students quickly learn the mechanics of writing checks and enjoy having their own checkbooks in class. Routine math drills are replaced with meaningful budgeting exercises—same skills, different approach. (I learned from the parents in my evening English class that many children were already writing checks at home, because this was the first thing the adults wanted to learn! However, the children had no idea how to balance the checkbook.) These activities compliment existing roles in the home and at times allow the students to become their parents' teachers.

Two sensitive societal issues that came up in the interviews also warrant curricular attention. The first is caring for aging and/or sick family members. Maritza and Carla's lives revolve around family activities. Every day they visit the extended family. When Lydia's stepfather became ill, visits to the hospital were routine. An awareness of caregiving responsibilities and the process of aging might help the girls cope with, and better understand, what is going on around them. A unit on aging could include easy-to-design simulations: petroleum jelly smeared on eyeglasses—cataracts; taped fingers—arthritis; earplugs—loss of hearing. Students assuming the role of an aging adult will need help throughout the day; thus the caregiver's role emerges as well.

Extemporaneous role-playing based on descriptions of specific situations would help students empathize with both the caregiver and the aging or sick family member. Moreover, second language development skills are enhanced through these types of activities.

The second issue is alcoholism. Because of this disease, the girls' father figure is no longer part of the household. The girls still love Marcos but do not like what he does to their mother. Giving him up after nine years is not easy.

Aging and alcoholism are both sensitive topics that I am certain play a part in many students' lives in Nogales. One possible way to introduce the issue of alcoholism is to invite someone from a local rehabilitation or counseling center to speak to the class. A former alcoholic recommended by the center also could serve as a resource of information for the students. Care must be exercised when addressing societal issues like these, but they cannot be ignored. At the very least, an awareness of the processes involved is essential.

Besides acquiring ideas on topics that can be integrated into the curriculum, teacher-researchers can assess which learning styles might work best for the child and what types of activities would be most appropriate. For example, Maritza and Carla would work well in cooperative groups building on their cooperative family life. Both could easily become group leaders and translators. I once asked Maritza, "Who do you translate for the most?" Her answer was, "My mother and my teachers." Maritza also knows how to use a dictionary. Whenever she is asked to translate a bill or a notice for her mother that contains a word she does not understand, Maritza looks up the English meaning of the English word. She said she uses the dictionary all the time. After reading a legal letter Lydia shared with me (a letter whose legalese I had difficulty deciphering), I became acutely aware of the obstacles Maritza must sometimes encounter. This evidence of leadership, maturity, and responsibility should not be ignored in the classroom.

Multiple possibilities exist for effective instruction that builds on Maritza and Carla's broad knowledge base. These few suggestions are just a beginning. Learning more about a student's home life and using that knowledge will enrich the teaching/learning experience and provide a smoother transition when children leave home in the morning and enter the cold, heavy doors of the institution we call school. Mediating the discontinuity that presently exists between home and school in many locations, particularly where Mexican or Mexican American children are involved, needs to be the focus of classroom reform.[6] Such reform, based on educational research, can then serve as a vehicle for larger social change.

Teacher Research as a Form of Advocacy

American ideology embraces individualism. Why then have our schools historically maintained that we must teach the same prepackaged curriculum to all students? Is this "equality" in education or is it a model reflecting one set of values, one interpretation, one history, to the exclusion of all others? If we taught everybody the same material, and by some miracle everyone learned at the same rate and by the same methods, we would have no experts. Can we not move beyond one view to encourage a blending of the dominant culture with the local one, to cultivate a sense of pride in both? A harmonious relationship between deeply rooted cultural identity and school life seems imperative. Schools that emphasize routine drills to teach skills do not capitalize on the wealth of cultural, social, and linguistic knowledge and experience that children bring with them to the classroom.

Advocating for our students comes with accepting and valuing who they are as human beings. Advocating means refuting the belief that there are subordinate ethnic groups. Advocating includes validating community and family life through a customized curriculum, eliciting productive classroom discourse. The growing hostility toward the Mexican immigrant population is an antipathy whose consequences for children on both sides of the border demands educational research—and corrective action. The findings of teachers' individual research projects in the homes of their students can lead to positive social transformations in the community and in society at large.

Throwing out all prepackaged curriculum is not my plea. Valuable information is presently available for classroom use. The question remains, however, do we want to remain receptacles for the research of others or can we exert our own strength and competence to delve below the surface, to teach more than cultural holidays and ethnic foods, to use priceless community expertise, to close the ever widening gap between home and school life? As teachers we are in the most logical position to combine research skills with pedagogy in the classroom and advocacy in the community. We can explore the diversity the families within our district retain, do something creative in our classrooms with the information we gather, and enhance the social dynamics between parents and educators via these positive interactions.

I visited the Silva family four times and spent many hours getting to know them. I also spent a lot of time analyzing the information they shared with me. Many teachers feel they do not have this time to spend. But the "work" that was involved was fascinating, engaging, and contributed to my own personal growth. We have a choice. We can spend our time collecting data and creating units that can be shared with other teachers, or we can spend the time creating remedial activities when our students do not learn from the rote skills promoted by many textbooks.

Entering a strange home to ask personal questions can be difficult, if not terrifying, the first time. But since that first visit I have found that parents are eager to share their perceptions, their dreams, their wisdom, in hopes that their children will benefit in school. *Vale la pena*. It is all worth it for the knowledge gained.

Endnotes

1. Denny Taylor and Cathy Dorsey-Gaines's research, documented in *Growing up Literate: Learning from Inner-City Families* (Portsmouth, NH: Heinemann, 1988) includes an in-depth look into the multiple ways print is used in family households. Their moving account helped me think about literacy in a more enlightened manner and nourished the initial stages of my research. **2.** The school's name was originally written in the title. The world "My" has been inserted for reasons of confidentiality. **3.** For a full description of the history of funds of knowledge research and models of collaborative work, see J. Greenburg, *Funds of Knowledge: Historical Constitution, Social Distribution, and Transmission* (paper presented at the annual meeting of the Society for Applied Anthropology, Sante Fe, NM, April, 1989); L. Moll, C. Amanti, D. Neff, and N. González, "Funds of Knowledge for Teaching; Using a Qualitative Approach to Connect Homes and Classrooms" *Theory into Practice* XXXI: 132–41 (year); N. González, L. Moll, M. Floyd-Tenery, A Rivera, P. Rendon, R. González, and C. Amanti, *Teacher Research on Funds of Knowledge: Learning from Households* (National Center of Research on Cultural Diversity and Second Language Learning, Washington, DC, 1993). I am grateful to Dr. Luis Moll and Dr. Norma González for their guidance and expertise throughout this research project. **4.** An excellent description of the definition of "educación" can be found in L. Reese, S. Balsano, Gallimore, and C. Goldenberg, *The Concept of Educación: Latino Family Values and American Schooling* (paper given at the annual meeting of the American Anthropology Association, Chicago, 1991). **5.** This quote is from Harry Wolcott, *Transforming Qualitative Data* (Thousand Oaks, CA: Sage, 1994). **6.** Excellent references of research exploring issues of discontinuity between home and school can be found in Jose Macias, "The Hidden Curriculum of Papago Teachers: American Indian Strategies for Mitigating Cultural Discontinuity in Early Schooling"; and Concha Delgado-Gaitan, "Traditions and Transitions in the Learning Process of Mexican Children: An Ethnographic View" (both found in G. Spindler and L. Spindler, eds., *Interpretive Ethnography of Education at Home and Abroad* (Hillsdale, NJ: Lawrence Erlbaum Associates, 1987).

This interview was conducted by telephone while Melanie was in Mexico.

Denny: Tell me about your job the year you visited Maritza's family.

MELANIE: The year before my visit I taught fifth grade. After that I was hired as a curriculum specialist in reading and environmental studies. But because the district didn't yet have a fifth-grade teacher to take my place, I stayed in the classroom for the first part of the school year. This is when I did the bulk of this project.

Denny: When you worked with teachers, did you share the study with them?

MELANIE: As much as I could. For the most part, teachers would ask me for curriculum suggestions and I would provide them with units of instruction. I spent time giving workshops, going into classrooms, and providing materials when they requested them. I did have an opportunity to integrate some of my findings into the units that I developed.

Denny: Teachers have said to me that they would never visit the families of the kids that they teach. They don't have time. One teacher said that the only time he visited a family was when there was an incident with a gun and that he didn't intend making any more visits. I think many teachers would like to visit families, but they are, understandably, a little nervous. Some are just plain scared.

MELANIE: As I said at the end of my article, it is scary the first time. But since my visits to Maritza's family I've visited numerous homes and I've asked very personal questions, and always, always, in every case, I've been warmly welcomed, graciously treated, and in the end thanked for showing interest in the families' lives.

Denny: What makes it work?

MELANIE: I think the key to success is to be respectful and appreciative of the time that family members give to you and to be appreciative of the opinions that are offered and the things that they tell you. If a teacher is there to learn—if she can maintain the attitude that she is there to learn and that the parents and other members of the family are the knowledge givers, that they are the authority—then the visit will work. The results will be both surprising and rewarding for the teacher and also for the family.

Denny: It's how you position yourself. Expert or novice. I think many teachers would be very comfortable assuming the position of novice and learning from families, but for some teachers it would be very difficult for them to give up their position of authority. Either way, it isn't that easy.

MELANIE: I can think of an analogy for me. It always seemed a very scary prospect to call my congressman and let my voice be heard. But it's really easy. All you do is call, and the secretary answers the phone, and you tell them what side you are on, and they record your opinion. The first time you do it is scary, but after that you realize how simple it is.

Denny: What you're saying is that whatever the situation, it is always more difficult the first time. After that it's less scary.

MELANIE: Exactly. Since the first visit, I've made so many home visits that it really is just a part of what I do, like any other aspect of teaching.

Denny: When I interviewed Nan Jiang he said that in China it is expected that teachers will visit the homes of every student in their classes. Sometimes teachers visit each family twice during the school year. That could mean that they make almost one hundred home visits.

MELANIE: Home visits are important. I learned more in that one visit to Maritza's family than I had learned in the entire previous year of asking kids questions about their lives. When I saw Maritza with her family, I gained a completely different perspective.

Denny: I want to ask you about the literacies at home and at school. It's a two-part question. What literacies have you found in family settings that you don't find in school? And what literacies are a part of the school curriculum that are not necessarily a part of the family's literacy?

MELANIE: Let's take a family like Maritza's, where the environment is completely bilingual. The literacy configuration of the family is bilingual. Then you enter the school, which in my case did not have an adequate bilingual program in place, and there is no comparison. I learned that we were working on two different planes. There was very little overlap between my students' home and school literacy experiences.

Denny: So school becomes an impoverished environment.

MELANIE: Yes, because families have many literacies that schools don't know about.

Denny: And don't recognize as important.

MELANIE: In school you have English textbooks based on Euro-American philosophies and outlooks, when so many children have very different outlooks. My whole reason for doing this kind of research is to help us value the differences.

Denny: Tell me a little more about the ways in which the literacies in the home differ from literacies in the school.

MELANIE: From what I found in this project, the literacies in the home were real-life literacies based on real problems and real experiences. The literacies in school seemed to me to be more forced. It's one size fits all.

Denny: How did your students look on standardized tests?

MELANIE: Not good. They hated them. They really dreaded them. [*Laughs*] We used to buy them M&M's to make them feel better. [*Serious again*] Their results were poor. But the results were not a reflection of their knowledge. Instead they were a reflection of their language development in English. A lot of the students would have been able to answer the questions had they been written in Spanish or in a combination of Spanish and English. In particular it was very difficult for them to understand written math problems on standardized tests. They may have had a basic vocabulary, but it's the small words, the use of prepositions, that really confused them, and then they were unsure which math process to use to figure out the problem.

Denny: I was at the International Reading Association's annual convention a few weeks ago, and we were talking about the importance of providing opportunities for students to become literate in their home language and of the ways in which literacy in the home language helps a student become literate in the dominant language of a country. This upset quite a prominent researcher, who said her parents had come to this country and they had to learn the language and that others should do the same. Nan says that this argument confuses the issue. As an immigrant from mainland China he believes it his responsibility to learn the language, but that does not mean that Chinese is not important, nor does it mean that he does not want his daughter to be able to read in Chinese.

MELANIE: I've heard the researcher's argument many times before, and I think it is related to ethnocentrism. There may be an argument about which comes first, the culture or the language, but there is a definite relationship between culture and language. When we force people to leave behind their home language we are forcing them to also forfeit their culture, their histories.

Denny: And that is the very essence of who they are.

MELANIE: Exactly. And it's my belief that diversity is what makes our world a fascinating and challenging place to live. It encourages us to think in more than just one way.

Denny: Tell me how you have extended this early project into your doctoral research.

MELANIE: I see the entire thing as an ongoing project that started with one home visit. I began with very surface-level questions, but that to me was not enough. And so I went for three more visits, this time with more in-depth interviews. And for me that was still not enough. I wanted to learn more, so I came here to Mexico to research children's sociocultural experiences.

Denny: Tell us what you are doing.

MELANIE: I'm working in a rural community in a multigrade school. The community is mostly women, children, and elderly, because many of the fathers are working in the United States.

Denny: Are they documented?

MELANIE: Many documented, and many undocumented.

Denny: How big is the school?

MELANIE: The school has three teachers, for grades one through six, with a little more than one hundred students. I began by observing in the school and slowly integrated myself into daily activity. Because one teacher has had to have surgery, I'm actually teaching forty-seven second and third graders.

Denny: [*Laughing*] How are you doing?

MELANIE: [*Also laughing*] Right now I have a headache!

Denny: I know you have also been visiting families.

MELANIE: Right. I'm also looking at the children's experiences in their homes. I'm living in the community, and I'm conducting in-depth interviews with the mothers, some fathers, the children, and the elderly.

Denny: What do you hope the outcome of your research will be?

MELANIE: I hope in some way to help people back home learn more about the lives of children and their families in rural Mexico and to help them understand why so many Mexicans try to come to the U.S. But as you know, this is ethnography. I don't attempt to generalize. However, there are certain common attributes within rural communities that we can recognize and use in order to facilitate and ease the transition for Mexican children when they enter schools in the United States.

Denny: You're going to be able to provide teachers with some important information that will help them find ways to support not only Mexican children but children from other countries who have emigrated to the United States.

MELANIE: I hope so. It's interesting; since I've been here it seems from the news I get from the U.S. that there's been a big increase in the difficulties that Mexicans and Mexican Americans are experiencing in the U.S. I think egocentrism is reaching dangerously high levels in our country. We no longer value anything that isn't U.S. made, and that includes people born in other countries, which is sad.

Denny: How would you describe yourself as an advocate? I hear you advocating on a world level as well as the local level.

MELANIE: I've been an activist in my community for years—mostly dealing with environmental problems. I try to work at the local level in areas where I see a need—where I feel I can help. And I guess at a more macrolevel, I try to do what I can to fight what I see as grand social injustices. I enjoy working at the local level, but I would also like to have some input into policy making at the state or national level.

Denny: [*Laughing*] You're not going to run for office are you?

MELANIE: [*Also laughing*] Absolutely not.

Denny: How does the work you do as an advocate translate into action in school?

MELANIE: I truly believe that teachers in general enter the profession because they want to try to make the world a better place. They are interested in social service. They possess a compassion for human life and a concern for social injustice, and I don't believe they want to contribute to the problems—though some teachers inadvertently do. We have to raise our level of consciousness, and analyze what it is that we are doing in our classrooms, and decide what we can do in order to expose the oppression that our bureaucratic system perpetuates in our schools. The responsibility lies with us as teachers, because we are the ones who are with the kids for seven hours a day or more. If we take an active role and learn about our students' sociocultural experiences and prior knowledge and incorporate our findings in our methodologies and curriculum, we validate their lives and become advocates at the classroom level. We have the power to make a difference.

Francisco

CARYL G. CROWELL

When I first met Francisco, he was a first-grade student assigned to my bilingual multiage classroom, known as the Sunshine Room, as a mainstream student whose primary placement was a self-contained cross-categorical bilingual (CCB) special education class. He was cheerful and friendly, willing to try new experiences, and very talkative. He stuttered, especially when he was excited and eager to tell us some important news. He wore thick glasses that dangled from a blue band purchased for him by Renée, my teaching assistant, because his glasses were often in his mouth or being spun by one of the temples. His handwriting was wobbly, and his drawings difficult to interpret at times, because of his undeveloped muscle tone. However, his mind was active, bright, and creative. Rosalie, his assigned special education teacher, admitted she did not understand why Francisco had been placed in her class, which consisted mostly of physically disabled, hearing-impaired, and otherwise noncommunicative children.

I'm presenting Francisco's story chronologically to better highlight the chain of events that resulted in his being placed in special education. The information about Francisco's kindergarten year was drawn from his cumulative record folder; his special education folder; Lisa, his speech therapist; his parents; Alisa, the teaching assistant in his kindergarten class and subsequently in my own classroom; and Francisco himself.

Francisco Begins School

When Francisco enrolled in school, an Elementary New Student Screening Report was automatically generated, as it is for all students new to the district. Teachers check A for each category in which the student exhibits "no observable problem," and B to indicate that "help might be needed." On September 23, 1993, Francisco's teacher checked B in three categories, and included a brief explanation for each:

motor development, "has difficulties with fine motor skills"; visual development, "wears glasses"; and speech development, "has difficulties with articulation, was receiving services through Tucson Medical Center (TMC)." The categories of social development, general health, and academic development were all checked A. At the bottom of the form, the teacher indicated that a referral to child study was necessary, but no follow-up is indicated on the form. A brief handwritten note in Francisco's cumulative folder reported on a vision screening done in September. Vision using both eyes was 20/40, 20/70 in each eye alone. The hearing screening done on November 8, 1993, was passed in both ears. By the following month, an evaluation for speech and language services was underway.

Francisco had received speech therapy for his stuttering before he began public school, through a program at Tucson Medical Center. Since I did not have access to these records, I relied on Lisa, Francisco's school district speech and language therapist, for information about these early services. Lisa first evaluated Francisco in the fall of kindergarten (October 26, 1993). Her evaluation differed significantly from the testing at TMC six months earlier. She described him as friendly and cooperative, interacting easily with her, and found the length of Francisco's utterances to be age appropriate. Although she thought his content area vocabulary to be somewhat low, she felt that his exposure to new experiences at school was expanding his vocabulary adequately. The articulation differences he produced at the time of the testing were determined to be developmental. Lisa recommended that she work with Francisco only on his fluency problems, characterized by "repetitions and prolongations, with secondary characteristics of averting eye gaze and accompanying head movements during dysfluent moments." Lisa's evaluation corresponds with the results of the Language Assessment Scales (LAS), required of all new students who speak a language other than English, which were administered when Francisco registered for school. Although this measure is not recommended by the publisher for children in kindergarten, Francisco scored a 4, or proficient, in Spanish, his native language, and 2, or limited, in English.

On December 7, 1993, Lisa, Francisco's kindergarten teacher, and another speech pathologist met to discuss the language-test results and recommend his placement. Their recommendation was that Francisco remain in his regular classroom and receive thirty minutes per week of resource services in Spanish from Lisa. Two days later, on December 9, a formal meeting was held at which Francisco's mother signed the Individual Education Plan (IEP) and Placement Notice. At this point, Francisco was labeled speech and language impaired. The IEP's long-term goal was to improve his fluency skills through short-term objectives of achieving oral fluency in the production of memorized materials (name, family members, counting), answering questions fluently, and beginning statements with "easy onset." Lisa began seeing Francisco weekly, usually on a pull-out basis, although occasionally she worked with him in his classroom.

There was very little in Francisco's cumulative folder to show what kinds of activities went on in his half-day kindergarten or what he was able to do. A teacher-made screening checklist for knowledge of numbers, shapes, colors, letters, and counting was dated August 30, 1993. On that day, Francisco knew some numbers between 1 and 10, some shapes, and some colors. He was able to count to eleven. Additional check marks on the checklist seem to indicate that Francisco made progress in these areas, but there were no additional dates by which to document it. Additionally, Francisco was asked to write his name following the teacher's model. His first attempt, I assume at the beginning of the year, was carried out as a continuous, unbroken line of hills, similar to a cursive *m*. The second entry showed conventional letters, about half of which are actually in Francisco's first and last names. The appropriate letters were in relatively correct positions, with other real letters used as fillers. The writing was mostly uniform in size and spacing, although just one letter, a lowercase *e*, fell precisely on the line. There was an appropriate space between first and last names.

The cumulative records folder also contained a series of journal entries, dated about a week apart. There was nothing to indicate why these particular pieces were placed in the folder or what Francisco's teacher thought they showed about his learning. A few had sticky notes attached with the words Francisco had used to describe his drawings. All the pages were quite similar, showing a face, or sometimes a body, with writing below a line drawn across the page. Despite the roughly drawn pictures, Francisco's understanding of how picture books look was evident. Like his journal entries, picture books often have illustrations above the written text.

On an entry dated September 24, 1993, Francisco used separate marks that, considering his difficulty with small motor movements, may well have been his effforts to produce real letters. His drawing on this page was just a head. On October 13 (see Figure 1), Francisco drew an entire body, with a head smaller than the torso, and arms and legs coming from the torso. The writing consisted of a continuous line of up-and-down movements. On October 18, he drew what appears to be another head, with similar squiggly-line writing below. Francisco described it to his teacher as "una cara de fantasmas," the face of ghosts, a very logical explanation for there being no body. On October 22, Francisco drew a picture of his mother, described to his teacher as "la cara de mi mamá." It showed lots of wavy hair and earrings, an accurate representation. Once again, squiggly-line writing was present.

On November 3, there was an important difference in Francisco's journal entry. His drawing (see Figure 2) was of a male figure with eyes, hair, ears, and a smile. As usual, below the line he had drawn across the page, was writing. This time conventional letters were written, an *F* and an *O*, the first and last letters of Francisco's name. Although this entry represents a very important step in literacy learning, there were no teacher notes indicating any interaction with Francisco about what he had accomplished. Unfortunately, there was only one more journal entry in the cumulative folder, dated December 8—a much smaller face with a vertical line descending from it. A capital *F* was written at the bottom of the page.

Interpretation of Francisco's November 3 journal page as an important breakthrough was supported by a self-evaluation done October 20. On eight of thirteen categories, Francisco rated himself "Casi siempre," or almost always. These included listening to others and to stories, learning and playing with friends, helping

Figure 1

Francisco's October 13
journal entry

to keep the room and his things clean and organized, and participating with confidence. Four other areas were marked "a veces," or sometimes, including reading with friends, reading alone, working quietly and independently, and recognizing colors. Only one item, "Puedo escribir mi nombre," I can write my name, was marked "todavía no," not yet.

Francisco's first-semester report card showed satisfactory progress in all areas of communication, personal and social growth, motor development, and work habits. Counting and recognizing numbers was marked as an area of difficulty, and reading and writing were marked as showing improvement. Additionally, the teacher's comments indicated that Francisco enjoyed listening to and talking about stories. An English-language learning observation matrix was also scored and was consistent with Francisco's LAS scores. It was typical of a child who was just starting to learn English, showing listening comprehension preceding oral production. Nevertheless, it is important to remember that Francisco's contexts for speaking English were decidedly limited (his kindergarten was only half a day) and that the oral production rating probably also reflected his stuttering and articulation difficulties. Francisco's second-semester report card gave him marks of N, needs improvement,

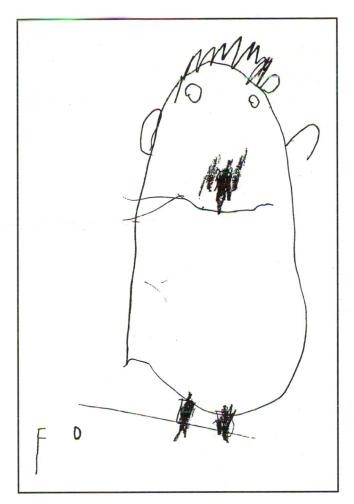

Figure 2

Francisco's November 3 journal entry

in reading, writing, and math; otherwise it was the same as the first semester. The teacher's comments addressed his enthusiasm and positive attitude toward school and how well he got along with others. It also mentioned that he liked to work on the computer.

Francisco's teacher referred him for a special education evaluation on March 15, 1994. Her reasons included slow academic progress; difficulty identifying colors, numbers, and letters; and hesitancy about writing his name. She also mentioned that he required one-to-one support from adults to accomplish most tasks. The steps she noted as having been taken to support Francisco included one-to-one attention from her and Alisa (the teaching assistant) and a request that his parents provide extra help at home.

Since Francisco's folder provided so little information about what his kindergarten experience had been like or what Francisco was able to do, I needed to look for other sources. Francisco's kindergarten teacher had left the school; however, Alisa, the teaching assistant in Francisco's kindergarten class, had recently been hired as a teaching assistant in my classroom. Alisa was also enrolled part-time in the College of Education at the University of Arizona. She was competent and knowledgeable in her work within our classroom. Therefore, I felt she would be able to provide valuable information regarding Francisco's learning during his kindergarten year compared to his subsequent progress within the Sunshine Room.

Alisa described Francisco's kindergarten as quite traditional in terms of teaching styles and learning activities. All children in the class were expected to perform at the same level, at approximately the same rate. Activities were usually not adapted to meet individual needs. Alisa described several activities as typical.

For one thing, the children in the class were expected to be able to write their full name, using upper- and lowercase letters appropriately, within the lines, by the end of kindergarten. There was daily practice. Each child received a lined paper with his or her name written once by the teacher. On the next line, the child's name was written in broken script to be written over by the student. The third line was blank, on which the child was to write the name on his or her own, copying the teacher's letters. This activity had to be done before other activities. Francisco did this name-writing activity every day. It was not adapted in any way to accommodate the difficulty he seemed to be experiencing with small motor coordination. Predictably, he did not meet with much success or appear to enjoy the task.

Journal writing was also a daily activity. The children drew in their journals and did any writing they chose. The teacher did not interact with the children while they were writing or immediately afterward. Once a week, the teacher selected a page from the journal and asked the child to "read" what had been written or tell about the picture. The teacher wrote the child's comments on a Post-it and attached it to the page. The page was photocopied for the child's portfolio. Francisco drew in his journal willingly.

I asked Alisa why the journal writing appeared to have stopped at the end of the semester. She wasn't sure, but said that Francisco's teacher had left near the end of March to have a baby and spent the rest of the year on maternity leave. The class had had a substitute teacher for approximately two weeks before the teacher of the morning kindergarten class took over Francisco's class as well. This teacher did not speak Spanish. Alisa interacted with Francisco in Spanish when she worked with him. Otherwise, all instruction and activities, including literacy and math, took place in English. Stories read aloud were in English, as were shared book readings, writing, and classroom discussions.

I also asked Francisco what he remembered about his kindergarten class. He described a listening center and, when asked, said that most of the stories he listened to were in English. Francisco's mother brought in a few examples of work from kindergarten that she had saved. They included several art activities and two examples of monthly calendars, made by tracing numbers written by the teacher and pasting the calendar onto a sheet of construction paper. No special dates were marked on either calendar, suggesting that its purpose was purely for practicing numeral writing. Francisco's mother and Alisa agreed that these few samples were typical of the work done in the class.

Alisa observed that activities and materials for Francisco's use and engagement were not modified in any way to accommodate his particular learning style, strengths, or difficulties. Furthermore, most of the work appears to have been rote practice. Journal writing was about the only time children could write for themselves, with the teacher as an occasional, delayed audience. There was no significant modeling of the writing process by the teacher.

Alisa noticed that as a kindergarten student, Francisco appeared to learn new ideas quickly. He remembered earlier activities and things he had learned and connected them to new concepts. He recognized the names of his classmates on their crayon boxes and cubbies. He appeared to understand directions, but liked to confirm that understanding by first observing other children as they worked. This is not unremarkable for children who are dealing with directions given in their second language. Alisa reported that Francisco got along well with other children in the room and was cooperative with adults. He was friendly and kind toward others.

In general, Francisco's kindergarten year seems to be one in which he was expected to do—or perhaps not to do—what everyone else was doing—work that in my professional opinion lacked authenticity, purpose, and meaning. It's not hard to see why Francisco might have been hesitant to write his name and have eventually given up the effort, knowing he would not be able to produce the letters, neatly written on the lines, with both upper- and lowercase letters correctly made. His obvious physical and communicative differences came to be regarded as intellectual deficiencies, and not much was done to alter his learning contexts and activities. It also seems that no one other than Alisa took much note of his literacy-related accomplishments.

The Evaluation for Special Education

Francisco was tested during the summer between kindergarten and first grade. The tests were administered in his neighborhood school on two separate days and were broken down into fifteen- or twenty-minute sessions. All of the people who tested Francisco were strangers. For each test Francisco was alone in the room with the tester.

The context of the testing is very important; the administrators of the psychological and diagnostic tests and the speech therapist described Francisco as "anxious," "distracted," "shy," and having "difficulty maintaining" eye contact." Francisco's mother said he was very nervous before and during the tests. He chewed on his fingers and tongue and asked her repeatedly not to leave him alone with strangers. Given this information, his behavior is not nearly so aberrant as it is typical of a frightened six-year-old who does not understand the purpose or meaning of what is happening to him. Even though the testers acknowledged the behavior, they did not consider that the difficulties Francisco experienced in the testing situation might be socially constructed.[1]

Considering Francisco's limited experience with schooling, the psychologist and diagnostician administered an impressive battery of instruments. Their phase of the testing took place on June 6, 1994. According to the bilingual diagnostic team's placement summary and the psychologist's report, the tests included:

Weschler Preschool and Primary Scale of Intelligence—Revised (WPPSI-R)
    Verbal Scales: Information
                    Similarities
                    Arithmetic
                    Vocabulary
                    Comprehension
    Performance Scales: Picture Completion
                    Geometric Design
                    Block Design
                    Object Assembly
                    Mazes
                    (Animal Pegs)
Raven's Coloured Progressive Matrices
Vineland Adaptive Behavior Scales
Bender Gestalt
Beery Developmental Test of Visual Motor Integration
Draw a Person
Kinetic Family Drawing
Bateria Woodcock-Johnson
    Cognitive Tests: Broad Cognitive Ability
                    Oral Language
                    Reasoning
                    Processing Speed
    Achievement Tests: Reading
                    Mathematics
                    Written Language
                    Skills

Also given weight in the psychologist's report were earlier measures, including a Vocabulario en Imágenes Peabody (the Spanish version of the Peabody Picture Vocabulary Test [PPVT]) and Francisco's earlier speech and language evaluation.

The speech therapist made the following assessments on June 20, 1994:

Narrative Language Sample
Prueba de Expresión Oral y Percepción de la Lengua Española (PEOPLE)
    Auditory Association
    Sentence Repetition
    Story Comprehension
    Encoding
Spanish Articulation Measure (SAM)

There were notable inconsistencies in the test results, and problems with the tests themselves. Although the psychologist noted some of these inconsistencies and problems in her report, the test results were still considered in determining Francisco's ultimate classification and placement.

The most serious problem was with the WPPSI-R. The Spanish translation of this test is considered to produce invalid results because it has not been normed for Spanish speakers and because it is a translation. Figueroa notes that translating psychometric properties from one language to another is difficult, if not impossible.[2] A word in English may not be a word of similar difficulty when translated to Spanish. On the WISC-R, a test similar to the WPPSI-R but geared for slightly older children, words that appeared early on the vocabulary subtest were easier in Spanish. But after item 16, the opposite occurred. Moreover, even when Spanish norms are available for intelligence tests, they are usually normed on monolingual Spanish-speaking populations, such as the Mexico City tests.[3] Such instruments fail to take into account the complex factors associated with becoming bilingual and the interplay between language loss and language acquisition among bilingual children in the United States.[4]

Francisco's scores on the WPPSI-R were considered an underestimation of his ability, given these test limitations. The bilingual diagnostic team ultimately decided on a label of severely learning disabled for Francisco, as opposed to the mildly mentally retarded label that would normally be made based on low scores on the WPPSI-R. Nevertheless, the scores were still listed on the Summary of Placement Form, a document that could be viewed by anyone examining the cumulative record folder. The implications here are not to be dismissed lightly. When the occupational therapist who worked with Francisco interviewed me about Francisco's performance in my classroom, she asked me whether I considered him to be a "meemer." She had to explain to me that it meant mildly mentally retarded (MMR). Even though the MMR label is nowhere to be found on the placement documents, that was the interpretation she made after reviewing the test results.

Of further interest with regard to the WPPSI-R was Francisco's relative strength in visual spatial reasoning as measured by the object assembly subtest and picture completion subtest. His average score on Raven's Coloured Progressive Matrices was further evidence of this strength. Yet, on other tests, notably the Bender Gestalt and VMI, visual processing was found to be moderately to severely impaired. In spite of these inconsistencies, Francisco was found to have visual motor deficits. Francisco also scored within the average range on the vocabulary subtest, yet the speech therapist cites weaknesses in receptive and expressive vocabulary.

Tests with similar problems between English and Spanish versions are the Peabody Picture Vocabulary test and the Woodcock-Johnson Psychoeducational Battery. Francisco was given both of these tests, even though some special education professionals feel that the Woodcock-Johnson is not appropriate for kindergarten children. On the Woodcock-Johnson, Francisco scored in the first and second percentile in all subtests of the cognitive battery. His scores on the achievement tests were higher, particularly on the reading subtest, where his score fell within the average range. Yet only the low scores were given any weight in the overall diagnosis. The reading subtest score was dismissed as most likely inflated.

Lisa, the speech therapist who had worked with Francisco during the second semester of kindergarten, did not administer the testing done during the summer before first grade. However, at the placement conference, she questioned the interpretation of test results. Originally, Francisco's IEP for speech dealt only with fluency. Lisa felt that the articulation problems observed in kindergarten were most likely developmental, or at the very least, that it was too early to tell. By the end of kindergarten, Francisco had partially met all objectives listed on his IEP. By the time Lisa reassessed him the following September, he had totally met two of three objectives.

I did not question that Francisco needed help developing strategies to assist him with fluency and perhaps articulation. (I thought it was still too early to make a decision about articulation, since Francisco was missing three front teeth at the time he began working in the Sunshine Room.) Francisco's anxious state of mind also most likely had some impact on the speech and language testing. He had a tendency to stutter more when he was excited or upset. Additionally, the interpretation of moderate to severely impaired language skills seemed inconsistent with the test results. On the Prueba de Expresión Oral y Percepción de la Lengua Española (PEOPLE), Francisco scored within the mean on three of the four subtests: auditory association, sentence repetition, and encoding. On the story completion subtest his score was one standard deviation below the mean. Furthermore, his problems with lexical specificity related to words that are learned in contexts that may not have been within the range of Francisco's experiences. The errors listed under "sentence types" and "types of errors" did not conform to standardized Spanish, but are acceptable in the dialect of most of the bilingual children attending school in this area.

Interestingly, the speech therapist recommended a "language enriched program with speech and language services" for Francisco. It's quite a contrast from the placement that was made: a self-contained, special education classroom where several of the students did not communicate orally at all.

Francisco's overall evaluation report found him to have severe visual motor and auditory processing problems based on test results. He was labeled severely learning disabled and speech and language impaired. Although a classroom observation was done, it was obvious from the date on the observation form (September 7, 1994) and the observer's comments that the decision to place Francisco in a special education track had already been made. The observation was done the day of the formal placement conference,[5] for only thirty minutes. There was no description of the activity going on in the classroom at the time, other than the word *seatwork*. The only comments were, "Observations were consistent with referral reasons. Needs small-group classroom setting with special assistance." While the report from the psychologist regarding intellectual, processing, and achievement testing occupies five singled-spaced, typewritten pages, this brief one-page observation checklist was the only nontest data presented at the placement meeting held September 22, 1994. On September 27, Francisco was withdrawn from his neighborhood school and bussed to Borton, the school where I teach, and assigned to the special education classroom.

The tests only described what Francisco was able to do in a testing context, with strangers, under considerable pressure and anxiety. They in no way described

Francisco as a learner within a classroom or outside school. Furthermore, the administrators of the tests failed to question the appropriateness of the education program that had been offered to Francisco. During over a year in school, little effort had been made to expand the range of activities or accepted responses to activities in order to allow Francisco to experience success. For whatever reason, there are few records of what Francisco was able to do in his classroom and none of these formed part of the placement report.

My purpose in describing the testing in such detail and pointing out inconsistencies in scores is not to discredit the overworked diagnostic team. I hope only to create enough doubt about the adequacy of such measures to encourage us all to ask and seek answers to a wider range of questions about the learning of children. Clearly, once Francisco had been referred for testing, all the evaluation data was interpreted pathologically. The only question was which label and how severe.

I Meet Francisco

Before I was introduced to Francisco, I met with Rosalie, his teacher in the cross-categorical bilingual (CCB) special education class to which he had been assigned at the beginning of first grade. Rosalie explained that Francisco appeared to have good language and social skills that would enable him to participate comfortably in our multiage primary class. Also, Francisco knew Jessica, one of my students who Rosalie saw as a resource student and who worked as a cross-age helper in Rosalie's class. She was sure that Jessica would be able to help Francisco adapt to new children and situations, and Jessica was more than happy to oblige.

We agreed that Francisco would join us for free time, on Fridays, and during interest centers, when activities were usually quite open ended and often carried out collaboratively. He would start by mainstreaming for one hour a day, and we agreed to expand the time if he met with success.

The first day Francisco came to the room, near the end of September, Rosalie accompanied him. We were studying chemistry, beginning with explorations of bubbles and the three states of matter. Francisco joined us for an activity that involved sorting solid objects by criteria determined by the children, describing the sorting characteristics, and coming to some conclusion about the properties that define solids. Interacting with Rosalie, and occasionally with Jessica, Francisco sorted his collection of objects into two groups. After sharing with others at his table his rules for sorting, he drew pictures of his objects on a Venn diagram. Rosalie helped him label the groups by showing him which words to copy from the list of properties on the chalkboard. Then she wrote his name on a piece of scrap paper and watched as Francisco copied his name onto his paper.

We all rated this first mainstream experience highly successful. Francisco enjoyed himself and smiled broadly when told he could return the next day. Rosalie was delighted with the kinesthetic aspect of the activities and their potential for Francisco's learning. I was pleased that he was able to participate meaningfully and make a contribution to the group's growing body of knowledge about solids. Jessica proudly and helpfully offered to place Francisco's paper in her folder until we could prepare one for him.

The following day, Rosalie brought Francisco to me at pledge in the patio. She asked if Francisco could go into the Sunshine Room for our opening story, while she attended to some other students. She promised to join us by the time we began our science work. Francisco entered and sat near the center of the group, where he listened politely and with interest to the story.

Rosalie joined him for the start of the day's science work. We continued the previous day's sorting, this time using more than one criteria at a time, such as "red and plastic." When Rosalie observed that Francisco seemed engaged, she left, assuring Francisco that she would return for him shortly. She reminded him that Jessica was nearby and would help if needed. This time, Francisco spent a considerable period of time watching his tablemates work. Finally, he completed the activity for himself. As we finished, he noticed that the pencil we had given him to use had his name on it. Letter by letter, he copied his name onto his paper. Jessica showed him how to file his work into a folder of his own that Renée had prepared. When Rosalie returned, he talked excitedly about what he had done.

Francisco joined us daily for our science centers for the next two weeks. He needed help making use of resources like word lists and labels in the room, but he never hesitated to try anything that any of the children were doing. He watched them carefully to see how to proceed. During one exploration that involved sorting small solids (like beans) by sifting them through different-size mesh screens, Francisco was able to identify which screen would be needed to sort out any particular solid. He was able to do the sifting and particularly seemed to enjoy running his fingers through the beans. Following my modeling on the chalkboard, he was able to draw pictures of the different gauges of mesh into his science journal. His pictures were immature and somewhat uncontrolled, but there were noticeable differences in the sizes of openings among the screens he drew. I noticed he did not look at his pencil when it came time to write his name on his paper.

Francisco's early participation in the class was so successful that Rosalie and I expanded the time he spent with us. By late October, he began coming in for math, art, and music, although he still spent most afternoons in the CCB class for language arts. Rosalie revealed that, from the very beginning of the year, she had felt Francisco's placement in self-contained special education was inappropriate. My own observations of Francisco in our regular classroom convinced me of that, too.

By the end of November, Rosalie and I had decided to request that Francisco's placement and Individual Education Plan (IEP) be changed, assigning him to my classroom, with Rosalie providing daily resource assistance, a sort of reverse mainstreaming arrangement. Rosalie called the regional service center and was told that services to Francisco could not be disrupted, that the mainstreaming needed to occur in a single-grade class at his grade level (meaning a straight first grade rather than my multigrade class), and that no one from the service center would be able to meet with us for at least two weeks. Rosalie was flushed and upset.

At this point, Rosalie talked with the principal, who, after talking with me, made this decision (his note to Rosalie is dated November 29, 1994):

> We will maintain Francisco in Caryl Crowell's classroom for the present. It functions as a multiage primary bilingual classroom. Another student, Jessica, is at a similar level and sees you for resource. We would have to disrupt two other children and classrooms who have bonded already—and we will be moving from this building in several weeks. I don't think a move would be prudent or beneficial. I've spoken with the bilingual speech and language teacher and mainstream teacher as well.

Rosalie documented her position in this letter, dated December 4, 1994:

> To Whom It May Concern:
>
> I have been Francisco's classroom teacher since approximately September 26, 1994. Since the day I met Francisco, I felt he demonstrated good comprehension skills, social skills, and command of the Spanish language.
>
> I have conferred with several people on Francisco's abilities and classroom placement. I have met with the speech and language therapist, Lisa; the mainstream teacher, Caryl Crowell; the principal; my program specialist; the psychologist; and Francisco's mother. I have shared that Francisco's classroom observations and work indicate that he should primarily be placed in a regular classroom. He has demonstrated difficulty in eye-hand coordination, visual motor tasks, and visual perception. However, for a child his age, I do not feel there has been enough time for us to determine how much Francisco will be able to compensate for his difficulties.
>
> Francisco is functioning well most of the day that he spends time in his multiage regular bilingual classroom. His progress will be documented at a meeting that will be held December 12.
>
> I feel the copies of the testing you will be receiving are an inaccurate portrayal of Francisco's abilities. I am aware that Francisco has some difficulties, but in his mainstream classroom he appears to be an asset to the group and often makes valuable contributions. Observations show Francisco is able to do the work others are working on, experimenting with hands-on activities.
>
> If you would like to talk further with me, please call me at Borton Elementary School.
>
> Sincerely,

Lisa, the speech and language therapist assigned to work with Francisco, supported our decision. Her written comments, dated December 9, 1994, were:

> Re: Francisco
>
> I questioned his placement in the self-contained classroom at his IEP meeting. Francisco's language skills were severely delayed enough to require additional service in a self-contained classroom, but the psychologist was looking at Francisco's whole profile. There have been more severely language-impaired students (both at his home school and here at Borton) that weren't considered for self-contained placements, but received or will receive resource support. Francisco's comprehension of language, in Spanish and even in English, is good and he is now answering wrong on purpose (and laughing!) which makes it difficult to instruct other language-impaired students.

When the December 12 meeting was canceled by the regional service center staff, we decided to go ahead with our plans for reversing Francisco's mainstreaming arrangement. He would become a regular member of our class. Rosalie would continue to work with him on a resource basis, in our classroom whenever possible. Occasionally, she would ask him to come to her classroom, when her full-time students could not be in their mainstream classrooms. Additionally, she felt that Francisco would be a good model for the other children.

After the winter break and our move to a village of portables while our building was being renovated, I began to collect Francisco's work. His parents gave me permission to examine his special education records that were on file at Borton, both in his cumulative file and in the file that Rosalie maintained for him. I hoped to understand what Francisco's kindergarten year had been like and how he came to be placed in the CCB classroom. Alisa turned out to be an invaluable resource. I asked her to be sure to spend time working with Francisco whenever she was in our room, since her earlier experiences with him would provide a good perspective on his progress. I also interviewed her at length to find out more about his learning in kindergarten and the types of experiences and support offered to him in that classroom.

Alisa described Francisco's first-grade, mainstream classroom, the Sunshine Room, as being different from his kindergarten classroom in just about every way possible. The Sunshine Room is a multiage bilingual classroom that reflects a whole language approach to learning. The defining characteristics of this classroom have been identified as offering a high level of intellectual activities and expectations, symmetrical power and trust relationships among students and adults, authentically purposeful and meaningful learning, and additive bilingualism.[6] The children in the Sunshine Room have the right to negotiate their curriculum with the teacher, define their own questions for investigation, and enjoy learning and expressing their learning to authentic audiences for real purposes. They make use of many ways of knowing and sharing their knowledge, which include all sign systems and academic disciplines. Such practices are atypical of the learning environments usually found in classrooms that serve low-income minority children and children identified as learning disabled or mentally handicapped.

However, classrooms like the Sunshine Room are exactly what has been recommended for children caught up in the special education track. A recently developed curriculum guide in California, *The Optimal Learning Environment Curriculum Guide: A Resource for Teachers of Spanish-Speaking Children in Learning Handicapped Programs*,[7] identifies nine instructional principles grounded in research on bilingual children in special education programs:

1. Take into account student's sociocultural backgrounds and their effects on oral language, reading and writing, and second-language learning.
2. Take into account students' possible learning handicaps and their effects on oral language, reading and writing, and second-language learning.
3. Follow developmental processes in literacy acquisition.

4. Locate curriculum in a meaningful context where the communicative purpose is clear and authentic.
5. Connect curriculum with the students' personal experiences.
6. Incorporate children's literature into reading, writing, and English-as-a-second-language (ESL) lessons.
7. Involve parents as active partners in the instruction of their children.
8. Give students experience with whole texts in reading, writing, and ESL lessons.
9. Incorporate collaborative learning wherever possible.

As a teacher-researcher with twenty years experience in the classroom, I stand firmly behind my belief that these principles should be the foundation of curriculum for any child, not just exceptional learners. Moreover, I advocate that all children should have access to multiple sign systems for learning and the expression of learning. Verbal expression and literacy are not the only modes of expression in our world, yet they became the only modes of evaluating Francisco's progress in school. Goldberg writes,

> Teachers and learners bring with them to school a great variety of cultures, experiences, and histories. They also bring with them varied methods of expression. By restricting students to traditional ways of expression—and thus to traditional means of evaluation—teachers may be preventing these students from fully working with and displaying their knowledge. By widening their vision of acceptable expression and ways of knowing, teachers can begin to create a community in which students have the essential freedom to learn.[8]

Other studies of bilingual children identified as exceptional learners, like Francisco, recognize the situational variability in the performance of such children. Rueda and Mehan found that their study subjects displayed both competence and incompetence in reading and writing, depending on the way that the tasks were organized.[9] Competence was observed in situations that were more like out-of-school experiences. Willig and Swedo found more task engagement when students participated in classroom events that encouraged the expression of personal interests, experiences, and language backgrounds.[10] Trueba, on the other hand, identified classroom characteristics that resulted in a deterioration of student performance: a time-tabled rate of instruction, fragmented settings and activities, and unconcern for the children's cultural adjustments to school.[11]

That the Sunshine Room offered the very educational environment advocated by recent research in the field of bilingual special education was most likely a factor in Francisco's early mainstream success. It was certainly a consideration in the decision to expand Francisco's mainstream experience, essentially making the Sunshine Room his regular classroom, supported by extra resource help from Rosalie, the special education teacher.

No standardized, norm-referenced tests were given to document Francisco's progress in first grade. Instead, the adults who worked with him took the time to study his work and make careful, thoughtful observations of him in a wide variety of educational contexts. Additionally, we sought out anecdotes from his parents that attested to his literacy learning and other growing bodies of knowledge outside school.

Francisco Writes His Name

Writing his name from memory, a task that Francisco could not, or would not, learn in kindergarten, was quickly accomplished in the Sunshine Room. From the time he used his labeled pencil as a resource to write his name independently in October, Francisco's progress was steady and unrelenting. By November, he was using capital- and lowercase letters appropriately, although with reversals on e and b. These reversals, common to children well into second grade, were already beginning to change by January.

Thanks to a wealth of tactile and manipulative experiences that crossed the curriculum, Francisco was also gaining better control over his handwriting. By January, he was able to write his name in the space provided on a library card. He still preferred to use unlined paper, or to write in boxes rather than on lines. Because the emphasis of learning experiences was on coming to know and sharing that knowledge, Francisco was assured access to the materials and procedures that provided him success.

Even Francisco's drawings improved in detail and accuracy. His nature journal entry of December 8 (see Figure 3) shows a carefully drawn representation of the fountain in the bird sanctuary. It is easy to identify the rocks lining the banks of the artificial stream, the water trickling over the small boulders that conceal the pipes, and even the sun on this particularly bright day. A pop-up book he constructed in February includes several tiny, detailed sketches of ants on a movable strip and a small star on the chest of a policeman who comes to investigate a downed saguaro. Moreover, Francisco's drawings correspond to and support his text, as dictated to an adult, a text that reveals his understanding of the environmental and legal consequences of destroying this giant of the desert.

The adults, and even other children in the room, took care to ensure that Francisco's difficulties with handwriting and small motor tasks did not interfere with opportunities to acquire and express knowledge. When mathematics, science, or some other content area was the focus of learning, adults and peers assisted Francisco in recording his ideas. Sometimes we took dictation, other times we helped him sound out words or use a phonetic alphabet chart. At times, we gave him alternative materials. For example, in a mathematics activity that made use of mirror symmetry to portray addition doubles, rather than having him trace the pattern block shapes he used in his designs, we gave Francisco cutouts of the shapes, which he glued to paper. In this way, Francisco was able to demonstrate an understanding of both mirror symmetry and the addition.

Similar accommodations were made whenever the task involved tracing, coloring, or cutting. As part of a study of geometry, the class made tessellations in the style of M. C. Escher. Francisco used cardboard and sharp, Fiskar scissors for children, rather than paper and the plastic scissors young children are usually given.

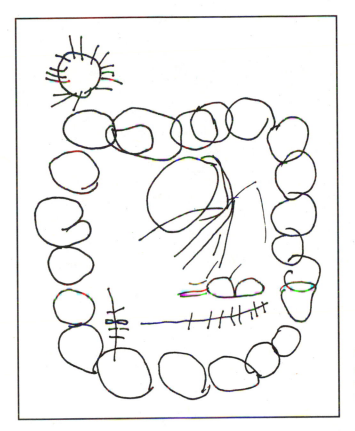

Figure 3

Francisco's drawing of a fountain and stream in the bird sanctuary

An adult held his tessellation piece in place while he traced. When it became apparent that coloring the resulting design was frustrating Francisco, we took discarded kindergarten crayons, broke them into inch and two-inch pieces, and removed the paper wrappers. By rubbing the sides of the crayons across the paper, Francisco was able to color his design more quickly and with more control.

Francisco's literacy was also developing steadily. Throughout the year, he had many opportunities to use literacy, both reading and writing, in a wide variety of contexts and genres. He enjoyed predictable materials, such as Sunshine Books and Story Box books in Spanish. Francisco was able to identify individual words in these books, often using beginning sounds to help him. He also made regular use of picture cues and wrote his own versions of the patterned language presented in these books. Toward the end of the year, rather than dictate these variations of patterns to an adult, Francisco began to write them in his own hand with an adult or classmate helping him spell the words. Songs and nursery rhymes that he knew became the content for these books. At the end of April, Francisco was observed reading Spanish predictable books that he knew to John, who read to Francisco from English predictable books in return.

Francisco also participated in literature study groups of his own choosing. An adult or a peer buddy needed to read the books to him, but he enthusiastically joined in the discussions. He routinely recognized characters, recalled plot details, and made connections to other books he had been read. His developing sense of story was most evident in the stories he authored and dictated to adults, times when he could focus on the story meaning and not on the labored process of writing it down.

Throughout the year, his stories got longer and he used more narrative and poetic devices. A creation story written in early February contains the characteristics of the genre, including a sustained metaphor of pianos as the creators of music and the givers of musical knowledge. The story contains five compound and complex sentences, with dependent clauses and appropriate subject-verb, noun-adjective correspondence. A story about dinosaur footprints from March (see Figure 4) reflects Francisco's understanding of the scientific theory regarding the evolution of dinosaurs into birds. He assumes a role as a character in the story and includes details of the setting. In April, he chose to author a self-initiated story about the stars, our topic of study at the time. Alisa took his dictation for this story,

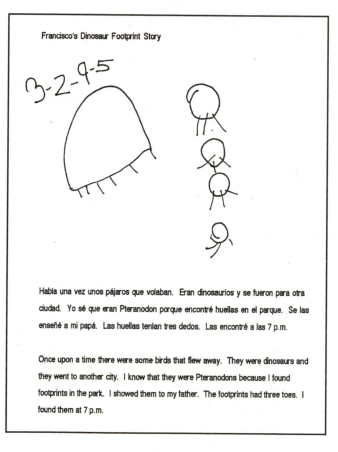

Francisco's Dinosaur Footprint Story

3-2-9-5

Había una vez unos pájaros que volaban. Eran dinosaurios y se fueron para otra ciudad. Yo sé que eran Pteranodon porque encontré huellas en el parque. Se las enseñé a mi papá. Las huellas tenían tres dedos. Las encontré a las 7 p.m.

Once upon a time there were some birds that flew away. They were dinosaurs and they went to another city. I know that they were Pteranodons because I found footprints in the park. I showed them to my father. The footprints had three toes. I found them at 7 p.m.

Figure 4

Francisco's dinosaur footprint story

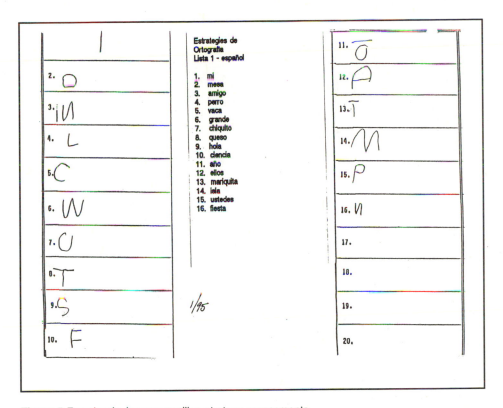

Figure 5 Francisco's January spelling strategy assessments

in which a character from the Greek legends we had been reading, Orion, combines forces with Batman to make the stars shine brighter.

The previous fall, Francisco knew the names and sounds of some letters, but not enough to help him identify many beginning sounds in a brief spelling strategies survey, done in early January (see Figure 5). Later that month, on a trip to the optometrist, Francisco was able to read the letter chart in both Spanish and English. His mother was quite surprised. She and her husband were discovering that Francisco knew things they were not aware of. Francisco's mother also told me that his favorite pastime on shopping excursions was reading signs. Mervyn's was the first sign that she was aware he could read. If he didn't immediately recognize what the signs said, he spelled out the letters and tried to sound out the words. I encouraged her to support this activity even though it sometimes slowed them down when they were in a hurry. The pragmatic context of Francisco's environmental literacy was an important factor in his early reading development.

Proof that Francisco was transfering this knowledge to classroom contexts came with his performance on a spelling strategies assessment on April 26 (see Figure 6). With the support of his phonetic alphabet chart and an adult to help him focus

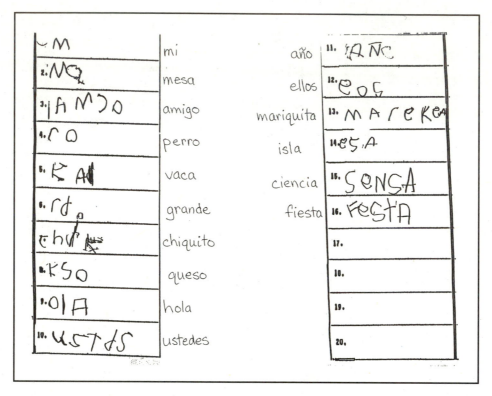

Figure 6 Adults helped Francisco move from one syllable to the next. He used an abc chart as a reference.

on the sounds of successive syllables, Francisco was able to write many of the letters in the words. Some spellings approached conventional spelling, especially toward the end of the survey, suggesting that he was learning more about how to spell as the work proceeded.

Despite this success, Francisco was still reluctant to write, perhaps because early demands for success had been unreasonable given his difficulty with small motor movements and the lack of authenticity and audience in the writing assignments. In what little time was left in the year, we hoped to be able to convince him that he had made sufficient progress to assume this new level of control over his learning. A subsequent observation convinced me that my optimism was not unfounded. Francisco was Alberto's partner on a research project about Pluto. I helped both boys locate appropriate information about the planet and helped Francisco sound out the name of the planet to write on his paper. Together Francisco and I worked on some other details to record, and I moved on to work with other children, leaving Alberto with Francisco. At last glance, both boys were working. The following day, a teaching assistant from the CCB class came in to help Francisco. I explained what we were working on, and left to attend to other students. When I glanced over to see how things were going, the teaching assistant was holding the pencil and Francisco was looking disinterested. When she left the room, Francisco got up from the table and spent the next ten minutes wandering the room. I remarked at how much more engaged he was when he had control and ownership in the process.

Francisco as a Conversant in the Room

Francisco's verbal and communicative development was just as noticeable as his academic growth. He talked often in many contexts, in one-to-one conversations with adults and children and in small- and large-group discussions. He often shared his experiences outside school. We noticed that when he was calm and took a moment to think, he spoke much more fluently. Stuttering was worst when he was excited and eager to tell us something. Everyone in the room was willing to wait to hear what he had to say. Only rarely, did we have trouble understanding him.

The stories that Francisco dictated to others revealed his enriched vocabulary and poetic sensibility. His participation in classroom discussions also highlighted his use of language to convey meaning. During a lesson with our counselor on the similarities among people and the differences that make each of us unique, the children were asked to compare a banana and an orange as an example. The class suggested characteristics for lists entitled Same and Different. Eventually the "same" list included "they both are plastic, they both have seeds, they're both fruits, they both have skin, you can eat both." "Anything else?" the counselor asked. Francisco raised his hand and contributed, "Los dos tienen olor" [They both have a smell.]

Francisco was also able to make choices about whether to use Spanish or English in a given situation. Most often, audience determined his language choice. The children had made 3-D thank-you notes shaped like crystals for Erin's father, a chemistry professor, to thank him for his help with our crystal-growing experiments. Jenny, a monolingual native speaker of English, and I were assembling the shapes to hang from a mobile. By the time the class began to clean up at the end of the day, we had successfully managed to balance about half of the shapes. They spun smoothly around the central string when we gave the sticks a light touch. Francisco came over and remarked, "It looks like a ballerina dancing."

Francisco as a Learner

Throughout the year, it was clear that Francisco used some learning processes that made him different from others. He learned by watching others, meaning that providing demonstrations for him to observe was crucial to his success. Although his small motor skills had improved, he needed to be accommodated with different materials or ways of working. The computer proved to be a very useful support for Francisco's emerging literacy. It enabled us to enlarge the print of Francisco's self-authored books and other reading materials, such as puppet-play scripts, so that they were easier for him to read.

In other ways, Francisco was like nonlabeled learners. He made use of his life experiences to support his learning and connected previously learned information to new ideas. He expressed new information through writing, art, mathematics, and conversation. Two of my favorite anecdotes from the year exemplify his ability.

In early February, Francisco and several other students received large stamplike stickers as a reward for bringing their evaluation portfolios back to school from home. Carlos asked if he could use the stamp to mail a letter. I explained that he could cover a letter with these stickers and the post office would still not deliver it, that he would need to buy special stamps at the post office to mail a letter. Francisco, who had been listening, raised his hand and told us that it was like the little boy who covered his baby sister with stamps because he wanted to mail her away. I asked him what the boy's name was. He replied, "It was really funny." "Fudgie?" I asked him. He said yes and explained he had seen it on TV. It's also a scene from *Superfudge*, by Judy Blume. When I told his mother about the incident, she remembered how amused he had been when he saw this episode over a year earlier. He certainly remembered and made an appropriate connection.

In April, we began working with our artist-in-residence, Debra Stevens, an actor from Childsplay, a Tempe dramatics group. After helping the children discover what tools an actor uses—body, voice, and imagination—Debra used her voice to show how a character being portrayed could be different from the person doing the acting. The children guessed she was Cinderella's stepmother or an evil queen. She affirmed she was a queen and asked the children which one. Some children guessed the queen in *Snow White*, the witch in *Sleeping Beauty*, or the witch in *Wizard of Oz*. Francisco correctly identified the character as the Queen of Hearts from *Alice in Wonderland*. The other children, adults, and Debra, were duly and audibly impressed.

Recommendations for Francisco

By the end of his first-grade year, I hoped that next year Francisco would return as a second-grader with the Sunshine Room as his full-time classroom. In this utopia that I constructed in my imagination, there would be no special education labels. In the Sunshine Room, and at Borton School, Francisco was most definitely not regarded as mildly mentally retarded, severely learning disabled, or language impaired. Francisco was supported as a learner in whatever ways he was best able to take responsibility for his own learning. He received help for his fluency problems from the speech and language therapist, within the context of the classroom.

For a brief time, Francisco received additional support from the Literacy Assistance Project (LAP), a program that provides regular, focused support in the use of reading and writing strategies for children who appear to have difficulty acquiring these processes. Francisco was invited to join the LAP group in my class during the spring, for about a week, when one of the other members was absent. He enjoyed the experience and felt successful, as it appeared to meet his needs for learning new literacy ideas.

Francisco's parents were made to feel they were partners in his learning—after all much important learning takes place outside school. And Francisco continued to be offered a rich learning environment where multiple intelligences and ways of knowing were recognized and fostered, the kind of context often reserved for so-called gifted students, which Francisco may very well be. Who knows?

The Year-End Review

On May 1, 1995, Francisco's annual placement review was held after school. I was prepared to support my view of Francisco as a successful student within the regular classroom. I came armed with a thick folder of his collected work and several copies of this case study. It was my hope somehow to convince the representative from the bilingual diagnostic team to reconsider the wisdom of their decision without personally offending anyone. I wasn't convinced I'd be able to do it.

Fortunately, it wasn't necessary. The bilingual diagnostic team was too overwhelmed with other referrals to attend. The regional service center did not send a representative, and the psychologist assigned to our school called in sick. The only people present were Rosalie, Lisa, Francisco's mother, and me. We wasted no time disposing of our agenda.

We shared many examples of Francisco's progress with his mother. I reviewed the testing that had been done the previous summer and explained some of the inconsistencies that I had noticed and the problems with the tests that had been documented by other researchers. Lisa supported my conclusions by showing how her evaluation of Francisco had differed from the one done by the other speech and language therapist. Rosalie noted that the progress Francisco had made in first grade was accomplished in a regular classroom, since he spent very little time during the year in the special education classroom. All of us agreed that Francisco should not be a special education student. On the last day of this school year, Francisco was dropped from special education. He would continue to receive support from a speech and language therapist, but only for fluency and, later, for articulation, if necessary. The language-impaired label was removed. Unfortunately, Francisco would no longer be eligible to receive services from the occupational therapist for muscle tone and motor coordination. However, the types of activities provided by this specialist could easily be accomplished at home and in a regular classroom setting.

Francisco's mother was eager for him to return to Borton for second grade. Unfortunately, Rosalie was assigned only kindergarten and first-grade students. Since the family did not live in the Borton School neighborhood and Francisco was a minority student not eligible for magnet status, he would be unable to return without special consideration from our district's central administration. Francisco's mother wrote a letter to the school principal, outlining her request and reasons for wanting him to continue at Borton, in the Sunshine Room. The principal was supportive and directed the request to the appropriate person in central administration.

While we awaited a response, Francisco's mother visited second-grade classrooms at the neighborhood school, hoping to find a place that would nurture her son. At our urging, she also made an appointment with the regional service center to ask that all documentation related to the special education testing and placement be removed. I offered to prepare a version of this case study for her, since she wanted it to be included in his file. On last day of school, I told Francisco, "I hope I'll see you in August."

Epilogue

The following August, the school district granted permission for Francisco to return to Borton School, and he was assigned to the Sunshine Room for second grade. He bounded in the door of the classroom and announced to a few newcomers that he would be able to help them since he had been a Sunshine Room student the year before.

Throughout second grade, Francisco has continued to receive help with articulation and fluency from the same speech and language therapist, Lisa. She has worked with him almost exclusively within the classroom and usually joins in the work of the class with Francisco and his group members. Since Francisco is no longer classified as a special education student, he has been eligible for inclusion in the Literacy Assistance Project (LAP). His stuttering is noticeably improved. Recently he was overheard defending himself to a child who had been teasing him. Francisco scolded the other child, "Don't make fun of me. I have good things to say. You should listen." Francisco is also quite bilingual and uses both Spanish and English throughout the day with both children and adults.

Remarkably, Francisco's normal growth has reduced his problems with nearsightedness enough that he no longer needs his glasses. He is currently undergoing physical therapy to strengthen his eye muscles in the hopes of avoiding surgery. Although the lack of tone in his eye muscles makes it difficult for him to fix his gaze on a page of print, he is emerging as a reader and writer.

All year, he has met three days a week, for thirty minutes each day, in a group of four students, with a special tutor who supports literacy development through contextualized reading and writing activities. On other days, he can often be found reading on a bean bag in the library corner, surrounded by a number of his favorite books. He still requires adult help to focus on his writing long enough to complete a story. However, when an adult reminds him to slow down as he sounds out words, he is able to produce spelling close enough to conventional spelling that others can read his work. His small motor skills have improved enough so that he was recently able to contribute to the production of an animated film, hand-drawn on bleached-out 8mm film with fine-point permanent markers.

Last week, Francisco presented his evaluation portfolio to his mother. He removed each piece of work he had selected for sharing from his folder and told his mother why he had chosen it and what he had learned. His progress since our first meeting at the beginning of his first grade year was undeniable.

Francisco will still need extra support from peers and caring, knowledgeable adults for a while longer. However, I believe he has adequately demonstrated, over the last two years, that he does not require a restrictive, or sheltered, special education classroom. In a regular classroom that offers a stimulating, literate environment and many ways of constructing meaning, Francisco can reveal himself as a learner.

Endnotes

1. D. Taylor, *From the Child's Point of View* (Portsmouth, NH: Heinemann, 1993). **2.** R. A. Figueroa, "Psychological Testing of Linguistic-Minority Students: Knowledge Gaps and Regulations," *Exceptional Children* 56 (2): 145–52 (1989). **3.** R. A. Figueroa, G. L. Delgado, and N. T. Ruiz, "Assessment of Hispanic Children: Implications for Hispanic Hearing Impaired Children," in *The Hispanic Deaf: Issues and Challenges for Bilingual Special Education*, edited by G. L. Delgado, 124–53 (Washington, DC: Gallauder College Press, 1984). **4.** R. A. Figueroa 1989. **5.** A conference with teachers and specialists to review test results and recommentations. The formal placement conference includes the parents. Test results, IEPs, and recommended services, including labels, are signed. **6.** K. F. Whitmore and C. G. Crowell, *Inventing a Classroom: Life in a Whole Language, Bilingual Learning Community* (York, ME: Stenhouse, 1994). **7.** N. T. Ruiz, "An Optimal Learning Environment for Rosemary," *Exceptional Children* 56 (2): 130–44 (1989). **8.** M. Goldberg, "Expressing and Assessing Understanding Through the Arts," *Phi Delta Kappan* 73 (8): 619–23 (1992). **9.** R. Rueda and H. Mehan, "Metacognition and Passing: Strategic Interactions in the Lives of Students with Learning Disabilities," *Anthropology and Education Quarterly* 17: 145–65 (1986). **10.** A. Willig and J. Swedo, *Improving Teaching Strategies for Exceptional Hispanic Limited English Proficient Students: An Exploratory Study of Task Engagement and Teaching Strategies.* Paper presented at the April annual meeting of the American Educational Research Association in Washington, DC, 1987. **11.** H. T. Trueba, "Cultural Differences or Learning Handicaps? Towards an Understanding of Adjustment Processes," in *Schooling Language-Minority Youth, Vol. III. Proceedings of the University of California Linguistic-Minority Research Project Conference*, 45–47 (Los Angeles: University of California, 1987).

Denny: One of the things you focus on at the beginning of your essay is all of the tests that were done and all of the official documentation. I think a lot of teachers get overwhelmed by the officialness of paper in kids' cumulative records or in their special education folders. If I were a young teacher and there was a kid that I was really concerned about, and I wanted to get into his folder and try to understand what's in there, and not just take it as truth, what would I do?

CARYL: First, you'd have to realize that if the child has already been in special education or if a referral has been made, there are two separate folders. That was one of the first things I discovered, because the only thing that I found related to the special education evaluation in Francisco's regular cumulative folder was the report from the placement meeting and a copy of his IEPs. All of the other things, like the tests and the written-out psychologist's report, were kept in a special education folder at the regional service center, and only the adaptive education teacher had access to it. The speech therapist also had a folder. So here we have a child who is six years old in first grade, and if you stacked all the folders up together they'd be inches thick, literally.

Denny: There were at least three folders?

CARYL: Yes, at least three. The psychologist's report wasn't too bad to get through. That's written out as a narrative. You start looking at the other tests, and scores, percentiles, standard deviations, and then the kind of language that's used to describe the results of the stuff; I just didn't understand. I found myself having to go and talk to the special education teacher and the speech therapist: Tell me what this means in real language with a real kid sitting in front of me. What does it mean to a student? The other thing that was interesting to me was just learning about the context for the testing. I think that's something that I probably wouldn't have considered before I took your class. Although I knew they took kids off to a little room, I hadn't really thought a lot about the impact that would have on a very young child: Francisco was stuck in a room with people he didn't know. Those children are very unlikely to talk a lot to anybody. That was a concern to me. What I tried to do was cut around all the myth that surrounds that.

Denny: Not to take them as the truth, but as documents that have been developed in ways that may not have anything to do with what happens when this kid is in a regular classroom?

CARYL: Well, that's an issue I've had for quite some time with the kind of testing that goes on, because I've seen this battle before with kids who supposedly weren't learning to read. And when you look at what's actually given in the form of a reading test, it's a short paragraph, maybe a cloze paragraph, and a few questions. There is no great length of text to support building meaning, no opportunity for a child to retell a story, which might give you other kinds of information. It's nothing like the activity that goes on in a classroom. So I would question, naturally. Obviously the kinds of things I was finding out that supposedly were problems for Francisco based on test results didn't fit the picture I was seeing in the classroom, and I wasn't the only one thinking that. His adaptive education teacher had the same kinds of questions. His speech therapist, who had worked with him in kindergarten, didn't agree with the placement at all, because she had known him even before the referral. It wasn't fitting together; we had two very different views of this child. When I started gathering up real classroom work for us to look at . . .

Denny: And comparing it to what was in the cumulative folder, you had a much different picture?

CARYL: He was obviously learning. And true, he did have vision problems at the time, and he was stuttering. But if you were able to get him calm so that he could get control of his speech, and you were really willing to listen to what he had to say, you found out that you had a child who understood language, who communicated effectively in spite of his articulation and stuttering problems, who was becoming bilingual, who made jokes and riddles that were like every other first and second grader's jokes and riddles: not really much different. And he had a lot of things to say. He had a lot of knowledge about the world, remembered stuff that had happened a long, long time ago, and was able to fit pieces together.

Denny: A new teacher who really is very concerned about a particular child in her room first of all has to find out how many folders there are. I know when I was working with Patrick, we'd asked for and we used to get the files, and this folder was never given to us. We'd been working nearly a year when his mother found this folder in the special education office in the administration building. It wasn't until she'd specifically asked, "Are there any other folders?" that someone said, "Oh, yes. The director of special education has another folder." So finding those folders becomes a quest.

CARYL: Because I was working together with the special education teacher in this situation, she knew.

Denny: This is a wonderful example of collaboration between a classroom teacher and a special education teacher.

CARYL: Well, this was a special education teacher who essentially had a whole language classroom. I mean, the kinds of things she did with her students, even though they were hard of hearing or physically impaired, were the same kinds of rich activities that you would do in any classroom for young children. She shared a lot of beliefs with the other teachers on the faculty and really got her children involved in life at school, to as great an extent as they were able. Of course, Francisco, the child in this particular piece, was much more able to be a part of a regular classroom and probably should have been. A much more appropriate decision would have been to give him resource support, rather than pull him out of a classroom and put him in a place where he wasn't going to have children who could communicate with him. Even though her classroom was a wonderful place for kids, it wasn't a suitable place for him.

Denny: For each of the authors in this book, one of the things that's been most important is to be able to get the official documentation and to be able to in some way deconstruct it. And yet it's very clear that a lot of that documentation is hard to come by; even if the teacher is resourceful, some information is not available, whether it's in a special education file that someone doesn't tell you about or it's held by other agencies. Probably for very legitimate reasons they feel that they cannot give you the information, but making educational decisions becomes incredibly difficult for teachers when they don't have access to the information they need to make these decisions.

CARYL: You're making decisions based on, well, I hope the assumptions I'm making about this situation are accurate or at least close. With Francisco I had access to documents because I knew this special education teacher. But I also knew that if the parent went down and demanded them, she had a right to see them.

Denny: So if a teacher was working with the parents in the way that I was when I was working with Patrick, then some advice for a teacher to give is for the parents to go and ask, and that parents have a legal right to everything that is in the special education folder; although a teacher might not be able to access that folder very easily, if he or she is working with the parent it becomes much easier.

CARYL: Well, I don't know about easier. When we held Francisco's year-end placement review, when no one from the bilingual diagnostic team showed up at our school and the psychologist assigned was sick, it was just me and the speech therapist and the special education teacher and his mother. At that time we made a decision to drop the learning-disabled and the severely language-impaired labels. The special education teacher told the mother, "You have a right to remove documents from his file," and she gave Francisco's mom a list of what she could take out, and she showed her copies.

Denny: Parents have a right to remove things from the folders?

CARYL: Yes. He wasn't in the program anymore, and she could remove the documents related to his testing.

Denny: Because he had left the program, she could remove them. If he were still in the program?

CARYL: Probably not. I'm guessing about that, but probably not. But she called the regional service office at the end of the year, and they gave her the runaround for a long, long time. She should have been able to just walk in there and ask to see the folder. Instead, they gave her a whole lot of rigmarole about making appointments, and needing to talk to this person and the other. When I ran into her close to the end of June—school had been out for a month—she still had not been able to get into that office to see his folder, so I gave her the home telephone number of a special education teacher that worked with us and said, "You need to call her, and she'll help you get in there and see that folder." They weren't going to ultimately deny her right to see that folder, but they were going to make it difficult for her, and she doesn't speak English. I think sometimes people make it difficult for parents like that. Sometimes we have parents that aren't here legally and they won't get involved with that stuff at all because they are scared to death that they might get sent back across the border. In our school right now we have parents who won't come to the school. They're afraid to come out of their homes because they're afraid they might get deported; it's hard for those parents to get involved in their kids' education.

Denny: Many teachers find themselves with children in their classrooms who are learning English, it's their second language, whose parents are still speaking the first language at home. I had an interesting conversation at IRA with a community worker working in an adult literacy program that begins by teaching mothers to read in Spanish, which is their first language. Then once they are fluent in reading Spanish, they move on to English. Someone was talking to her at IRA, who should have known better, who said, "My parents came to this country not speaking English, and they learned to speak English. Why should we worry about the first language, we all have to speak English." And I'm sure that's a prevalent idea in society. I'm not so sure how prevalent it is within schools, but there are some real serious issues around second-language learning. How did you deal with that with this little boy, whose mother does not speak English, who finds himself in special education and who might have been tested in . . . what language was he tested in?

CARYL: He was tested in Spanish, but researchers have found a lot of problems with those tests. One of the ones given was translated from English, the Peabody Picture Vocabulary test. When words are translated they're not necessarily at the same level of difficulty. I know when we were doing a state-required third-grade performance test, they had translated an article on tarantulas into Spanish for the Spanish kids to read and go through the same process. But when they translated the word *poisonous*, which is a rather common word in English, its direct translation, *ponzoñoso*, is a more scientific kind of word. It has a higher load to it. The most common word for *poisonous* in Spanish is *venenoso*, which would correlate to venomous, which is a higher-level word in English. And the Peabody Picture Vocabulary test ended up being like that too. You had a word that was so-called easy in English, but when it got translated into Spanish it was much more difficult. The Spanish translation of the WISC-R was normed on children in Mexico City, who live in a community where there's not a whole lot of second-language learning going on. The Spanish-speaking kids coming into schools here have a whole set of problems that Spanish speakers in Mexico City don't face. Because these children are learning two languages. Growing up, a lot of the time they're learning both simultaneously, especially if there are younger children in the family.

Denny: Sometimes losing one language?

CARYL: Sometimes the families are already losing one. The statistics now aren't very much different from when my grandparents came to the United States not speaking English. By the second generation the native language is usually gone. I have a little boy right now in my class who can't talk to his grandfather. His grandfather speaks Spanish, but he doesn't. He has some receptive understanding, but he doesn't speak it. And I think about what a loss that must be. I couldn't imagine my children not being able to talk to their own grandparents. How hard that must be for a family, all the family stories and the wisdom that just stops, gets lost. And so our Spanish-speaking children in school have a lot to deal with; and yet the tests are not normed on those kinds of kids, they're normed on kids who grew up totally in a Spanish-speaking community. It's not to demean the children here, because I see plenty of kids growing up speaking two languages and they're doing a fine job of it, even learning to read and write both languages at the same time. And they can handle that, they're smart kids. But the way they look on formal kinds of tests is very different, at least for a certain period of time. Those were the standards used to measure this child's learning, on top of all the other things that were going on at the same time.

Denny: These are critical issues that I don't think we spend enough time talking about, helping teachers understand how first-language loss, for example, affects families, and what happens to kids when the mother speaks the home language and the child is already fluent in English, and the mother and the child no longer are able to communicate because the child—for very complex reasons—has given up the first language. Those issues create very particular problems for teachers who wish to advocate for a child like Francisco. Was he bilingual at this point?

CARYL: Very Spanish dominant, although there is some English in the home. He has an older teenage brother, his father speaks some English, and his mom knows some but not a lot.

Denny: How much of that was a factor here?

CARYL: Other than the way it would affect the normed results of tests, I don't think it was that much of a factor. Bilingual education is pretty well supported in our school district. It certainly isn't available as much as it needs to be, because we're in a minority district, but there's plenty of people around with positive attitudes about bilingualism. The team of diagnosticians who worked with Francisco are in bilingual special education. The clientele they deal with are all bilingual children. It's not the same team that would evaluate a child who is English speaking. I don't think they saw bilingualism as a liability, but I've run into that, too, in special education. I haven't referred any child for a long time for special education. [*Laughing*] I told Bob, our principal, "We need to change child study. We need to change what we're doing with these kids. When we refer them, even though we think we are brainstorming and looking for other solutions, they always end up getting tested. I don't want to do that." I spend a lot of time with my students reminding them that it's really important to be bilingual. Yes, it's important to learn English, but it's really special to know more than one language.

Denny: I agree. The only other area that I think I'd like to cover is the paper trail that you've created in the letters that you wrote. First of all you documented it. You keep records on all the kids in your class, but you also kept copies of all letters you wrote and the special education teacher wrote, so you were creating a much different paper trail from the one that existed as part of his record. Were you aware of this?

CARYL: Yes. Bob was aware of that, too. We tend to do a lot of things differently at our school. We try to put something in writing. When parents have special requests of Bob, he asks them to put it in writing. When we are going to do something a little bit different, then we need to make some statement of our rationale for doing that, and it's usually written down. These notes about Francisco were just handwritten notes. They weren't anything on letterhead, but just some evidence of the date, the decision, and this is why we're doing it and who we talked to. And in terms of Francisco's work, all the children in the class keep portfolios of their work as their evaluation, and we use a narrative report card. When Francisco first came into my class we had just begun to work with the narrative report card, so keeping lots of pieces of children's work was very important. One of our goals was to have kids be able to look at work from earlier in the year later on, and actually be able to see the difference themselves. They'd pick up the stuff from September and go, "Oh, I didn't write that." So they really could see the difference, and you could see the difference in Francisco's work. We have examples of his work from early in the year and all the way through the year as evidence of his learning: Yes, he did learn to write his name, and here it is.

Denny: You also mentioned that areas of difficulty singled out in his special education file were areas you focused on in the classroom, and you documented those areas: speech, literacy.

CARYL: Small motor skills were difficult for him.

Denny: So you were collecting counterevidence in a way?

CARYL: One of the kindergarten teacher's reasons for referring him was that he hadn't learned to write his name. So we went back and looked at that. It was a stroke of pure luck that the teaching assistant in the kindergarten class ended up being my teaching assistant that year, because she was able to describe the kinds of activities that went on around the task of writing your name in the classroom: every morning the kids would be given a model of their name written by the teacher on lined paper, using upper- and lowercase letters, and the children were to trace it and then copy it. Well, given Francisco's visual problems and motor skills at the time, that was an impossible task for him. He wasn't allowed to engage in other activities until he had accomplished that or made the effort. But he eventually just gave up. The conclusion was he couldn't learn to write his name. Maybe the decision by him was, I don't want to write my name. There were activities in the classroom going on like children making up books, or setting up a grocery store, things you didn't need to have your name on. But when he first came into my class, the kids had some recording sheets and records they needed to keep as part of their science work, and he had no trouble writing his name. The special education teacher who sat with him that whole day helped him copy it. The next day we gave him a pencil that had his name written on it, and he noticed that. It was all caps, which is the way most kindergartners learn to write their name. He'd look at the letters and copy them down. A couple of weeks later he didn't need the pencil anymore, he was just writing his name down. But even if you go back to the journal he kept in the former class, he'd made an F and an O, which are the first and last letters of his name. But that was lost; I don't know if anybody ever recognized it or celebrated it.

Denny: Do you recognize yourself as an advocate?

CARYL: I certainly do.

Denny: I think that's a wonderful place to end.

Inventing Learning Disabilities

ALAN D. FLURKEY

Special education, by whatever name or organizational structure, is inherent in the bell-shaped distribution of many human learning characteristics. Regular education, even reformed or renamed, is a system that by its very essence is group oriented. Even if it were to adopt an individualized approach to the group enterprise, that individualized approach would be less than maximally effective and appropriate for the students at the extremes, the outliers.

BARBARA BATEMAN[1]

Introduction

Any review of the current literature on learning disabilities (LD)[2] reveals bubbling controversies ranging from the need for more precise research methodology[3] to the efficacy of subtypes[4] to the validity of intelligence testing[5] to intractable problems with definition.[6] As a researcher and former learning disabilities resource teacher, I share these concerns and harbor doubts of my own. However, unlike professional researchers, my concerns do not arise from trying to make sense of conflicting interpretations of large bodies of empirical data or contradictory findings of metastudies. Rather, my concerns are informed by observations of my students as learners, musings about their lives within their classrooms and outside school, and the forces that propel local, state, and federal educational policies.

My experiences have led me to recast learning disabilities as an artifact stemming from mechanistic conceptualizations of curriculum and learning theory, an invention that is both personal and social and that is maintained as an educational construct through its popular acceptance as a social/educational convention.

Teaching and [This] Teacher['s] Education

Challenging the prevailing beliefs in a given field is generally hazardous. Penalties include having one's motivations questioned, seeing one's competence challenged, or being dismissed out of hand.[7] But when one's observations are in conflict with one's model of the world (in this case, my model of learning disabilities), the most reasonable course is a sincere reappraisal of the field.

As an LD resource teacher in a large school district in the Southwest, a conflict between observations and models arose soon after I became familiar with my students and the requirements of my position. As a first-year resource teacher with an MA in special education, my optimism and enthusiasm were tempered early in the school year by events I had not anticipated and could not explain.

Mickey[8]

Mickey was a fourth-grade boy of fair complexion, light brown hair and brown eyes, and a small, light frame compared with other boys in his classroom. He lived with his mother and younger sister in a house that was a brief walking distance from school. He had been diagnosed as having a learning disability while in second grade and was currently receiving resource services primarily because of difficulties in reading, writing, and spelling. He was frustrated to tears when pressed to keep up with classmates—especially on tasks that required reading. In the spring of that year Mickey's reading quickly began to improve, and it was apparent to his fourth-grade teacher and to me that he had begun to read with a new confidence. By early in fifth grade, Mickey returned to the classroom full time and his resource services were terminated.

I was somewhat baffled by these events, because I could not explain them. Mickey had received the same skill-oriented instruction as my other students, who did not show the same improvement. I did note, however, that in the early spring his mother married a man who was nurturing and supportive of Mickey, and I could not escape the conclusion that this was a key event in changing Mickey's life as a reader.

This observation was significant for me because it suggested that events outside the classroom can often have a bearing on students' in-school performance—specifically, by ameliorating a learning disability. But this left me with a question. How can events outside school affect a learning-disabled student whose low achievement is caused by an organically based processing deficit or neuropathology?

I now realize that this question had propelled me into an arena of debate about the theory and nature of learning disabilities. But my experiences with Mickey were not the only ones that raised questions. Consider the following observations:

• Students who are learning disabled in one school district do not qualify in another when they move.

- Most of the same teachers refer most of the students for LD testing most of the time and after a short time.
- The critical factor in whether a teacher refers a student for LD services is not simply low achievement, but whether the teacher can tolerate behavior that reportedly disrupts classroom life.
- Flurries of referrals come at certain times of the year: usually two months after school begins or two months before summer break.
- A student who is LD in one classroom ceases to be handicapped in another (this is perhaps the most important observation).

One might be tempted to conclude that these observations are particular to my geographic or demographic area, but the professional literature supports the contention that they are endemic in the field.[9]

A researcher might counter that to cite these observations as providing evidence that questions the validity of the construct of learning disabilities naively ignores that these are all issues that can be resolved by greater precision in how learning disabilities are identified. However, I recount them to suggest the variability of interpretations: differences in perception that reflect socially organized forms by which student failure is recognized.

Learning from Learners, Learning About Learning

When I think about those persons who have most influenced my thinking as a learning disabilities resource teacher, I think first of my students. As I trace the evolution of my thinking about schooling and learning, I realize that my observations and discussions with them were instrumental in my reexamining the meaning of learning handicaps. Consider these two profiles.

Elena

Elena is in the fifth grade, the youngest of six children in a home where Spanish is spoken by the parents and eldest siblings, and English is the preferred language of the younger siblings. She was placed in a learning disabilities program in the second grade—referred by her teacher because of difficulties in reading and writing. For the past three years she has received pull-out instruction in reading and writing.

In preparation for her three-year reevaluation conference, Elena is given a battery of intelligence and achievement tests. While the results of intelligence testing reveal a profile that is within normal limits (Weschler Intelligence Scale for Children—Revised [WISC-R] standard score of 102), her standard scores on the achievement tests administered by the school psychologist still show a significant academic deficit.[10] Her standard scores on the reading and writing achievement subtests of the Woodcock-Johnson Psychoeducational Battery—Revised are shown in Table 1.

At the child study team meeting designed to brainstorm solutions for Elena's

Subtest	Standard Score
Letter-Word Identification	82
Passage Comprehension	83
Word Attack	80
Reading Vocabulary	84
Dictation	82
Proofing	76
Writing Sample	86
Writing Fluency	80

Table 1 WJ-R achievement subtests and standard scores (mean = 100; standard deviation = 15)

classroom difficulties, her classroom teacher describes her as a hard worker who has difficulty keeping up with the rest of the class. She cites "appalling spelling and mechanics" and "poor reading fluency" as the main impediments to Elena's performance. However, her teacher also reports that when Elena contributes to the class conversations, her comments show that she is paying attention to what is being said and also reflect a reasoned perspective that is slightly different from that of her peers. Following a discussion of homelessness, her teacher said, "She sees the odd angles of things in a way that less mature kids don't."

We decide to continue Elena in the LD program for two reasons: (1) her achievement scores do not warrant termination from the program, and (2) we are uncertain how she will fare in middle school; labeling her LD is a type of "failure insurance."

Elena confides that she doesn't like being away from her classmates but she also thinks the schoolwork she is given in her homeroom class is difficult for her.

Maria

Maria, also a fifth grader, is a talented writer and thoughtful reader. She lives with both parents and is a resident of an adjacent Yaqui community that my district serves. She is the youngest of six brothers and sisters. She is much younger than the next child in her family's birth order and has been living alone with her parents since the fourth grade. The primary language spoken at home is Spanish. Maria's parents understand some English but use it little inside or outside the home, and all our parent/teacher conferences require an interpreter. Maria reports that her oldest brothers and sisters are fluently bilingual, but that she herself understands and uses little Spanish. She is, however, proud of and knowledgeable about her Yaqui/Hispanic heritage.

Maria has just begun to think of herself as a writer, and she fills language arts time producing stories and poetry and commenting on the novels her group has chosen to read. Two frequent themes of her writings are social issues and the nature of personal relationships. Her poetry reflects this:

Home Sweet Home

Leaving my house was no fun
for me.
Knowing that my parents
don't care for me.
Coming home from school and
finding myself alone and nothing
to do.
I hate this feeling.
Leaving was too easy for me.
Now I know how it is in
the dark cold street at night
trying to live and fighting all day long.
My eyes are filled with cold
tears.
My friends call this place
   HOME SWEET HOME

Maria consistently writes thoughtful, sensitive pieces, and I am impressed by the strength of her voice and her directness. Particularly intriguing is the sense of authority, empowerment, and personal connection that she brings to her writing, as well as to the literary discourse inside our classroom.

Maria is also an avid reader of many types of fiction available to most fifth graders: mysteries, adventures, serials like the Babysitter's Club. On her own she has studied authors that she likes: William Steig, Gary Paulsen, and Joe Hayes, to name a few.

Maria's stories feature adventurous experimentations with genre and literary devices. And it is not difficult to see how her writing reflects the influence of some of these authors she has read. After reading several books written by Joe Hayes, author and storyteller of southwestern folktales, Maria produced a Spanish folktale in the same spirit. Her story *The Traveling Cricket* is a quintessential folktale complete with an unexpected angst-filled ending. The excerpt below resonates with Joe Hayes's style of storytelling, including the provision of an English translation alongside Spanish dialogue that is embedded in a Spanish folktale told in English.

From *The Day It Snowed Tortillas*[11]

On winter mornings the old woman would wake up cold and call to her son to get up to see if the fire was still burning: "Juanito, levántate, por favor. Mira ver si hay lumbre."

Lazy Juan would call the cat, "Pssst, psst." And when he felt that the cat's side was warm, he'd know that the fire was still burning. "Si, mamá," he would yawn. "Si, hay lumbre." And he'd roll over and go back to sleep.

From *The Traveling Cricket*

The cricket said, "Haven't you ever seen a cricket that talked?"

She nodded side to side that meant "No."

> The cricket said, "Mi nombre es Estevan." That said, "My name is Steven." "Como te llamas?" "What is your name?"
> "Mi nombre es Veronica." "My name is Ronnie."

By now the course I've chosen to present my argument may be clear: the profiles I've called "Maria" and "Elena" are of the same student—or perhaps it would be better to say the two names represent different ways of viewing the same student. (From this point Maria/Elena will be referred to as Maria only.) I have chosen to make a comparison in this fashion to lend support to the idea that as teachers and researchers, the way in which we perceive students and their academic competence is grounded in the beliefs we hold about schooling, curriculum, learning, and language processes—the social construction of literacy competence—not in objective measures.

As a teacher I could not help but wonder how a student could produce writing like Maria's and also perform on writing achievement subtests to produce standard scores in the 75–85 range (see Table 1). As I came to know Maria as a reader, I found myself raising the same question with regard to her reading achievement scores. In the following excerpt, Maria and some other fifth and sixth graders who have been classified as learning disabled for most of their school careers are discussing a number of books written by William Steig:

SHARI: In a lot of them, there are animals.

MARIA: I like the pictures in it. I mean, to me it's just like, like this one right here and this one right here. The pictures are great—I think they're great. I don't know why. They [the stories] look short, but actually it's really long. The stories are short, but they look long to me.

ME: What else did you notice about the stories aside from looking short but actually really being long?

SHARI: [*Her words come all at once; she moves her hands rapidly, smiling and trying hard to express her complex thoughts about her response to the literature*] He makes the stories—you think it's short and then you read it and then you really see it's long, and then you think, god, I really want to get into it. You get really—he makes it—he knows you're going to think this—that he knows you're going to want to put it down but you can't. Like this book [*The Amazing Bone*]. It sounded really boring at first, but then when you get to the part where the wolf is going to eat them, then you really get into it.

MARIA: It really doesn't describe the person—the character—it just describes what's going to happen. You do it really quick, I mean, maybe he doesn't care about the characters or the people, but he's really good. Maybe he's getting into telling the story.

SHARI: [*Jumping in after Maria*] Yeah, he's saying stuff and you know that it's going to happen. He uses this like—if you haven't read one of his books; you read this and he takes you out of reality. He takes you into another world; animals and all that.

MARIA: It doesn't really bother me, I mean not knowing so much about the characters. You know that *he's* a doctor, as the character [*Dr. DeSoto*], and that he's pulling teeth out and everything. I don't know; I guess the pictures are telling us what's going on.

SHARI: I sometimes wonder if things like *Caleb and Kate* really happen—

MARIA: I liked that story—that was a *good* story. Maybe he [William Steig] wants people to communicate with animals and see their languages. Like the book *CDC*. That was a *weird* book.

ME: Yeah, it makes you wonder, doesn't it, about what his intention was in making these books. We don't know very much about him except what we read on that little biographical thing. And we found out that he is, what . . . that he's eighty-one now? He's eighty-one, right?

SHARI: Oh my gosh!

ME: And that he's still alive—he's got two sons and a daughter and they're all artistic. And that a few of them are authors and they're all illustrators. But as far as his reasons for doing the stories the way he does, we don't know too much about it.

SHARI: It's like you wonder if maybe some of these things have happened in his family. Or some of these couldn't have happened. Some of these are way out, maybe in another world.

MARIA: Yeah, maybe there are things that happened to him—that the characters are animals, but they're people.

SHARI: Yeah, if they were all people, it would be really boring. You got to use your imaginations in these things.

MARIA: Yeah, these are kids' stories.

SHARI: But they're not *really* even kid stories.

LINDO: What makes you think they're kid stories, Maria?

MARIA: Most of them look like kids' stories. But like this one . . . and this one [*Caleb and Kate*]—you got to use your imagination, but it really could happen. I mean like, breaking up, marriage and all that. That is true. That can happen. I've seen that before. And another one, for instance [*Rotten Island*]. Where's the other one . . . this one. It's—it's the same thing as the dinosaurs and everything.

In this short excerpt, Maria and her peers shine—they show what they know about making personal connections with text, that they indeed are *capable* readers. When these students are engaged in constructing personal meanings and are given the opportunity to negotiate the meanings of text communally, the affectations of possessing learning handicaps begin to fall away. For example, Maria shows that she knows the difference between a tale whose purpose is to recount an adventure and a more involved story in which the development of a character is a main feature. She recognizes that an author, in constructing a text that tells a story, is continually faced with choices. (She has learned this from her reflections of herself as a writer.)

Not satisfied by simply stating that authors make choices as they write, she also conjectures why the author made his choices:

> This book [*The Amazing Bone*] really doesn't describe the person—the character—it just describes what's going to happen. You do it really quick, I mean, maybe he doesn't care about the characters or the people, but he's really good. Maybe he's getting into telling the story.

Recognizing that one is engaging in a personal transaction with an author, as Maria has done here, is a hallmark of an effective reader.[12]

Shari, excited by Maria's comments, shows similar insights:

> Yeah, he's saying stuff and you know that it's going to happen. He uses this like—if you haven't read one of his books; you read this and he takes you out of reality. He takes you into another world; animals and all that.

In her follow-up to Maria's remarks about authoring, Shari shows that she has become familiar with the pattern of story that lies within Steig's tales—the way he creates a false sense of calm before introducing a conflict ("Yeah, he's saying stuff and you know that it's going to happen"). In addition, she reveals the pleasure of self-discovery that she is able to engage in a reading experience and create a new, imagined reality (". . . if you haven't read one of his books; you read this and he takes you out of reality. He takes you into another world. . . .") In this instance, Shari gives form to what Rosenblatt would call reading with an aesthetic stance; a most personal form of engagement with text—a "lived-through expression"[13] and one that is indeed another hallmark of an effective reader.

I hasten to add that even though their comments about their reading seem sophisticated and insightful, in my experiences Maria and Shari are not unique among those classified as LD. I do not wish to cast them as the "gifted LD" students about whom we occasionally read[14] and who are contrasted with typical, poorly achieving LD students. Nor do I mean to suggest that Shari, Maria, or any other students do not face challenges in their reading, but I do mean to say that our LD programs are populated with students just like them in schooling systems that, by virtue of their daily operations, fail to recognize or understand the contributions these students have to offer.

Revaluing

As the resource room teacher, I began to appraise the work of students like Maria and Shari differently as a result of viewing learning and the use of language processes from a different perspective. Rather than seeing them as learners who did not possess certain skills, such as the ability to punctuate sentences correctly or read lists of isolated nonwords or read a passage accurately and fluently or produce cursive writing at an age/grade-appropriate rate with correct slant and formation, I saw them as producers of meaningful oral and written texts. Clearly these were readers who realized that reading was an enjoyable activity in which they were able to participate. As readers, they were able to construct personal meanings from the books they chose and enjoyed. As writers, they were able, some for the first time, to produce pieces of writing that had personal meaning—books, correspondence, personal journals. It was clear that some of my students had inadvertently (or even deliberately) learned poor strategies for dealing with meaningful construction of texts and, at the same time, had failed to learn helpful strategies that would enable them to deal with text more easily. But instead of seeing them as poor users of language, or disabled users of language, I saw them as thinkers who were grappling with achieving control over the conventions of language—always "in process," always moving forward if given choices and encouragement. Contrast this linguistic strengths-oriented profile of Maria as a learner with that of "Elena," which is dominated by the interpretation of her scaled scores on commercial standardized tests.

Ken Goodman calls this shift in thinking about learners *revaluing*.[15] Revaluing is a shift toward viewing learners as purposeful users of language processes and a corresponding shift away from relying on reductionistic, diagnostic tests that promote a deficit-oriented view of learners. How can a writer perform so as to receive standard achievement scores in the 75–85 range and yet produce crafted writing and articulate statements about what she reads and about herself as reader? A perspective on the answer to this question comes from reflecting on the nature of the tools used to measure achievement.

A variety of authors from different disciplines in education have written at length about the reductive properties of standardized tests.[16] To summarize without going into the science of test construction, test developers are faced with the task of producing an instrument that is quickly and easily administered and that reliably and validly discriminates between those who have mastery over the target skills or domains of knowledge and those who don't. The goal of the test maker is to produce a profile of scores that are obtained from a representative norming sample and that are normally distributed. To accomplish this, test makers must place restrictions on what is in the test (typically a brief question or stimulus) and what the student produces (typically a brief response). A central criticism of this enterprise is to question the extent that the constraints placed on what is tested and sampled limit what can be interpreted from the test results. In other words, can a timed performance reading a word list or writing on a topic determined by the test maker really tell the interpreter anything relevant about the test taker's competence in authentic reading and writing? Test makers would argue yes. So would many researchers, including Barbara Bateman, whose words begin this essay and who would have us believe that the learning disabled are found in the shadow of the left tail of "the bell-shaped distribution of many human learning characteristics." But documentation of the strength of Maria's and Shari's reading and writing suggest otherwise.

Revaluing is the alternative to depending on the interpretation of standardized tests to inform those concerned with a student's academic well-being. Revaluing begins with an honest look at how students are using language processes and whether or not the strategies they use are serving them properly and enabling them to use language processes to meet their needs as users of language. But there are two things that inhibit teachers, parents, and all those concerned with the welfare of children as learners, from taking this honest look and revaluing certain learners. Surprisingly, these reasons have little to do with the learners themselves. They are (1) outdated views of curriculum and (2) the nature of language processes.

How We Systematically Fail to Recognize the Strengths of Students

Curriculum

For a beginning LD teacher, determining what or how to teach is never difficult and never involves a great deal of choice. School districts provide scope and sequence curricular charts that specify academic objectives to be demonstrated by each learner in every content area. A similar list is provided by each of the publishers of the programmed reading, writing, math, handwriting, and language materials purchased by the district's special education department. (It seems reasonable to assume that the situation is similar among nearly all districts in the country.)

The important thing to remember about curricular checklists, scope and sequence charts, and programmed materials is that none of the decision making about what is to be taught and learned is made by the teacher or learner.[17] Thus it is impossible for student and teacher to create classroom conditions and personal transactions in which either has a personal interest or control.

This, in turn, has a chilling effect on motivation. Consequently, teachers must then resort to the gimmicks and tricks of behavior plans and reward systems. While some teachers and researchers argue that such behavior plans can be well crafted and effective, few will disagree that when the plan is withdrawn, the symptoms related to lack of motivation return. And few will disagree that a motivational plan that relies on external contingencies is a poor way of promoting independent, lifelong learning.

Indeed the issues of skill transfer and generalization from simple to complex tasks (e.g., the subject is trained to identify a list of words but is unable to read the same words in a passage) and maintenance after a contingency program is withdrawn are recognized as longstanding, intractable problems.[18]

But there is a more pervasive problem related to the practice of relying on sequences of curricular outcomes to determine what is to be taught and learned. The problem is that alternative conceptualizations of curriculum are precluded. The history of educational curriculum,[19] or more specifically, the shape that curriculum has taken for the better part of this century in schools in the United States, can be described as a linear, sequenced set of content-specific outcomes that learners are required to learn and teachers are responsible to teach at each grade level. Typically, it is the determination of whether or not a learner can demonstrate satisfactory performance of these outcomes that decides if a learner can proceed to the next educational level.

This is particularly poignant for the field of LD because, since its inception thirty years ago, the field has subscribed to this linear interpretation of curriculum. It could not have been otherwise, for in the mid-1960s, for the field to define a learning disability, educators had to distinguish what "normal" learners did in school from the academic performances of learning-disabled students. Therefore it was necessary to appropriate the conceptualization of curriculum as it popularly existed in education. In other words, if a chief characteristic of a learning disability was a failure at school, the question to be answered was, a failure at what? how is failure operationalized, measured? Indeed, it can be argued that it makes no sense to talk about failure without relating it to a linear curriculum.

This line of reasoning has been a mainstay of learning disabilities all along. Learning is taken to proceed in an incremental, elemental, stepwise fashion in which identified skills are encountered in sequence. It turns out this is a simple way to characterize learning—straighforward and incremental. In recent decades, such thinking about curriculum has traditionally directed what and how we teach, observe, and evaluate. It provides our frame.

It is also wrong. Natural learning does not proceed in this fashion, as several writers and researchers have shown us.[20] Learning proceeds in a fashion that might appear to be helter-skelter but is, at all times, directed by the learner. Vera John-Steiner describes how learners often go on "binges"—intently focusing their energy on an item of interest until they have had their fill, then moving on to another item they find interesting.[21] It simply is not possible to predict what items a particular person is going to find interesting and when. We cannot know in which direction a learner will skitter, much less designate a time frame in which learning is to take place. Learning is nonlinear.

This is the crux of the problem—traditional curriculum is a linear vision of ordered learning for which there is no real match in the world outside school. Classroom experiences support this. For example, there is a widespread belief that children should be reading by the time they finish first grade; however, first-grade teachers know that many children come into first grade already reading, many begin reading while in first grade, and many will begin to read sometime in second or third grade. Another example: a "poor" reader (i.e., one whose oral reading is slow and labored), on finishing a story, is able to construct a theme and relate the story to his or her personal life.

Both examples are commonplace, yet both run counter to traditional beliefs about curriculum, either in terms of time constraints or skill sequencing. When children fail to meet milestones at expected times or deliver poor surface perform-ances, they are judged to have failed to meet the expectations of the curriculum. I concur with Altwerger and Bird,[22] who suggest that it is the curriculum, which has been informed by an inappropriate, outdated view of learning, that is at fault.

Traditional, linear conceptions of curriculum have encouraged deficit-oriented explanations for school failure. Indeed, such notions have created a space for the existence of school failure all along. A linear view of curriculum systematically excludes portions of the broad spectrum of how various learners go about con-structing their own knowledge. In the traditional scheme, students who gain control of language processes at different-than-expected rates or who fail to pro-

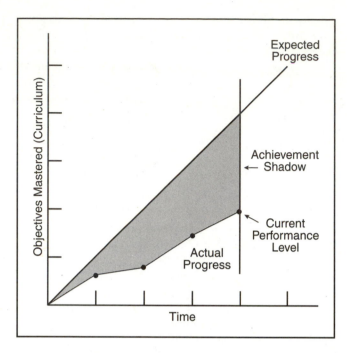

Figure 1

Linear Curriculum

duce performances in the prescribed manner are deemed to possess an achievement deficit. A linear view of learning and a linear view of curriculum influence each other to cast an "achievement shadow" (see Figure 1) in which personal deficits are created.

Whole language provides an alternative perspective on learning (and ultimately on interpreting the world)[23] that is characterized by a search for and construction of meaning that is both personal and social. In this frame, all learning takes place within a social context: forces of personal invention (which include the need to satisfy one's needs) drive the search for meaning and the forces of social convention influence the form those inventions will take if they are to be effective for the inventor. For example, all humans need to learn language. "Need" is a force of personal invention; the language they learn depends on the culture, neighborhood, and family in which they are raised—forces of social convention.

This personal-social perspective not only provides an elegant explanation of how learning works for individuals, it also has a broader application. Historical beliefs about deficits that are fueled by linear, incremental beliefs about curriculum play both roles of invention and convention in the creation of learning disabilities. Both are responsible for the creation of the concept and for the form it takes.

In addition to encouraging deficit-oriented interpretations of a student's academic value (a force of social convention), this linear view of curriculum steers teachers away from considering alternative organizations of curriculum that are personally meaningful to students and generated by the learners themselves. These alternative curricula not only better serve the interests of the learner, but also bring to the surface the strengths and experiences particular to each student.[24]

It is crucial that educators realize that a linear organization of well-defined outcomes is only one among a variety of curricular organizations. Further (like the reductive nature of standardized tests mentioned earlier), this view of curriculum is particularly restrictive because it masks what can be known about students by reducing the possibilities of what qualifies as evidence of learning to a measurement of performance on outcome measures. Redrawn and reinterpreted, the "shadow" in Figure 1 is conceptually the same shadow in which learning disabilities are found: under the left tail of "the bell-shaped distribution of many human learning characteristics."

The Language Processes

Curriculum and learning are interwoven concepts—beliefs about one are reflected in the other. If a teacher believes that a child learns to read by systematically being exposed to a series of printed words or by systematically blending together the sounds represented by letters of the alphabet, then she or he will choose materials or design activities that are consistent with those beliefs. Or to work from the other direction, if a teacher believes that effective teaching produces optimal learning and, further, that effective teaching results from the use of materials or activities organized around the sequential presentation of lessons that target the acquisition of specific skills, then she or he will tend to look at reading in terms of the component parts that can be defined as skills and taught sequentially.

But these beliefs about curriculum and learning are based on simplistic interpretations of complex processes. Real learning, regardless of its setting, requires a more complex description than simply a one-to-one match between what is taught and what is learned. In the case of language processes, simple behavioral explanations are particularly ill suited to describe the complexity of language learning and language use across a variety of settings.[25]

These simplistic beliefs about curriculum and language processes have, working together, resulted in the systematic failure of the field of LD to recognize the varied strengths and learning experiences that students bring with them to school. Unable to recognize strengths, the field has mistakenly attributed reasons for poor performance to an individual's possession of a learning disability.[26]

It goes something like this. A teacher determines that a child is having difficulty keeping up with other students. ("Keeping up," of course, means failing to make progress commensurate with peers at demonstrating mastery over sequenced curricular outcomes.) When a student has been identified as having difficulty reading and it is suspected that the cause is a learning disability, then reading achievement tests are administered—in most cases by the LD teacher or psychologist. And from the way the achievement tests are organized and the results interpreted, we can infer that like curriculum, the LD field views reading as a linear, incremental process.

For example, among the reading achievement tests used to establish an ability-achievement discrepancy for special education service classification purposes, the Woodcock-Johnson Psychoeducational Battery—Revised is clearly the most popular, and its minor psychometric faults notwithstanding, it was recently described in a review of psychometric tests and measurements as having high concurrent validity with similar achievement tests.[27] The following is a list of the WJPB-R reading subtests: Letter-Word Identification, Passage Comprehension, Word Attack, and Reading Vocabulary. A review of the subtests and the descriptions supplied by the test manual[28] reveals that according to the test maker, normal reading is characterized as:

- The accurate and rapid identification of words and nonwords arranged in lists.
- The ability to identify the meanings of words accurately.
- The ability to read a short paragraph and then correctly choose answers to questions that relate to the paragraph's content.

But thirty years of model building and research in psycholinguistics and cultural anthropology have provided a conceptualization of reading that is much different from the linear, behavior-oriented representations that were on hand to orient the original thinking in the field and that continue to dominate the field today. An alternative to a view of reading as word identification is a sociopsycholinguistic transactional model[29] that focuses on reading as a process of constructing meanings that are unique to each reader and are at once both personal and social.

A meaning-construction model of reading can explain why readers like Maria are able to construct rich, personal meanings for themselves when reading authentic, engaging literature of their own choosing and yet exhibit an intelligence/achievement discrepancy based on a profile composed of standard scores that suggest the possession of a learning disability. It can also explain how other purportedly learning-disabled students, who do not appear to be constructing personal meanings when they read, actually engage in the same sociopsycholinguistic transactional reading process but misapply, inconsistently apply, or misunderstand the same reading strategies that efficient readers employ without difficulty. Finally, a sociopsycholinguistic model of the reading process recognizes the complex linguistic resources, life experiences, and literacy experiences that every reader brings to each engagement with print and addresses how such resources and experiences can be used to support and develop more efficient application of the reading process.

Revaluing Gastón

I began to work with Gastón when he was in sixth grade. He had recently moved from another district where he had been classified as learning disabled and had been receiving resource pullout services for reading for four years. A review of his most recent achievement and I.Q. scores showed a typical discrepancy of eighteen points—a principal justification for his continued classification as LD. His sixth-grade homeroom teacher acknowledged that when he listened to Gastón's oral reading, Gastón seemed to experience severe reading difficulties.

My initial evaluation of Gastón painted a different picture. His responses to the

Burke Reading Interview[30] suggested that he believed himself to be a poor reader and lacked confidence and self-esteem. As the interview proceeded, the low, wavering tone of his voice suggested that the questions touched on issues that were very sensitive for him:

ME: What would you like to do better as a reader?

GASTÓN: Say all the words. Sometimes I don't know all the words and I can't, uh, sound them out.

ME: Anything else you'd like to do better as a reader?

GASTÓN: Read faster. I can't think of anything else.

ME: Are you a good reader?

GASTÓN: [*Pauses*] Not that good.

ME: Not that good. Why do you think that?

GASTÓN: I don't know all the words . . . [*Pauses*] And I'm not very fast. That's all.

Following the interview, I asked Gastón to read aloud *Jumanji*,[31] a picture book that he hadn't read previously. Although Gastón seemed to hold himself in low regard as a reader, a miscue analysis[32] of his oral reading and retelling revealed a pattern of strengths. Superficially, Gastón's oral reading sounded labored and slow as marked by his production of several miscues and regressions; however, he was also able to produce a comprehensive retelling of the story, including major and minor details, plot summary, character analysis, and a statement of the theme (see appendix). Equally surprising was the quality of the miscues he produced:

0315 ⓒ "Not really," (said) Peter. "I'm sure somebody left it here be-

0316 cause it's ~~so~~ boring."

pestered
0317 "Oh, come on," protested Judy. "Let's give it a try. ⓡ Race you home."

On line 0315 Gastón omits *said*, most likely in reasonable anticipation of the name *Judy*. "Not really, Judy" is the alternative structure that Gastón may have been predicting, but after producing the text word *Peter*, he apparently realizes that something has gone amiss with his prediction and he doubles back to the beginning of the structure to self-correct. No meaning loss here.

On line 0316 Gastón inserts the word *so*, a term that functions as an intensifier in this context. There is no meaning loss in this structure: "I'm sure somebody left it here because it's *so* boring." In fact, it can be argued that the added emphasis provided by the insertion of the intensifier enhances meaning for this reader.

On line 0317 Gastón substitutes *pestered* for the text word *protested*. Grammatically, this miscue carries the same function as the text word, that is, as an attributive verb or dialogue tag—a linguistic element that is reserved for written narratives and oral storytelling. The miscue is every bit as sophisticated as the text word. It also looks somewhat like the text word, sharing graphic features in the beginning, middle, and ending. And like the insertion of the intensifier *so*, it can be argued that this substitution actually enhances the reader's meaning construction since *pestered* suggests the playful needling of an older sister—a conceptualization that is consistent with this particular passage of the story. No meaning loss results from this miscue.

Also on line 0317 Gastón repeats the word *race* one time before continuing. While repetitions (regressions) do not result in meaning loss, they can signal that a reader is trying to solve a perceived problem ahead in the text. We can't know what Gastón was thinking, but we can hazard a guess: he was surprised by the choice of *race* as a verb to begin a sentence. *Race* as a noun is certainly familiar to elementary school children, but its use as a verb in the beginning of a structure that differs from the explicit subject-verb-object pattern may have been unexpected.

In these examples, which were typical of Gastón's productions within this text (and across other texts), none of the miscues resulted in meaning loss—indeed, several enhanced meaning construction. In summary, 86 percent of all the sentences he produced in this text were grammatically acceptable, and 76 percent were semantically acceptable. Coupled with Gastón's detailed retelling, these figures are consistent with profiles of effective readers.

This brief analysis told me things about Gastón's reading that a battery of standardized achievement tests could not. As a reader, Gastón:

- Could construct meaning for himself.
- Could monitor his meaning construction.
- Possessed sophisticated knowledge of written language structures.

Gastón was not a poor reader, nor was he a learning-disabled reader. Rather, he was a reader who could focus on constructing meaning for himself and whose processing ranged from effective to ineffective because of the misapplication of some reading strategies and the overapplication of others.

This was information that nobody else seemed to have and that provided a picture of Gastón that nobody seemed to share. There was no evidence in Gastón's records that the psychologist who had reevaluated him had ever listened to a complete reading and retelling. And his classroom teacher told me she hadn't either. How different Gastón's educational experience could have been if his teachers and psychologists had been able to discuss his existing strengths and potentials!

Conclusion

School is nothing more than an arrangement we have made to foster our young. People can and have learned to read without schools and will continue to learn.

PAT CARINI[33]

I think the spirit of renewal and invention implied in this statement can be a source of inspiration to both regular and special educators. Although one might be tempted to interpret the phrase "people can and have learned to read without schools" as a call to explore alternatives to public education, neither Carini nor I would suggest that course. On the contrary, she seems to be calling our attention to the simple fact that the current educational organization in the United States is merely a social convention with a real history, dominant leaders, theoretical assumptions, folk beliefs, and traditional practices, and that like language itself, there is nothing intrinsically meaningful about its structure. When the possibilities of what "can be" are informed by fresh thinking about curriculum and language processes—when we envision the rich experiences that can be afforded all children—it becomes clear that the limits that we place on educational experiences are ultimately self-imposed.

The field of LD needs to engage in a critical examination of outdated, linear, behavior-oriented beliefs about reading in light of current sociopsycholinguistic perspectives. This is crucial if we are to discover, value, and build on the linguistic strengths and literacy experiences that our students already possess when they enter our classrooms.

As a teacher, I no longer subscribe to simple, deficit-oriented, in-the-head pathology-based explanations for what educators in the field call learning disabilities. And while I do recognize that there are readers who are experiencing real and severe reading difficulties, I argue that what we are calling LD is a constellation of factors relating to the failure of school.

Instead of characterizing LD as solely the property of an individual, we need to recognize that a learning disability is socially constructed by the learner and all others involved in his or her education. It is constructed through a complex arrangement of personal experiences and social expectations ranging from early exposure to literacy activities, personal constructions of how literacy works, a reader's appraisal of his or her relationship to literacy as a means to solve problems and as a means to provide enrichment and recreation, and the ascription of competence or noncompetence by those who the reader believes have the power to determine such things.[34] All of these factors have a bearing on one another in the particular variety of school failure and failure-of-school that we call LD.

If the field of LD continues to ignore current sociopsycholinguistic theoretical and practical ideas about curriculum and language, then students like Maria, Shari, and Gastón may never have the value of their musings appreciated, and they themselves may never know the value of their own contributions.

Appendix

Gastón's Retelling of *Jumanji*

ALAN: You really worked hard on that, didn't you. Let's stretch for a sec.

GASTÓN: My back popped.

ALAN: Me, too. That was really nicely done. I really appreciate all the hard work you put in on that.

GASTÓN: That was a hard story.

ALAN: What made it hard?

GASTÓN: The words . . .

ALAN: Did you understand it?

GASTÓN: Not really. 'Cause I didn't know most of the words or anything.

ALAN: But I didn't—Sounded like you were coping with those words real well. Why don't you tell me everything you can remember about the story.

GASTÓN: I remember the mom—that the parents left them and they took out the toy chest and took out all the toys and started playing. And after that, they got bored of playing. And they went outside to the park and they fou—and they were chasing each other. The girl was right on his heels when they raced 'em home after they found the box. And they went in and they played it, played the game. They got all worried when they saw that most of the animals coming out of the stuff. She explained to him, um, to Peter that they had to finish the game in order for everything to go away. So she fin—she told him that they had to get, like, 12 to win the game. And she got a 6 and that helped her, and she got to the City of Gold and won. The room got darker and the mist—the steam got thicker and she couldn't see across the table to him so, like she says something that—in the story that—the windows and the doors suddenly open and the cool breeze blew the steam away. And they ran—the threw the game pieces into the board and everything and ran back outside and threw the game under the tree and ran back home. Then the parents came home and they were asleep. And they woke 'em up and they were going to try to tell them what happened and, uh, the parents interrupted them. Then after that they, the kids, their two, oh I don't know whatever her name was went out and was telling the kids, Judy and Peter, that their kids never read instructions—always started puzzles and never finished them. So, they had the game under their arm and then were probably going to play it at their house. They probably would have left the game started and they would be running all over the place if they didn't read the instructions . . . That's all that happened.

ALAN: That's everything that happened. That's a marvelous retelling, Gastón. Now what did you say before we started, I think you said, "I didn't understand the story?" [*Laughs*] I mean you retold *everything*. You even told me the funny ending to it, which was, you know, what happen to Daniel and Walter because of what their mom said. You got this stuff cold. Tell me a little bit of detail about what kinds of stuff showed up in the house once they started playing the game.

GASTÓN: At first the lion appeared. The kids thought that's all that was happening. And then when his sister was scared, or something, she looked and whispered to him and told him to turn around. There was a lion there, and after it was her turn the monkeys came out in the kitchen. And after that he rolled, I think, the guide came out—the man on the house—the little house, he came out—the guide. And after that, um, it was the rhinos. The rhinos, the snakes and uh, the mos—those bugs. Sleeping gas or something. And volcanos. The volcano that erupted or something and started sprinkling.

ALAN: Yeah, what do those bugs do?

GASTÓN: They sting you and then they make you fall asleep or something.

ALAN: And the volcano and then . . . Uh, I was thinking about what you were saying. I don't know if I heard you talk about the, uh, there was the lion . . . and did you mention the monkeys?

GASTÓN: Yeah.

ALAN: And then that guy?

GASTÓN: Um hm.

ALAN: Who was he?

GASTÓN: The guide.

ALAN: Okay. What was his problem?

GASTÓN: He was lost.

ALAN: Okay. So you mentioned him. You mentioned the sleeping sickness. Did you mention the rain?

GASTÓN: Um hm.

ALAN: How about—go ahead.

GASTÓN: The, um, the, what was it? Not April showers, but some kind of storm they said it was. I can't remember.

ALAN: Yeah, yeah. It stormed and uh . . .

GASTÓN: . . . thundered and everything. The wall shook.

ALAN: Okay, that's . . . what was it about the instructions at the beginning of the game that Judy read. You said that, you know, they got the game and then you said that—then you went on but could you tell me about the instructions a little bit? What's the trick to the instructions or what's the deal about them.

GASTÓN: Once you start a game that—when you start a game, not to—you have to finish it or something. That game probably taught them something. So now everything they play they're going to read the instructions and, uh, finish the game.

ALAN: Oh, yeah.

GASTÓN: They probably won't want something happening like that.

ALAN: That's—that's what I think the theme is. Uh . . . what was the adult's reaction to them. I think you told me, but why don't you be more explicit. What did the adults think. Yeah, the mom came home, what did she say to them?

GASTÓN: She—they interrupted them by laughing, so they just stayed quiet. She said something that, they got—they did get sleeping sickness and she told them to go upstairs and get their pajamas on and come downstairs and finish the puzzle and eat dinner.

ALAN: So the adults, what did they think about—

GASTÓN: They didn't believe them or something.

ALAN: I—I—This is just a fantastic retelling. You really understand what you read really well. [*Stop tape*]

Endnotes

1. This quote is taken from B. Bateman, "Who, How, and Where: Special Education's Issues in Perpetuity," *Journal of Special Education* 27 (4): 509–20 (1994). Embedded in the worldview that Bateman espouses are the assumptions that I seek to question. **2.** Although the comprehensive construct of "learning disabilities" is the topic under investigation in this paper, I focus primarily on reading disabilities. This is reasonable because reading disabilities (currently and historically) make up the overwhelming majority of learning disabilities classifications and special education placements in the United States. See B. Keogh, "Definitional Assumptions and Research Issues," in *Learning Disabilities: Theoretical and Research Issues*, edited by H. Swanson and B. Keogh (Hillsdale, NJ: Lawrence Erlbaum Associates, 1990) 13–22. Similarly, the professional literature relating to both research and theory of LD is dominated by the topic of reading disabilities. These circumstances notwithstanding, I assert that the discussion and arguments presented in this paper are applicable to learning disabilities in the broader conceptualization. **3.** L. Moats and G. Lyon, "Learning Disabilities in the United States: Advocacy, Science, and the Future of the Field," *Journal of Learning Disabilities* 26 (5): 282–94 (1993); J. Torgeson, "Thinking About the Future by Distinguishing Between Issues that Have Resolutions and Those that Do Not," in *Research in Learning Disabilities: Issues and Future Directions*, edited by C. Bos and S. Vaughn (Boston: College-Hill Press, 1987) 55–85. **4.** S. Forness, "Subtyping in Learning Disabilities: Introduction to the Issues," in Swanson and Keogh, 194–200. **5.** K. Kavale, "A Critical Appraisal of Empirical Subtyping Research in Learning Disabilities," in Swanson and Keogh, 215–22; L. Siegel, "I.Q. and Learning Disabilities: R.I.P.," in Swanson and Keogh, 111–30. **6.** See B. Keogh, "Definitional Assumptions and Research Issues," in Swanson and Keogh, 16, for a statement of the organic/pathological basis for learning disabilities. See C. Smith, *Learning Disabilites: The Interaction of Learner, Task and Setting*, 3d ed. (Boston: Allyn & Bacon, 1994) 35, for a representative operational definition of learning disabilities. **7.** The series of exchanges beginning with the research article by R. F. West, K. F. Stanovich, and H. R. Mitchell, "Reading in the Real World and Its Correlates," *Reading Research Quarterly* 28 (1): 35 (1993), and followed by Taylor's commentary: "Commentary: The Trivial Pursuit of Reading Psychology in the 'Real World': A Response to West, Stanovich, and Mitchell," *Reading Research Quarterly* 29 (3): 277–88 (1994), and Stanovich and West's response to Taylor, "Reply to Taylor," *Reading Research Quarterly* 29 (3): 290–91 (1994), provide an example of the manner in which "worldview challenge-and-response" are played out in research journals. **8.** To preserve confidentiality, the names of all of the students in this paper have been changed with their permission. **9.** Moats and Lyon; C. Sleeter, "Literacy, Definitions of Learning Disabilities and Social Control," in *Learning Disability: Dissenting Essays*, edited by B. M. Franklin (Philadelphia: Falmer Press, 1987) 67–87, provides a critical treatment of regional and local discrepancies in the classification of learning disabilites and implementation of learning disabilities services. **10.** Local criteria for severe discrepancy based on an ability-achievement model: standardized guidelines as representing a discrepancy of 1.5 standard errors of estimate between a full scale IQ score (M=100, SD=15) and standardized administered tests of word identification and passage comprehension. **11.** J. Hayes, *The Day It Snowed Tortillas: Tales from Spanish New Mexico*, 3d ed. (Santa Fe, NM: Mariposa, 1985) 60.

12. The theoretical perspective on reading that has informed this paper is drawn from K. Goodman's model of the reading process. For a detailed discussion of a meaning-construction model of reading, see K. S. Goodman, "Reading, Writing and Written Texts: A Transactional, Sociopsycholinguistic View," in *Theoretical Models and Processes of Reading*, edited by R. B. Ruddell, M. R. Ruddell, and H. Singer (Newark, DE: International Reading Association, 1994) 1093–130; See L. M. Rosenblatt, *The Reader, the Text, the Poem* (Carbondale, IL: Southern Illinois University Press, 1978), for a seminal explanation of the construction of personal meaning as transaction with text. **13.** Rosenblatt 68. **14.** C. Clements, "Serving the Gifted Dyslexic and Gifted at Risk," *Gifted Child Today* 17 (4): 12–17 (1994); T. Ellston, "Gifted and Learning Disabled . . . A Paradox?" *Gifted Child Today* 16 (1): 17–19 (1993). **15.** See K. S. Goodman, "Revaluing Readers and Reading," *Topics in Learning and Learning Disabilities* 1 (4): 87–93 (1982), for a detailed description of revaluing as a conceptual alternative to traditional thinking about evaluation and assessment. **16.** Moats; Goodman 1982; M. Poplin, "Holistic/Constructivist Principles of the Teaching/Learning Process: Implications for the Field of Learning Disabilities," *Journal of Learning Disabilities* 21 (7): 401–16 (1988); F. Smith, *Insult to Intelligence* (New York: Arbor House, 1986); K. Stanovich, "Discrepancy Definitions of Reading Disability: Has Intelligence Led Us Astray?" *Reading Research Quarterly* 27 (1): 7–29 (1991); D. Taylor, *From the Child's Point of View* (Portsmouth, NH: Heinemann, 1993). **17.** K. Goodman, P. Shannon, Y. Freeman, and S. Murphy, *Report Card. The Basal Readers* (New York: Richard C. Owen, 1988); P. Shannon, "The Struggle for Control of Literacy Lessons," *Language Arts* 66: 625–34 (1989). **18.** L. Gelzheiser, M. Shepherd, and R. Wozniak, "The Development of Instruction to Induce Skill Transfer," *Exceptional Children* 53 (2): 125–29 (1986); M. Poplin, "Self-Imposed Blindness: The Scientific Method in Education," *Remedial and Special Education* 8 (6): 31–37 (1987). **19.** L. Tanner, "Curriculum Issues in Historical Perspective," in *Critical Issues in Curriculum*, edited by L. Tanner (Chicago: National Society for the Study of Education, 1988) 1–15. **20.** Smith 1986; K. S. Goodman, *What's Whole in Whole Language?* (Portsmouth, NH: Heinemann, 1986); V. John-Steiner, *Notebooks of the Mind* (Albuquerque, NM: University of New Mexico Press, 1985); J. Kinchloe and S. Steinberg, "A Tentative Description of Post-Formal Thinking: The Critical Confrontation with Cognitive Theory," *Harvard Educational Review* 63 (3): 296–320 (1993), provides an excellent account of post-formalism as it compares to the positivism and reductionism of Cartesian-Newtonian formality; Poplin 1988. **21.** John-Steiner 1985. **22.** See B. Altwerger and L. Bird, "Disabled: The Learner or the Curriculum?" *Topics in Learning & Learning Disabilities* 1 (4): 69–78 (1982), for a wonderfully conceived rethinking of curriculum from a holistic perspective. **23.** Goodman, K. S. 1986; Y. M. Goodman and K. S. Goodman, "Vygotsky in a Whole-Language Perspective," in *Vygotsky and Education*, edited by L. C. Moll (Cambridge, UK: Cambridge University Press, 1990) 223–50, provides a comprehensive framework for viewing the socially constructive nature of schooling and the role of the teacher in supporting learning. **24.** Goodman, K. S. 1986; K. Goodman, F. Smith, R. Meredith, and Y. Goodman, *Language and Thinking in School: A Whole Language Curriculum*, 3d ed. (New York: Richard C. Owen, 1987); See K. Short and C. Burke, *Creating Curriculum: Teachers and Students as a Community of Learners* (Portsmouth, NH: Heinemann, 1991), for a comprehensive discussion of inquiry-oriented alternatives to traditional linear-oriented curriculums. **25.** Poplin 1988; Goodman and Goodman 1990; L. C. Moll, Introduction to *Vygotsky and Education*, edited by L. C. Moll (Cambridge, UK: Cambridge University Press, 1990). **26.** Taylor 1993. **27.** R. Webster, "Review of Woodcock-Johnson Psychoeducational Battery—Revised," in *Test Critiques*, Vol. 10, edited by D. Keyser and R. Sweetland (Austin, TX: Pro-Ed, 1994) 804–13. **28.** R. Woodcock and M. Johnson, "*Woodcock-Johnson Psychoeducational Battery—Revised* (Allen, TX: DLM Teaching Resources,

1989). **29.** Goodman 1994. **30.** Y. M. Goodman, D. J. Watson, and C. L. Burke, *Reading Miscue Inventory: Alternative Procedures* (New York: Richard C. Owen, 1987). **31.** C. van Allsburg, *Jumanji* (Boston: Houghton Mifflin, 1981). **32.** Goodman, Watson, and Burke 1987. **33.** P. Carini, personal communication, April 12, 1993. **34.** See R. McDermott, "Acquisition of a Child by a Learning Disability," in *Understanding Practice: Perspectives on Activity and Context*, edited by S. Chaiklin and J. Lave (New York: Cambridge University Press, 1993); D. Taylor, *Learning Denied* (Portsmouth, NH: Heinemann, 1991); and D. Taylor, *From the Child's Point of View* (Portsmouth, NH: Heinemann, 1993), for discussions of the socially constructed nature of learning disabilities.

Denny: Your essay fascinates me. I've read it a number of times now. I've always been interested in the way in which you're portraying learning disabilities. You talk about learning disabilities as an invention, and I'm intrigued by how it got invented. I'm really interested in documentation and how we develop ways of thinking about particular people. Do you see learning disabilities as a paper trail?

ALAN: I see learning disabilities as both a paper trail and as something being perpetuated by a paper trail. So, I see it being both things at once.

Denny: So, once there was an invention on paper, then researchers—in particular test makers, I guess—expanded upon that image.

ALAN: That's just it; the way I see this working is that learning disabilities really came into being as a way to explain school failure from a psychological perspective. The conditions in psychology and education were historically moving in certain directions. They had a certain momentum. At a certain point, conditions were right for this particular explanation to carry meaning with a group of people who had a certain orientation toward learning.

Denny: And once that explanation was put forth within the educational community, it became reified.

ALAN: It very quickly became reified. It became a convention. And now people use it. They've adopted the convention without questioning . . .

Denny: Without questioning whether there are such phenomena as learning disabilities.

ALAN: That's how invention and convention work. That's why I think it's a marvelous explanatory tool.

Denny: And because the views of learning in this country are linear, the definitions of learning disabilities were also linear. It fit within the dominant model.

ALAN: That's why it became very easy to reify. It made it smack of a certain sensibility. And that's why it got adopted so quickly, because it fits within this deficit model of learning and of curriculum.

Denny: So if you don't believe that learning is linear, automatically a teacher should be questioning the notion of learning disabilities. Because the whole of the foundation of the concept fits within a linear paradigm?

ALAN: If you challenge those assumptions, then the whole thing begins to unravel. That's why I had to attack this notion, telling the story of this particular kid in this way. It's the only way that I knew to tell her story so that I could make sense of it myself. When I first started teaching in special education, very quickly things didn't add up. Things didn't reconcile with what I had been taught about learning and about the nature of kids. I had to begin trying to make sense of what it was that was going on with these particular kids. It was much more reasonable for me to reject the assumption that there was something flawed with these kids, and to accept that my job was somehow to find better teaching practices to reach them, to boost them to where they should be in the curriculum, because those flaws weren't evident to me. I simply saw them as being learners. And I appreciated that whatever difficulties they were having were much broader than anything that could be measured by any test. So in order to make sense of it, I had to frame the paper the way I did.

Denny: One of the really helpful things here is that you provide two images of this one child. One of them is linear, within the traditional model of learning disabilities, and the other is holistic, looking at learning as something that's systemic and far more complex; and it's in that juxtaposition that you begin to see that it's really problematic to try to reduce learning to stages or any kind of linear framework.

ALAN: It's that reduction, that perspective, that creates the place for the learning disability to exist.

Denny: So how does a teacher come up with alternative views? I mean, he has thirty or thirty-five children in a room, and here's this child who comes in with an IEP, and some sort of learning disability is being described, and the teacher has to say, Wait a minute, I need to get my own perspective here. How does a teacher do that?

ALAN: It's not easy, because the very nature of schooling and the way school is organized within school districts really works counter to everything that you try to pull off holistically. When you're told by your principal, I don't care what you do with your kids, just make sure your test scores are higher at the end of the year, how do you deal with those kinds of pressures?

Denny: How do you deal with the whole child and the family?

ALAN: Right. I'm not saying you can't do it, but the reality is, there are tremendous pressures that work counter to viewing kids in a holistic way. I just want to acknowledge that those pressures are there.

Denny: And naming those pressures, I think, becomes important, because once you can get ahold of the documents and you can begin to deconstruct them and say, This isn't true, this isn't reality, this is just one perspective that's come out of the testing situation. The kid is doing very different things in the classroom. And then move into somehow countering the perspectives that are in the folder. We know, for instance, from Debbie's work with Valerie, that it's a tremendous effort for a teacher to make that counterargument.

ALAN: You come to know the pressures once you understand how language works and how curriculum works with language holistically.

Denny: So a teacher has to have a theoretical base?

ALAN: Yes, first and foremost.

Denny: To understand learning, a teacher must have a philosophical framework within which to work?

ALAN: Yes, and the boundaries of what it is you're trying to do become clear, and you begin to see where the pressures come from and why they are there. And how they are, indeed, socially constructed.

Denny: And you can frame the argument. I know from my own experience in working with teachers in New Hampshire that one of the biggest difficulties they faced was that while they had very detailed notes, and they had collected lots of examples of children's work, and they could counter the perspectives presented in tests that were in a child's folder or at an IEP meeting, they had tremendous difficulty in orally framing the argument. They fell into the other paradigm; as soon as they went into a meeting, they began talking within the framework of the psychologists and within a linear learning disabilities model. It took them a long time to reach a point where they could frame their arguments within their own theoretical framework. In fact I got a phone call about this one night from a teacher who said, "I think we've got this worked out: we keep putting our documentation into their framework, and it doesn't work." That's where the notion of having your own theoretical framework and being able to articulate it comes in.

ALAN: Once you do that, Denny, then you can take the argument of this linear perspective and circumscribe it, set it within your own theoretical framework. What I am arguing is that a holistic orientation of language and learning is much broader than this linear perspective. It has much greater explanatory power to address what it is we see is going on with the kid, both inside and outside the classroom. Once you have a sense of that, then you can begin to frame the argument, get a handle on it. Because you've really walked around the theoretical perspective that you're arguing against.

Denny: Do you see this as an advocacy model of teaching?

ALAN: Well, yes, but—that was a yes-or-no question, so yes. [*Laughter*] In what way is it an advocacy model? Everything about a holistic perspective, really, orients you toward what a kid's linguistic strengths are and what a kid brings into the classroom. Without a doubt, every kid brings all kinds of strengths that you can build on. Dewey was one of the first people that I read that pointed that out, that every kid has experience, every kid has language that you can build on. And that's a much more helpful perspective.

Denny: I think within a holistic advocacy model, there is an implicit assumption that observation is not enough. We have a number of teachers in our schools that are really extraordinary in what they are doing with kids, and the way they work with kids, and who can stand up and talk about a particular child for two hours. Without any trouble, at the drop of a hat, they can go through the work. But we're at a point where that is not enough. The piece that's important to advocacy is the documentation. Teachers need to be note takers in their classrooms and create an alternative paper trail. So within that framework—and here's my next question—where does miscue fit into this analysis?

ALAN: Miscue analysis is a crucial piece; it's foundational to understanding how language works and how learning works as a transaction. All the evidence I needed to understand that has come from miscue analysis. So it's central for me. And I'm arguing that you can't fully appreciate whole language without understanding miscue analysis.

Denny: I agree with you.

ALAN: And you can't really respond to a linear, word-recognition paradigm and what goes along with it, which is this linear construction of curriculum, without understanding the transactional nature of language, which you get the deepest appreciation of from miscue analysis. I see it as being a wellspring, that's what it is for me.

Denny: I think miscue analysis is incredibly complex. I've sat in on the course here for two semesters, and I'm actually going to take it next semester, because in my own work miscue has become essential. For me, one of the pieces that's been missing is that incredible description of what children are doing when they're reading.

ALAN: And the sense that they are making in any particular reading, the strengths that they bring to using language—if you don't understand miscue analysis, all that is lost. Miscue analysis is the most elegant way to come to revalue a kid in what he's doing. It's a quicker way to seeing the sense that a kid brings to any particular activity that he's doing in school. It's faster than looking at his writing or at the variety of things that he does, because it's right there on paper. You see that a kid is making sense, whereas if you hadn't listened with a miscue analysis perspective, it sounds like a kid is having a difficult time using print.

Denny: And miscue analysis is something that a teacher can take into a meeting and share, put the transcript out on the table and talk about whether the miscue is an omission or substitution, whatever the patterns are, whatever the kid is doing, the quality of the miscues, and can talk about the retelling and the comprehension, what is it that the child knows about the story at the end in relation to what miscues there are. Sometimes it's so easy to make assumptions about a child's reading based on her so-called errors. The fact that a child may have an incredible retelling with a large number of miscues in the reading is something that needs to be discussed and put on the table in thinking about a kid's learning.

ALAN: For many people at this—let's say hypothetical—this hypothetical meeting, it's been my experience that having a kid produce retelling is not a thought.

Denny: Nor of reading the whole story. I know that when we've done some miscue before I came to Arizona, much of our work focused on writing and looking at whole texts that children have constructed is also something that is very new within some contexts where a child study team comes together. Because basically what gets discussed is the Woodcock-Johnson and the IQ tests. We've had this psychologist put an IQ test on the table after teachers have done an incredibly complex analysis of oral language and a child's response to a movie, then looked at his reading and his writing, and the psychologist puts the test on the table and says, Now let's look at the hard data. And we're back to how do teachers counter that, and it has to be through knowledge, through understanding, through the development of an alternative perspective, and being able to support that perspective in the documentation that they have.

ALAN: Which gets back to its being a very difficult thing to do. If you're sitting down at a table with a psychologist, or whoever is there, what you're essentially saying is, What we have to do is examine your epistemological assumptions. [*Laughing*] That's not going to go down very well at a meeting at three-thirty. But that's what you're saying.

Denny: It's a very good question. [*Laughing*]

ALAN: And so when a teacher brings in this evidence to a child study team meeting, it can go a number of ways. One, it can be a very enlightening experience for those who come to the table; the other piece, and I don't want to be negative, is that it will be rejected outright. Because, like you said, it's not considered hard data.

Denny: Psychologists and special educators who are interested in more holistic ways of doing things really become quite excited about the alternative perspectives that teachers are developing. And new relationships can be developed because of these kinds of conversations. That's the upside. The downside is that in many situations that's not going to happen. I don't think that's reason enough not to try. I think things will change, but it would be naive of us to imply that if you do develop a more holistic framework, if you understand miscue, if you're documenting a child's learning, and you go into the meeting, you will automatically be able to persuade those at the table that this is the approach that should be taken in supporting this kid's learning. And this book has examples of when that does not happen, Valerie being one. And then coming back always to this other piece of the puzzle, that being the social nature of the invention of learning disabilities, the social nature of our construction of what it is that kids can do. I think of LaFon and her son, Mark, who are also in the book. Mark had finished sixth grade and had done all the work, and was told that he couldn't go to the graduation ceremony. LaFon and her husband challenged that, and they were then told that he could not attend because of his behavior. Then they were told that he was going to be retained. It's not much of a leap to conclude the reason they decided to retain him was because they didn't want him to go to the graduation ceremony. It was sheer bloody-mindedness—no other English phrase fits better—and that's often an element of a political framework. Teachers are left having to walk a fine line, trying to negotiate an alternative perspective.

ALAN: We haven't talked much about what drives this whole system, this whole political atmosphere in which teachers find themselves, and how politics and educational policy—which is dictated in part by politics—have a hand in driving perspectives on curriculum and perspectives on language use. So another layer of complexity is added to all of this.

Denny: It's much more difficult for teachers to deal with than an alternative paradigm, because once you can frame the paradigm you do at least have an opportunity to negotiate, but the political circumstances of teaching are so intangible. And yet, they are part of everything that teachers do. The politics of teaching frames their lives, but it doesn't have a clear shape that you can get ahold of, articulate, think about, and then in some way counter.

ALAN: Right, and because the scope of this particular entity is so big, and it's part of the local community, it's part of the country as a whole, it is difficult even to begin to frame it. Among some circles, if you do you're viewed as a kook because how can you possibly say that. One of the things you're trying to expose is that the reason your kid is having problems has to do with politics. To many people, politics is so far removed that it's hard for them to see the impact that it has on what happens in the classroom.

Denny: Yes. It's hard for us to think of politics in our everyday life. Politics is something that happens at the state or national level. But all of our lives are political and what happens to children is political.

ALAN: Yet in some real ways it may be why you're budgeted to receive thirty fourth-grade workbooks, and you can't have two hundred dollars to buy a classroom set of literature. In some places that's the reason, it has to do with this political perspective and how it trickles down and finds its way into the classroom.

Denny: And learning disabilities are politically defined. In many states and at the federal level they're defined as disparity between individual IQ and, basically, a performance rating of some kind. So teachers are locked into this politically defined framework of what a learning disability is, as well as dealing with all the researchers who have ad infinitum done serious pieces of research that lead us to believe that there is a linear framework to learning. And if you take a sidestep out of that linear framework, then there must be something wrong with you.

ALAN: I guess I have some anger toward the way I've seen kids treated in school. Because kids make decisions about their life in part based on how they're treated in schools. And the way they're treated is based on this false set of assumptions and beliefs, and so, because of that, they make life decisions that are in a sense shortchanging their potential.

Denny: It's a reason to become an advocate and to believe that there is an opportunity for us to change. It might take us a long time, but the more we see, the more we know. And the more grounded we are within our own theoretical frameworks, and the more articulate we become, then the more opportunity we have to assume the role of advocate for children and, we hope, eventually to change the system.

ABOUT THE AUTHORS

Debbie Coughlin is currently teaching third grade at Gardendale Elementary Magnet School in Merritt Island, Florida. She is a doctoral candidate from the University of Arizona with a major in language, reading, and culture and a minor in teaching and teacher education.

Caryl Crowell, M.Ed., teaches a bilingual multiage class at Borton Primary Magnet School. She is a part-time graduate student at the University of Arizona and mother of two teenage boys. She enjoys desert living.

Alan Flurkey is an elementary school teacher who has taught both regular and special education. He is a doctoral candidate in the College of Education at the University of Arizona, where he is currently conducting research in retrospective miscue analysis with Regents Professor Yetta M. Goodman.

Nan Jiang is currently a Ph.D. candidate at the University of Arizona. He taught ESL in China and freshman composition for ESL students at the University of Arizona. His areas of interest include ESL, bilingual education, and bilingual memory organization.

Marge Knox is a primary multiage teacher and a member of a district literacy committee for conducting district-wide and school activities to promote literacy in California. As a teacher and reading specialist for more than thirty years in the United States, Luxembourg, and Egypt, she has conducted workshops and presented at conferences while advocating for children. Currently she is a long-distance graduate student in language, reading, and culture at the University of Arizona.

Joanna Marasco teaches reading and writing at the Desert Vista Campus, Pima Community College and is a doctoral student in language, reading, and culture at the University of Arizona. Her research focuses on the interconnection of the politicization of teen pregnancy and what happens in the everyday life of a teenage mother.

LaFon Phillips is a teacher of hearing impaired children in the Tucson Unified School District. She is a doctoral candidate in of language, reading, and culture at the University of Arizona.

Debbie Smith is a doctoral student in language, reading, and culture at the University of Arizona. For the last two years she taught at an alternative high school but is presently advocating for high school students who have been marginalized through the system.

239

Denny Taylor is an ethnographer and writer who has spent more than twenty years working with families, communities, and schools. Her awards include the Mina P. Shaughnessy Prize from the Modern Language Association of America, the Elva Knight Award from the International Reading Association, and the Richard A. Meade Award from the National Council of Teachers of English. Her latest book is entitled *Toxic Literacies: Exposing the Injustice of Bureaucratic Texts*. She is currently working on a biography of Ken and Yetta Goodman in Tucson, Arizona.

Melanie Uttech is a doctoral candidate in language, reading, and culture at the University of Arizona and the coordinator of a United States–Mexico teacher exchange program at the University of Guanajuato, Mexico. Her dissertation, an ethnographic study of a rural school and community in the state of Guanajuato, received the National Security Education Program award for international research, one of the first such awards given for research in Mexico. As a bilingual teacher in schools along the Arizona–Sonora border, Melanie developed an environmental science curriculum embracing the languages, life forms, and lifestyles of the Sonoran desert region.

INDEX

Other books from Stenhouse...

Peer Mediation
Finding a Way to Care
Judith M. Ferrara

For more than ten years peer mediation programs have been springing up in schools. Although they are begun with the highest hopes and best intentions, many programs falter in their second or third year, then disappear. What makes a program effective enough to endure year after year and become part of a school's culture?

Peer Mediation is the story of how one successful program started in an urban elementary school—how it was designed, implemented, and maintained. Teacher and mediator Judith Ferrara explains mediation, what it means to start up a program, watch it grow, change, and endure. At the heart of this book are the voices of the students who volunteered to become peer mediators, learned to understand the mediation process, and worked to help shape the program. Their thoughts and reactions to the peer mediation program, their tenacity, and, above all, their ethic of caring will leave a strong impression. *Peer Mediation* demonstrates the need to listen to students, observe their responses to the program, and work with them to revise it in order to maintain it.

1-57110-021-0   Paperback

The Writing Lives of Children

Dan Madigan and Victoria T. Koivu-Rybicki

How do children choose the topics they write about? Is their writing another step to literacy, or are they accomplishing something greater and more personal? Can a child's writing really be political? social? How does a child's social and physical environment influence his or her writing?

The answers are as different and as complex as the children, as Dan Madigan and Vicki Rybicki reveal in this compelling study of third- and fourth-grade writers in an inner-city school. The ten children they portray have found in the act of writing another way to express their lives, explore their ideas, and define the world about them. They are like children in any classroom, but there is a difference. They have space and time and a forum in which to present their writing. An atmosphere of encouragement and an attentive, thoughtful audience of their peers are the support they need—and use—to grow as articulate, thoughtful writers.

1-57110-011-3   Paperback

For information on all Stenhouse publications
please write or call for a catalogue.
Stenhouse Publishers
P. O. Box 360
York, ME 03909
1-800-988-9812